MAKE IT *Fast*, COOK IT *Slow*

MAKE IT Fast, COOK IT Slow

The
BIG
Book of
Everyday
SLOW
Cooking

Stephanie O'Dea

HYPERION

New York

Library of Congress Cataloging-in-Publication Data

O'Dea, Stephanie.
    Make it fast, cook it slow : the big book of everyday slow cooking / Stephanie O'Dea.
        p. cm.
    ISBN 978-1-4013-1004-2
    1. Electric cookery, Slow.   2. Gluten-free diet—Recipes.   I. Title.
    TX827.O35 2009
    641.5'884—dc22
            2009012246

Hyperion books are available for special promotions and premiums. For details contact the HarperCollins Special Markets Department in the New York office at 212-207-7528, fax 212-207-7222, or email spsales@harpercollins.com.

Book design by Shubhani Sarkar

FIRST EDITION

10 9 8 7 6 5 4 3 2

To my husband,
ADAM:
Thank you
for eating **slow-cooked** food
every day for a year,
and for doing the dishes.

CONTENTS

MAKE IT Fast, COOK IT Slow

INTRODUCTION

It Started With a Resolution

I went into 2008 with a New Year's Resolution: I would use my slow cooker every single day for a year and document my results daily on a personal Web site, crockpot365.blogspot.com. When I started my project, I didn't expect that anyone would make the food I attempted. I figured people might tune in to read about the process, but I wasn't expecting to come up with new uses or recipes for the slow cooker.

That changed on Valentine's Day, 2008, when I made crème brûlée in the slow cooker. I was flabbergasted that a delicate restaurant-quality dessert could be made with very little effort in a slow cooker—something many (myself included, at the time) think of as a glorified pot roast machine. When the crème brûlée came out perfectly on the very first try, I got excited. Really excited. I sent an e-mail about my success to *The Rachael Ray Show*—and hinted that they should have me on to show her audience how they, too, could make this dessert easily. When a producer from the show called two weeks later, I knew I was on to something.

That's when I decided to take my challenge to the next level: I became determined to "think outside the crock" and come up with innovative, fun uses for the slow cooker, along with an extensive array of family friendly meals. This book is a compilation of the recipes I prepared throughout 2008, minus the ones that just did not work.

Yes, I had some flops. I would not recommend trying to hard-boil eggs in the slow cooker: you'll end up with a horrid smell in the house and greenish eggs. I needed to air out the house for forty-eight hours after that catastrophe. I'd also recommend not experimenting with bacon-wrapped scallops, unless you're okay with tossing away $60 in fresh seafood after they become a rubbery mess in the slow cooker because they've swum in slimy bacon juice for six hours. I did learn through this challenge, however, that a really bad flop results in dinner out—certainly not a horrible outcome.

This book is a group effort. Scores of readers from all over the world sent me their favorite recipes to try in the slow cooker. Some were traditional slow-cooked meals, and some needed to be tweaked to work in the slow cooker. All of the recipes have been tested in my own home kitchen, with my own Crock-Pot® slow cookers, and tasted by my family: my husband, Adam, and my two girls, who were three and six years of age at the time. The dishes have also been tested in home kitchens around the world, with reader results posted in comment sections under each recipe on the Web site.

In order to save on publication fees and keep the purchase price of this book down, I've opted not to include photographs. If you would like to see a finished photo as well as preparation photos, please visit the Web site. Every dish has been well documented.

Unless otherwise indicated, you may use whatever variety and fat content of milk you desire.

Please note that children under the age of four should not be given hot dogs, nuts, seeds, popcorn, large chunks of meat, whole grapes, carrots, or any other food that may cause choking.

Save Money and Time

I received my first slow cooker when I turned twenty-one (along with a food dehydrator and pasta machine, which have since been freecycled). I still own my original slow cooker, and continue to use it about once a week. While I was in school I found that coming home to slow-cooked meals was a fantastic way to save money and stave off the dreaded "freshman fifteen." As newlyweds, my husband and I used to eat meals from a pot of beans or a roast for a week. We'd eat leftovers over rice or pasta to stretch the meal, or stuff it into tortillas for burritos.

When I had children, I quickly learned that it was much safer to chop vegetables and prepare our evening meal in the morning while still heavily caffeinated, than in the evening with tired kids hanging on my ankles. The slow cooker became a permanent fixture on our kitchen countertop. I loved how a forgotten and frostbitten roast from the back of the freezer could come back to life by cooking it in its own juices, or with a bit of help from a jar of pasta sauce. I was amazed at how tender chicken breasts could become when slow cooked, and how well our family could eat with minimal effort on my part.

Cooking with the slow cooker is quite economical. With its help you can stock the freezer with homemade broth, stock, and cream-of-something soup. You can freeze your own cooked beans. You can make yogurt, granola, and baby food. You can cook a whole chicken for meat, and use the carcass for broth. You can even make playdough, crayons, soap, and food gifts, such as spiced nuts and apple butter. I learned through this challenge that the average energy used for slow cooking is similar to that of a desk lamp: 75 watts on low, and 150 watts on high. This is much less energy use than an oven, stove, or barbecue requires.

Choosing a Slow Cooker

Although there are many different brands of slow cookers on the market, I have only personally used the original Crock-Pot® brand of slow cooker. All the meals in this book and on the Web site (crockpot365.blogspot.com) were prepared in Crock-Pot® brand slow cookers. Please refer to your owner's manual for proper use and care of your slow cooker and use your best judgment when in use. The cooking time is a range—if you know that your particular slow cooker seems to cook fast, stick to the low end of the cooking time. When preparing delicate dishes, and when baking, keep an eye on your cooker and don't venture too far away. I recommend keeping your pot two-thirds to three-quarters full for optimum performance.

I have quite a few Crock-Pot® slow cookers, and am pleased with the variety of sizes available. If you are in the market for a new slow cooker, consider purchasing one with an auto-warm safety feature. This type of programmable slow cooker lets the cook choose the cooking temperature (high or low) and the exact amount of time that the heating element is cooking. When the time has elapsed, the cooker will automatically stop cooking and shift to a lower temperature to keep the food warm until you arrive home and are ready to eat.

If you are cooking for 1 to 2 people, opt for a 2-quart cooker. For a family of 3 to 4, a 4-quart slow cooker is a great choice. For a family of 4 to 6, a 6-quart would work well, and a 7- to 8-quart cooker is ideal for large families, or for entertaining groups. The 1-quart and smaller models are ideal for desserts, fondues, or for keeping dipping sauces warm. If you only own a large slow cooker, you can still make all of the meals, appetizers, and fondues by simply inserting an oven-safe dish (Corningware®, Pyrex®) into your stoneware to create a smaller cooking vessel.

Get to Know Your Slow Cooker

You don't need to take your cookware on dates or for a stroll on the beach, but you do need to get to know your particular slow cooker. Start easy. Don't try out a complicated dessert or pasta dish, or Blue Cheese and Steak Roll-Ups (page 304) for one of your first slow-cooked adventures. The reason the machines come with a little book full of stews and soups is because they are easy and somewhat fool-proof. Once you get the feel for your slow cooker (which is why you should start with the easy ones) you will be able to determine how long things will take with your own machine, altitude, and humidity level.

If you are going to be out of the house, cook for the shortest and lowest cooking time possible. I know, it doesn't make sense. But if you are going to be out of the house for 10 hours, and the cooking time says 6 to 8 hours, don't set it for 10. Set it for 6, and your cooker will automatically switch to warm for the rest of the time you're gone. Worst case, the meal isn't quite done and you flip the cooker to high while you change your clothes and set the table. You *will* get a feel, I promise. I'm a complete dunderhead when I'm in the kitchen, yet I can slow cook. You can, too. I promise.

Everything Is Gluten-Free

The recipes in this book have been prepared completely gluten-free, due to a family intolerance. If you do not have to worry about gluten, feel free to ignore my notes, or file them away in case you ever need to cook for someone with gluten sensitivity. Gluten is found in wheat, barley, and rye. Please read all manufacturer labels carefully; ingredients sometimes change with little or no warning.

I use the following gluten-free foods and condiments in our home kitchen, readily found at neighborhood grocery stores, Trader Joe's, Whole Foods, or Amazon.com:

Barbara's Bakery Organic Brown Rice Crisps cereal
Bob's Red Mill Certified Gluten Free Whole Grain Rolled Oats
Coleman Natural chicken meatballs
Food For Life brown rice bread
General Mills Rice Chex

Glutino Pretzels

La Choy soy sauce, sweet & sour, and teriyaki sauce

Lea & Perrins Worcestershire Sauce, Made in USA (only the
    U.S.-manufactured is gluten-free)

Pamela's Baking and Pancake Mix

Redbridge beer (Anheuser-Busch)

San-J Tamari, Wheat-Free

Tinkyáda Brown Rice pasta (all sizes, including lasagna noodles)

Trader Joe's Gluten Free Pancake and Baking Mix

Whole Foods 365 Everyday Value Gluten Free baking products

*R*eal Life

I love how the slow cooker allows me to have wiggle room when preparing meals. I am not the best in the kitchen, and before this challenge, had no idea which spices went well together and why. I have certainly expanded my culinary expertise through this exercise, but I would never consider myself to be a good cook. I like having fun. I treat the slow cooker as an Easy-Bake™ oven for grown-ups.

I love that I can put something on and wander away without fearing the food will burn to a crisp or boil over (things that happen often when I cook using traditional methods). I also like that I can taste and tweak spices while cooking with plenty of time to "fix" anything that might happen. I've been known to accidentally add a tablespoon of salt instead of a teaspoon. The low and steady heat of the slow cooker gives me the opportunity to scoop out my mistake without burning my fingers, or the time needed to add more broth or ingredients to balance out my flub. I also appreciate that my children can sit on the countertop with me while I prepare meals and add ingredients without worry of being burned.

Cooking should be fun. When preparing dinner becomes a chore and it's no longer enjoyable, money is wasted ordering pizza or takeout. One of the reasons the slow cooker has become such an in-valuable tool in our house is because I can make do with pantry staples or with meat I buy on sale. Some of our favorite meals have occurred when I just started opening cabinets and dumping stuff in the pot. I urge you to do the same. Play. You might just surprise yourself with what you come up with!

BEVERAGES

MILK

$\mathcal{S}$erving hot beverages during a party, play group, or meeting is such a fun use for the slow cooker. Visitors will love lining up for their drinks, and the house smells marvelous while the beverage stays hot. When serving guests, provide a ladle and keep the slow cooker lid off with the pot turned to low. When the lid is off, the drink will not remain hot enough if on the warm setting.

CHAI TEA LATTE

HOLIDAY PUNCH (NONALCOHOLIC)

HOT BUTTERED RUM

GINGERBREAD LATTE

MULLED WINE

PEPPERMINT HOT CHOCOLATE/
PEPPERMINT MOCHA

PUMPKIN SPICE LATTE

WASSAIL

CHAI TEA LATTE

serves 2 to 4

The Ingredients

    4 cups milk
    1/4 teaspoon ground cloves
    1/2 teaspoon ground ginger
    1 teaspoon vanilla extract
    1 tablespoon sugar (I like baker's sugar because it dissolves nicely)
    4 cinnamon sticks (or 2 teaspoons ground cinnamon)
    4 cardamom pods
    4 tea bags (black tea)

The Directions

Use a 4-quart slow cooker. Put milk into the stoneware, and stir in the spices, vanilla, and sugar. Float the cinnamon sticks, cardamom pods, and tea bags on top. Cover and cook on high for 2 hours, or until heated through.

The Verdict

Of the different hot beverages I've made in the slow cooker, this is my least favorite, but it's because I'm just not a fan of tea. My husband, Adam, and I joked that a shot of espresso would really liven it up. But! If you like tea, and are spending $4 for store-bought lattes a few times a week, you should give this a try. I've gotten quite a few nice e-mails about this tea. Apparently it tastes just like the "real" thing.

HOLIDAY PUNCH (NONALCOHOLIC)

serves 6

The Ingredients

4 cups cranberry juice
4 cups pineapple juice
$1/3$ cup hot tamales candy
6 cinnamon sticks

The Directions

Use a 4-quart slow cooker. Combine the juices in the stoneware, and add the hot tamales. Cover and cook on high for 2 hours, or on low for 4 to 5 hours. Stir. The candy will pretty much dissolve, leaving just a hint of cinnamony flavor. Ladle the punch into mugs and garnish with a cinnamon stick if desired.

The Verdict

This is the easiest hot drink I have made in the slow cooker, and the kids liked it the most. They drank two mugs each after school, and another after dinner. I really liked it a lot, too, and had two servings while watching *Oprah*. Adam only got a taste; he should have come home earlier!

HOT BUTTERED RUM

serves 5

The Ingredients

4 cups warm water
1 cup dark brown sugar, firmly packed
4 tablespoons (1/2 stick) butter
pinch of salt (even if your butter is salted, go ahead and add it)
2 cinnamon sticks
3 whole cloves
1/4 teaspoon ground nutmeg, plus more for garnish (optional)

TO ADD LATER
shot or two of rum
splash of eggnog
ground cinnamon (optional)

The Directions

Use a 4-quart slow cooker. Add the water, brown sugar, butter, salt, cinnamon sticks, cloves, and nutmeg to the crock. Cover and cook on high for 1 to 2 hours, or until the butter has melted and the mixture is quite hot. Ladle into a mug with a shot or two of rum, and add a splash of eggnog. Garnish with a sprinkle more nutmeg and cinnamon, if you like.

The Verdict

We had this on Christmas Day, and it was delicious. My mother-in-law even liked this, and she usually doesn't drink alcohol. Keep in mind that if your eggnog is right from the fridge, it will make the butter harden in the mug if you add too much (ask me how I know this . . .). It would be better to take a bit out of the fridge and let it warm to room temperature while the butter and sugar cook in the crock. My sister-in-law was pregnant, and she enjoyed plain eggnog with the butter and brown sugar.

GINGERBREAD LATTE

serves 2 to 4

The Ingredients
    4 cups milk
    1 teaspoon ground cinnamon
    1/4 teaspoon ground cloves
    1/4 teaspoon ground nutmeg
    2 teaspoons ground ginger
    1/2 cup sugar
    2 teaspoons vanilla extract
    1/2 cup strong black coffee, or 1 freshly brewed shot of espresso, per serving
    Cinnamon sticks, whipped cream (garnish)

The Directions
Use a 2-quart slow cooker. Put the milk into the stoneware, and whisk in the dried spices, sugar, and vanilla. Don't add the coffee. Cover and cook on low for 3 hours, or high for 1 to 2 hours. The milk should be quite hot, but if your slow cooker tends to get hot enough to boil, keep an eye on it. Don't let the milk boil. Pour into hot coffee or espresso. Garnish with whipped cream, a sprinkle of nutmeg, and a cinnamon stick.

The Verdict
I think this might be my favorite coffee drink I've made. It really hit the spot on a cloudy day around 3:00 p.m. when I really, really wanted to climb into bed for a nap, but didn't have the time. After four or five sugar cookies and a latte, I was wide awake until 1:00 a.m. With any luck, you can have the same experience. The kids both had a cup of the warm milk mixture with whipped cream and were delighted. Adam didn't get to try any, but I did save my mug for him to smell—I'm thoughtful that way.

MULLED WINE

serves 10

The Ingredients

2 (750 ml) bottles dry red wine (I used Cabernet Sauvignon)
1 cup freshly squeezed orange juice (about 3 oranges)
3/4 cup sugar
1/4 teaspoon ground allspice
1/4 teaspoon ground cinnamon
4 cinnamon sticks
4 whole cloves
2 more oranges (one to float on top, and one for garnish wedges)

The Directions

Use a 6-quart slow cooker. Pour the wine into the stoneware, and squeeze the oranges to get 1 cup of juice. I'm sure you could get away with using store-bought juice, but the pulp floating around is what's kind of neat about mulled wine; it's more rustic this way. Stir in the sugar and ground spices. Float the cinnamon sticks and whole cloves on top. Slice one of the oranges in rings and float on top. Cover and cook on high for 2 hours, or on low for 4 hours. You want the wine to get as hot as a traditional hot beverage. Ladle the wine into mugs, and serve with a fresh orange wedge. When serving, leave the lid off and the slow cooker on low.

The Verdict

I liked this a lot. An awful lot. Maybe even a bit too much. The guests I've served this to have all been equally impressed. I like that you can use cheap wine (the wine I've used is between $2 and $4 per bottle) and it still wows even the toughest wine snob.

PEPPERMINT HOT CHOCOLATE/
PEPPERMINT MOCHA

serves 10 to 12

The Ingredients

FOR THE BASIC PEPPERMINT HOT CHOCOLATE

3 cups nonfat dry milk

1 cup confectioners' sugar

3/4 cup unsweetened cocoa powder

1/4 teaspoon kosher salt

1/2 cup milk chocolate syrup

1 to 2 teaspoons peppermint extract

7 cups water

marshmallows and candy canes, for garnish

FOR A "MOCHA"

Pour the cooked hot chocolate over a shot of espresso or a half cup of very strong coffee.

FOR AN "ADULT DRINK"

Omit peppermint extract and pour the hot chocolate over a shot of Peppermint Schnapps.

The Directions

Use a 4-quart slow cooker. Combine the dry ingredients in the stoneware and stir with a spoon. Squeeze in chocolate syrup, and add the peppermint extract. Add water a cup at a time, and stir well. The chocolate mixture will be bubbly and look powdery. It's okay—I promise it will cook together. Cover and cook on high for 2 to 3 hours, or until completely hot. Serve with marshmallows and candy canes. If guests serve themeselves, keep the pot on low with the lid off, and provide a ladle.

(CONTINUED)

The Verdict.

Very tasty. I tried it plain, and with a half cup of strong coffee. I did not try the Peppermint Schnapps version, but assume it would taste good (it was 10:00 a.m.). The kids thought that the 2 teaspoons of peppermint extract was too strong, but that 1 teaspoon was perfect. I recommend starting with 1 teaspoon, and adding ¼ teaspoon at a time to taste.

PUMPKIN SPICE LATTE

serves 2

The Ingredients

- 1/2 cup brewed espresso or 3/4 cup strong coffee
- 2 cups milk (I used 1 percent)
- 2 tablespoons canned puréed pumpkin
- 1/2 teaspoon pumpkin pie spice or 1/4 teaspoon ground cinnamon, 1/8 teaspoon cloves, 1/8 teaspoon nutmeg, and a teeny tiny pinch of ground ginger
- 2 tablespoons sugar
- 2 tablespoons vanilla extract
- whipped cream (optional garnish)
- 2 cinnamon sticks (optional garnish)

The Directions

Use a 2-quart slow cooker. Add coffee/espresso and milk to the stoneware. Whisk in pumpkin, spices, sugar, and vanilla. Cover and cook on high for 2 hours. Whisk again. Ladle into mugs, and garnish with whipped cream and additional cinnamon. You can add a cinnamon stick to be fancy.

The Verdict

This recipe really does taste like the real thing—except it doesn't leave a fluorescent orange stain when you dribble it down your sweater. I also learned that coffee-house pumpkin spice lattes may contain gluten, which is another reason to make them yourself!

WASSAIL

serves 8

The Ingredients

2 quarts apple cider
1 cup pineapple juice
$\frac{1}{2}$ cup honey
3 cinnamon sticks
2 whole cloves
1 orange, cut into rings
brandy (optional)

The Directions

Use a 4-quart slow cooker. This makes 9 cups of spiced punch. Put the cider, juice, honey, cinnamon, and cloves into the cooker. Wash the orange well, and cut off each end. Slice the rest into rings, and float on top of the punch. Cook on high for 2 hours, or on low for about 4 hours. You want the punch to be completely hot, and the flavor of the cloves and the cinnamon to have permeated the juices.

Ladle the punch into mugs. If you are going to add the brandy, put a shot into each mug, then top with the hot punch. If guests will be serving themselves, provide a ladle, and keep the slow cooker turned to low and the lid off.

The Verdict

Delicious and soothing. One of my kids had a sore throat, and she drank a lot (minus the brandy), and was happy with how it made her throat feel better. We drank our wassail out of mugs while we watched a *Murder, She Wrote* marathon on TV. I love Jessica Fletcher.

APPETIZERS

*E*ntertaining with the slow cooker is such a breeze. I love having a few little cookers plugged in with a variety of dips for guests to sample while I'm finishing up the main meal. The variety of slow-cooked appetizers is extensive. You can make the old standby of Cream Cheese, Sausage, and Rotel Dip (page 28) for the big game, or wow visitors with Tomatoes and Goat Cheese with a Cranberry Balsamic Syrup (page 39) at a fancy dinner party.

BACON AND CHEESE DIP

serves 4

The Ingredients

    ⅓ cup milk (I used soy milk)
    1 teaspoon gluten-free Worcestershire sauce
    2 slices American cheese
    2 slices cheddar cheese
    5 pieces cooked bacon, crumbled

The Directions

Use a 1-quart or smaller slow cooker. Add the milk to the crock, then add the Worcestershire sauce. Crumble in the cheese slices, and add the cooked bacon. Cover and cook for 1 hour. Stir to blend and serve with tortilla chips, bread cubes, or sliced vegetables.

The Verdict

We ate this at 9:15 a.m. on Mother's Day. I had just received the Little Dipper Crock-Pot as a gift from my mother-in-law, and was eager to test it out. Our dip had a great smoky flavor without being too greasy.

BAKED BRIE

serves 8

The Ingredients
    1 can refrigerated crescent rolls
    (If gluten-free, use the recipe listed on page 404 for crescent dough)
    1 (16-ounce) wheel brie

The Directions
Use a 4-quart slow cooker, with an oven-safe dish inserted for easy brie removal. Roll out the chilled dough or crescent rolls on a cutting board. Don't tear apart the little crescent roll triangles. I didn't use an actual rolling pin, I just squished the dough down with a piece of plastic wrap. Place the wheel of brie in the center of the dough and fold the edges of the dough together. If you have enough dough to cover the top, go for it. I did not, and left a peek-hole. Put the wrapped brie into the oven-safe dish, and insert into the stoneware. Cover and cook on high for 3 to 4 hours, with a toothpick wedged in the cover for just a bit of a vent. Your brie is done when the dough has browned on top, and begun to pull away from the sides of the dish.

BLACK BEAN AND GOAT CHEESE DIP

serves 4

The Ingredients

1 cup refried black beans
1 tablespoon freshly squeezed lime juice
2 garlic cloves, chopped
1 teaspoon cayenne pepper
1 teaspoon ground cumin
2 tablespoons chopped cilantro leaves
3 to 5 slices goat cheese

The Directions

Use a 1-quart or smaller slow cooker. Put 1 cup of refried black beans into your cooker. Add the lime juice. Top with the garlic, cayenne, cumin, and cilantro. Stir. Add the goat cheese. Cover the cooker and plug it in. Cook the dip for 1 to 2 hours, or until the goat cheese has melted and the beans are warm and gooey. Serve with corn tortilla chips.

The Verdict

Very tasty. I was quite pleased with the kick the dip had, and loved how the goat cheese was creamy and mellow. The cilantro gave a "freshness" that I really appreciated—it didn't just taste like a canned bean dip. The kids scooped most of the goat cheese off the top, but did try enough of the black bean dip to declare it spicy.

BRIE WITH APRICOT TOPPING

serves 6

The Ingredients
1 (16-ounce) round or wedge brie
½ cup chopped dried apricots
1 teaspoon balsamic vinegar
2 tablespoons brown sugar
2 tablespoons water
¼ teaspoon dried rosemary
½ cup chopped walnuts

The Directions
Use a 2-quart slow cooker. If your brie has a really hard rind, cut the top part off and discard. Put into the stoneware. In a bowl, mix apricots, balsamic vinegar, brown sugar, water, and rosemary together. Spoon on top of the brie. Sprinkle with the walnuts. Cover and cook on low for 3 hours, or on high for 1 to 2 hours, checking after 1 hour. Serve with your favorite crackers or apple slices.

The Verdict
I couldn't wait to dig in, so I removed the stoneware from the base, wrapped it up in a beach towel, grabbed a sleeve of crackers, and plopped on the couch in front of the TV. When Adam or the kids got near, I snarled and batted them away with my arm. This couldn't possibly taste any better. The flavor is delicious, and the brie got so gooey and amazing—I think I just drooled a bit, remembering.

BRIE WITH PECANS AND CRANBERRIES

serves 8

The Ingredients

1 (8-ounce) round brie
1/3 cup candied pecans
1/3 cup dried cranberries

The Directions

Use a 2-quart slow cooker. Put the brie into the stoneware, and cover with the pecans and cranberries. Cook on high for 2 hours, or until cheese is melted and gooey. Serve with crackers and sliced green apples. When we make this for friends, no one speaks because we're all too busy shoveling it into our mouths.

BUFFALO CHICKEN DIP

serves 12

The Ingredients

1½ cups diced cooked chicken

2 cups blue cheese salad dressing

¼ to ½ cup Tabasco sauce (depending on taste)

1½ cups shredded cheddar cheese

The Directions

Use a 2-quart slow cooker. Put the chicken into the stoneware, and top with the salad dressing. Add the Tabasco sauce and cheese. Cover and cook on low for 3 to 4 hours, or on high for about 2 hours. Stir well. Add more Tabasco sauce, if needed. Serve with celery sticks, bread cubes, and your favorite crackers.

The Verdict

I puffy-heart love buffalo wings, and can't ever seem to get enough of the vinegary sauce. This dip completely satisfies my wing cravings and is fun to serve at a party—it's always a hit with guests.

CHICKEN NACHOS

serves 6 to 8

The Ingredients

$^1/_2$ pound boneless, skinless chicken meat, diced

1 (32-ounce) package Velveeta cheese, cubed

1 (14.5-ounce) can tomatoes and chiles (Rotel) (do not drain)

refried beans, salsa, sour cream, sliced olives, jalapeños (optional)

The Directions

Use a 4-quart slow cooker. Put the chicken into the stoneware, and cover with cheese cubes. Add the entire can of tomatoes and chiles. Cook on low for 6 hours, or on high for 3 to 4 hours. This is finished when the chicken is cooked fully and the cheese has melted completely. Serve over your favorite chips and top with desired toppings.

CRAB DIP

serves 20

The Ingredients

1 pound shelled crabmeat (imitation crabmeat is not gluten-free. Go for the real stuff!)
3 (8-ounce) packages cream cheese
1/2 cup buffalo wing sauce or 1/2 cup jarred salsa
1/2 cup milk
1 (10-ounce) can tomatoes and chiles (Rotel), drained
2 lemons (optional)

The Directions

Use a 4-quart slow cooker. Sort through crabmeat to remove any extra bits of shell, and set aside. Cube the cream cheese and put it into your cooker. Plug the cooker in and turn to high to start melting the cream cheese. Add the buffalo wing sauce (or salsa), milk, and the tomatoes and chiles. Add the crabmeat, and stir gingerly to combine. Cover and cook on low for 2 to 3 hours, stirring every 20 to 30 minutes, or on high for no more than 2 hours, stirring often. Serve with your favorite crackers, cubed bread, or celery sticks. If you plan on serving the dip out of the slow cooker, you can "pretty it up" by placing lemon slices all the way around the edge of the dip in the crock. This feeds 20 people as an appetizer, or one cranky woman as a meal.

CREAM CHEESE, SAUSAGE, AND ROTEL DIP

serves 8

The Ingredients

1 pound breakfast sausage, browned and drained
1 (8-ounce) block cream cheese
1 (10-ounce) can tomatoes and green chiles (Rotel), drained

The Directions

Use a 2-quart slow cooker. Put the chopped sausage into the stoneware, and add the cream cheese. Add the tomatoes and chiles. Cover and cook on low for about 90 minutes, or on high for 45 minutes. Stir well, and eat with tortilla chips.

The Verdict

This dip is famous. This is The Internet's Dip. When I asked for help with hot dip recipes, I got no fewer than forty e-mails telling me about this dip. Pretty much everybody acknowledged that the ingredients were weird and shouldn't taste good together, *but they just do.* The Internet is right—this dip is amazing.

HOISIN CHICKEN WINGS

serves 6

The Ingredients

2 to 3 pounds frozen chicken wings or drumettes

1/2 cup prepared hoisin sauce (or your own, recipe below)

1/4 cup honey

4 to 5 garlic cloves, smashed and chopped

1 (1-inch) piece fresh ginger, peeled and grated

1 tablespoon sesame oil

THE HOMEMADE HOISIN SAUCE

4 tablespoons gluten-free soy sauce

2 tablespoons peanut butter

1 tablespoon molasses or honey

2 garlic cloves, chopped

2 teaspoons sesame oil

1 teaspoon hot sauce (I used Thai red chili paste; Tabasco or similar would also work)

1/8 teaspoon black pepper

The Directions

Use a 4-quart slow cooker. Put the chicken into the crock. Add the hoisin sauce, honey, garlic, ginger, and sesame oil. Cover and cook on low for 7 to 8 hours, or on high for 4 to 5 hours. Stir before serving.

The Verdict

These were great! I love chicken wings, and routinely skip the pizza when we order delivery and go straight for the wings. My three-year-old ate seven or eight, and asked me to make them for her birthday.

HOT AND SPICY ARTICHOKE DIP

serves 8 to 10

The Ingredients

    1 (12-ounce) jar marinated artichoke hearts, drained and chopped
    1/2 to 1 teaspoon crushed red pepper flakes
    1 (8-ounce) block cream cheese
    1/2 cup shredded mozzarella cheese

The Directions

Use a 2-quart slow cooker. Put the chopped artichokes into the stoneware, and add the red pepper flakes. I started with 1/2 teaspoon, then added a bit more for a kick. Add cream cheese and mozzarella. Cover and cook on low for 3 to 4 hours, or on high for 2 to 3 hours. Stir well and serve with your favorite chips.

The Verdict

If I ever live alone, I think I'd like to fill a bathtub with this artichoke dip and climb in with a bag of chips. It's that tasty.

JALAPEÑO POPPERS

serves 5

The Ingredients

10 whole jalapeño peppers
4 ounces cream cheese
1/3 cup shredded Parmesan cheese
1/4 cup sour cream
9 pieces of bacon, crumbled (I used turkey bacon)
1/3 cup water

The Directions

Use a 4-quart slow cooker and wear plastic gloves when handling the jalapeños. I ignored this advice and had pain for about three hours in all of my fingers, even after taking a high dose of aspirin and sitting with an ice pack. Jalapeños are very powerful creations. Anyhow, wearing gloves, cut the tops off the jalapeños, and scrape out and discard the membrane and all of the little white seeds with a knife under running water. Set aside. In a bowl, mix together your stuffing mixture of cream cheese, Parmesan cheese, sour cream, and crumbled bacon. Fill the empty jalapeño cavities with the stuffing. You could probably be fancy and pipe it in with a plastic bag, but fingers will work (you're going to wear gloves, right?). Put 1/3 cup of water in the bottom of your stoneware, and place the stuffed jalapeños on top. Cover and cook on high for 2 to 3 hours, or on low for 3 to 4 hours. The jalapeños are done when the skin starts to wilt and look wrinkly. Serve hot or at room temperature. I like them best at room temperature.

The Verdict

These are delicious, and aren't overly spicy—the heat was just right for me. I made them for my brother and sister-in-law, but didn't think to make them until right before we ate dinner. So we had them after dinner and dessert, which is a bit different. I was too full to enjoy them that night, but adored the leftovers, which I had for breakfast with coffee. Weird, I know.

NOT-TOO-SPICY BEAN DIP

serves 6

The Ingredients

1 (15-ounce) can refried beans
3 tablespoons taco sauce
handful of shredded cheddar cheese

The Directions

Use a 1-quart slow cooker. Pour the beans into the stoneware, and stir in the taco sauce. Add the cheese. Cover and cook on low for 3 hours, or on high for 1½ hours. Serve with your favorite chips. We used flaxseed chips so we could justify eating it for dinner. And then we sang the bean song.

ROASTED GARLIC

serves 6

The Ingredients
6 heads garlic
aluminum foil

The Directions
Use a 4-quart slow cooker. With a sharp knife, carefully cut off the top end of the garlic bulb. You want to keep it wrapped in the outer skin layers, and have just a bit of some of the cloves exposed. Wrap each bulb in its own piece of aluminum foil. Plop all the foil-wrapped bulbs into your cooker and cook on low for 4 to 5 hours. Unwrap the foil, and squeeze the bulb. If the garlic pulp squirts out (like a tube of frosting), it's done. If not, wrap it back up and cook for another hour or so.

The Verdict
Roasting garlic creates a mellow, somewhat nutty flavor. The softened garlic is easily spread on your favorite crackers or pieces of crusty bread, and makes a wonderful snack or appetizer. This is not only delicious, it will clear sinuses, and ward off vampires.

SPINACH AND ARTICHOKE DIP

serves 8 to 10

The Ingredients

1 (14-ounce) can artichoke hearts, drained and chopped
1 (9-ounce) bag baby spinach
½ cup sour cream
½ block (4 ounces) cream cheese
3 tablespoons jalapeño slices, chopped
1 cup shredded mozzarella cheese
1 cup shredded Parmesan cheese

The Directions

Use a 4-quart slow cooker. Put the artichoke hearts into the stoneware. Scrunch the spinach and chop it the best you can—you're mostly trying to get the long stems off. Add it to the cooker and put in sour cream, cream cheese, and jalapeños. Top with ½ cup each shredded mozzarella and Parmesan. Cover and cook on low for 2 hours, or on high for 1 hour. Stir. The spinach should begin to wilt. If it hasn't, cook some more. When the spinach is totally wilted, add the remaining ½ cup of mozzarella and Parmesan cheeses, and let them melt, with the lid off to allow the moisture to evaporate. Serve with your favorite chips, sliced veggies, or bread cubes.

The Verdict

I liked this a lot—the fresh spinach retained a bit of its crunch, and the cheeses and jalapeños complemented each other beautifully. This wasn't too spicy for my kids, and they both ate more than I would have liked, since they then were too full to eat dinner.

SUN-DRIED TOMATO DIP

serves 8

The Ingredients
    1 (8.5-ounce) jar sun-dried tomatoes, drained
    1 (8-ounce) block cream cheese

The Directions
Use a 2-quart slow cooker. Pulse the sun-dried tomatoes in a food processor or blender until finely chopped. Add to the slow cooker. Top with the cream cheese. Cover and cook on low for 3 to 4 hours, or on high for about 2 hours. Stir well and serve with your favorite chips, crackers, or cubed bread.

The Verdict
We were home, sick, for New Year's Eve, but it was okay because we had this dip. And Boggle. This tastes better than most things in the world, and I couldn't stop eating it. It even tasted good cold the next morning for breakfast.

SUPER DUPER GARLIC DIP

serves 8

The Ingredients

    1 (8-ounce) block cream cheese
    1/3 cup mayonnaise
    1 whole head garlic, peeled and minced

The Directions

Use a 1-quart or smaller slow cooker. Plug in the cooker to warm it up, and add the block of cream cheese. Add the mayonnaise and garlic, and cover. You won't be able to stir it until the cream cheese has melted a bit. After 30 minutes, stir well, and cook, covered, for another 30 to 45 minutes. Serve with your favorite crackers and celery sticks. If you leave the slow cooker plugged in for too long, the dip might separate a bit, and the garlic will brown. If this happens, unplug the cooker and give the dip a quick stir—it's definitely salvageable.

SWEET AND SPICY CHICKEN WINGS

serves 6

The Ingredients

    4 pounds chicken wings and tiny drumsticks
    1 (14-ounce) jar chipotle salsa
    1 (11-ounce) jar apricot preserves

The Directions

Use a 6-quart slow cooker. You can use frozen or thawed wings and drumsticks. Some people like to brown the wings before adding them to the slow cooker; I do not. Browning provides a bit of color and texture, but does not improve flavor. Put the chicken into the stoneware. Add the salsa and apricot preserves. Cover and cook on low for 8 hours, or on high for 4 hours. The chicken is finished when it is fully cooked and has reached the desired tenderness. (If your chicken is fresh and has been browned, it will cook faster.) These wings are a great change of pace from the tangy flavor of traditional wings, and are a bit "fancier" to serve to guests.

TERIYAKI DRUMETTES

serves 4

The Ingredients

2 pounds chicken drumettes
1/2 cup gluten-free soy sauce
3 tablespoons brown sugar
1 tablespoon dry sherry or tequila
3 garlic cloves, minced

The Directions

Use a 4-quart slow cooker. Plop the chicken into the crock. Add the soy sauce, brown sugar, sherry, and garlic. Toss with two large spoons to coat the chicken somewhat evenly. Cover and cook on low for 6 to 8 hours, or on high for 4 to 5 hours.

The Verdict

I served this with white rice, and my kids ate every single drumette I made. They were like savage beasts.

TOMATOES AND GOAT CHEESE WITH CRANBERRY BALSAMIC SYRUP

serves 6

The Ingredients

3 tablespoons balsamic vinegar

4 medium vine-ripened tomatoes

1 (6-ounce) log goat cheese

1/4 teaspoon kosher salt

1/4 teaspoon black pepper

1/4 cup dried cranberries

1 tablespoon sesame oil

The Directions

Use a 6-quart slow cooker. Swirl the balsamic vinegar on the bottom of the stoneware. Cut the to-matoes into thick slices, and top with rounds of goat cheese. Put them into the cooker (you may need to stagger-stack to get them all in). Sprinkle with the salt and pepper, add the cranberries, and drizzle the sesame oil over everything. Cover and cook on high for 2 hours, or until the goat cheese is melty and tomatoes start to pucker. Serve as an appetizer with some bread to soak up the juice.

The Verdict

Oh My Little Pony, these couldn't possibly be any better. Goat cheese is like a nice, creamy mild feta. This was the first time I had cooked with it, and now I buy it regularly. The kids loved these—I so wish they didn't, so I could have eaten them all myself.

TURKEY MEATBALLS WITH CRANBERRY BARBECUE SAUCE

serves 4 to 6

The Ingredients

1 (16-ounce) can jellied cranberry sauce

1 pound cooked turkey meatballs (store-bought or homemade; Coleman Natural are gluten-free)

½ cup bottled barbecue sauce

1 teaspoon soy sauce

The Directions

Use a 4-quart slow cooker. Slice the cranberry sauce, and lay the slices on the bottom of the stoneware. Cover with the meatballs. Add the barbecue and soy sauce. Cover and cook on low for 4 to 6 hours or on high for 2 to 4 hours. The cooking time will vary depending upon whether your meatballs are fresh or frozen.

The Verdict

I made my own meatballs for this dish. The proportions of the sauce are for 1 pound of meatballs, but I stretched it to cover 2 pounds. My dad thought they could use some more sauce, my husband thought they were plenty saucy, and one of my kids washed all the sauce off hers. Use your best judgment as to how much sauce to make for your family.

WHITE BEAN AND PESTO SPREAD

serves 4

The Ingredients

1 cup canned white beans, drained and rinsed (cannellini or white kidney beans)
1/4 cup prepared pesto

The Directions

Use a 1-quart or smaller slow cooker. Smash the beans; I used a handheld chopper, but you could squeeze them in a ziplock bag or use a tiny food processor. Mix with the pesto. Add the mixture to a mini slow cooker, cover it, and plug it in. I cooked our dip for about 45 minutes, and it was warm and gooey. Serve with pita chips, tortilla chips, or crostini.

I made crostini out of leftover brown rice bread. It was easy. Brush the pieces with a bit of olive oil, then sprinkle them with salt and pepper. Bake at 400°F until the bottoms are toasty, then broil until the tops are toasty, too.

The Verdict

This is such a yummy spread, and it is so easy; it practically makes itself. It must eat itself, too, because I have no idea where it went. I made a batch, took a picture, and then it disappeared. Keep the ingredients on hand for last-minute company. You will thank me when your guests' eyeballs roll back in delight.

BREAKFAST

*W*aking up to a hot breakfast is pretty much the best thing, ever. While a few of these can be cooked overnight, others can be assembled the evening before for an easy morning plug-in. Do yourself a favor and load up the coffeepot the night before, too!

APPLE BUTTER

APPLE OATMEAL

BAKED OATMEAL

BREAKFAST RISOTTO

EGG, FETA, AND MUSHROOM BREAKFAST
   CASSEROLE

GRANOLA

HASH BROWN BREAKFAST CASSEROLE

MEXICAN BREAKFAST CASSEROLE

OVERNIGHT BREAKFAST CASSEROLE

OVERNIGHT BREAKFAST POTATOES AND SAUSAGE

OVERNIGHT GRITS

PANCAKES

STRAWBERRY JAM

YOGURT

APPLE BUTTER

makes approximately 10 cups

The Ingredients

    12 to 15 apples (14 large apples fit in my 6½-quart cooker)
    1 tablespoon vanilla extract
    ¾ cup granulated sugar
    ¾ cup brown sugar, firmly packed
    2 teaspoons ground cinnamon
    ½ teaspoon ground cloves

The Directions

Use a 6-quart slow cooker. This is a two-day process. Peel, core, and quarter each apple. Put the apples into your crock, and add 1 tablespoon of vanilla. Cover and cook on low for 8 hours. When the cooking is done, mash the apples with a fork. Stir in the sugars, cinnamon, and cloves. Cover again and cook on low for 6 hours. If you prefer your apple butter to be velvety-smooth, blend with a handheld immersion blender, or in small batches in a traditional blender.

APPLE OATMEAL

serves 2

The Ingredients

1 cup rolled (not instant) oats (I used certified gluten-free oats)

1 green apple, cored and chopped

2 cups milk (I used soy milk; if using cow's milk, stick with 2 percent or lower fat content)

2 tablespoons brown sugar

1 tablespoon vanilla extract

pinch of kosher salt

ground cinnamon (optional garnish)

The Directions

Use a 2-quart slow cooker. Put the oats, chopped apple (I didn't peel it), and milk into the stoneware. Add the brown sugar, vanilla, and salt and mix to combine. Cover and cook on low for 2 to 3 hours, or on high for 1 to 2 hours. Check the consistency of the oats—some people like them chewy and some don't. Garnish with the cinnamon, if using. My oatmeal cooks perfectly on high for 1 hour, 15 minutes. It's creamy and milky, and the kids gobble it right up. I sometimes mix the ingredients in a bowl the night before, and then add them to the crock in the morning when I first wake up.

BAKED OATMEAL

serves 8

The Ingredients

    3 cups rolled (not instant) oats (I used certified gluten-free oats)

    1/2 cup brown sugar, firmly packed

    2 teaspoons ground cinnamon

    2 teaspoons baking powder

    1 teaspoon kosher salt

    2 tablespoons flax meal (optional)

    3/4 cup dried fruit

    1 cup milk

    4 tablespoons (1/2 stick) butter, melted

    2 teaspoons vanilla extract

    2 large eggs

The Directions

Use a 4-quart slow cooker. Put the dry ingredients into the stoneware, and add the dried fruit, milk, butter, vanilla, and eggs. Stir well to combine. Cover and cook on low for 3 to 5 hours, checking after 90 minutes. The oatmeal is done when the edges are brown and are beginning to crust, the center is set, and a knife inserted comes out clean. Let it sit in the cooling cooker for at least an hour before attempting to cut it. The longer you let it sit, the more set and brownie-like the pieces will be.

The Verdict

Baked oatmeal can be uber-healthy, or packed with sugar. I've cut the sugar and butter in half since I first started making it years ago. If you think your family will meet this with resistance, start with a full cup of brown sugar (no need to double the butter, there's plenty of moisture) and then cut sugar content back each time you make it. You can sneak in nuts (ground or whole), extra grains, fresh and dried fruit, and protein powder. The flavor is sweet, and it tastes like a huge oatmeal cookie. I like mine heated with morning coffee, Adam likes his crumbled in yogurt, and the kids enjoy munching on it throughout the day.

BREAKFAST RISOTTO
serves 4 to 5

The Ingredients
4 tablespoons (1/2 stick) butter
3 little apples (I used 2 green and 1 red)
1 1/2 cups Arborio rice
1 1/2 teaspoons ground cinnamon
1/8 teaspoon ground nutmeg
1/8 teaspoon ground cloves
1/4 teaspoon kosher salt
1/3 cup brown sugar, firmly packed
1 cup apple juice
3 cups milk (2 percent or lower in fat content)
dried cranberries or raisins, optional garnish

The Directions
Use a 4-quart slow cooker. Turn your cooker to high and add the butter so it can begin melting. Wash and cut up the apples (I didn't peel them). Set aside. Add the rice to the butter, and stir it around to coat it nicely. If the butter isn't completely melted, don't worry, mine wasn't either, and it didn't seem to make a difference. Add the apples, spices, and salt. Stir in the juice and milk. Cover and cook on high for 3 to 5 hours, or on low for 6 hours or so.

The Verdict
Oh my, this is delicious. The kids both had three small bowls, and I had more than I probably should have. It was very tasty. We added a touch more brown sugar at the table and sprinkled on some dried cranberries. The kids decided this was porridge and did a whole Bear and Goldilocks routine. My part was to sit on the couch and eat—good deal.

EGG, FETA, AND MUSHROOM
BREAKFAST CASSEROLE

serves 8

The Ingredients

1 pound sliced portabello mushrooms (or other "fancy" mushroom)
1 red bell pepper, chopped
1/2 tablespoon olive oil or butter
cooking spray
6 1/2 ounces feta cheese, in one piece
1 dozen large eggs
1/2 teaspoon black pepper

The Directions

Use a 4-quart slow cooker. Sauté the mushrooms and bell pepper in a large-ish frying pan over medium heat in a bit of olive oil or butter (I used butter) until they are wilted and tender. Spray the inside of your stoneware with cooking spray, and add the sautéed mushrooms, bell pepper, and any mushroom juice. Crumble in the entire block of feta cheese. In a large bowl, whisk the eggs with a fork. Add the pepper to the eggs and mix. Pour the eggs on top of the feta and veggies. Cover and cook on high for 2 to 4 hours, or until eggs have fully set and begun to brown on the top and pull away from the sides.

GRANOLA

serves 12

The Ingredients

5 cups rolled (not instant) oats (I used certified gluten-free oats)
1 tablespoon flaxseeds
1/4 cup slivered almonds
1/4 cup raw pumpkin seeds
1/4 cup raw sunflower seeds
1/4 cup unsweetened coconut
1/2 cup dried fruit (I used raisins and cranberries)
1/4 cup honey (see note below)
4 tablespoons (1/2 stick) butter, melted (see note below)
parchment paper

The Directions

Use a 4-quart slow cooker. Put all the dry ingredients into the stoneware. Add the honey and butter. Toss well.

Cover, but vent with a chopstick. Cook on high for 3 to 4 hours, stirring every so often. If you can smell the granola cooking, give it a stir. It will burn if you don't keep an eye on it. But it won't burn as quickly as it does in the oven! (Ask me how many batches of granola I've had to throw out after burning in the oven. Go ahead, ask. It's seven. I've burned at least seven batches in the oven, ugh.)

Cool the granola on a sheet of parchment paper. Eat with milk like cereal, warmed with milk like oatmeal, or as is. Store in an airtight container or in a ziplock freezer bag. Granola freezes well.

Note: If you use this amount of honey and butter, the granola will be cereal-like, and not trail mix–like. If you'd rather have the granola clump together in pieces, you'll need to use 3/4 cup of both the honey and butter.

HASH BROWN BREAKFAST CASSEROLE

serves 6 to 8

The Ingredients

cooking spray

1 (30-ounce) package of plain frozen hash brown (shredded) potatoes

12 large eggs, whisked

1 cup skim or fat-free milk

1 teaspoon kosher salt

1 teaspoon black pepper

1½ cups shredded cheddar cheese

4 cooked sausages, or leftover ham, diced (I used chicken and apple sausage)

½ onion, diced

1 green bell pepper, diced

The Directions

Use a 6-quart slow cooker. Spray the inside of your stoneware with cooking spray. Dump in the whole package of hash browns. Spread them out with your fingers to break up any clumps. In a mixing bowl, combine the eggs with the milk, salt and pepper, cheese, cut-up sausage, and diced vegetables. Pour everything on top of the hash browns. Cover and cook on low for 6 to 8 hours, or on high for 3 to 4 hours. The casserole is done when the eggs are fully cooked and the edges start to brown a bit. If you want the cheese to brown and get a bit crispy on the sides, cook it longer.

MEXICAN BREAKFAST CASSEROLE
serves 8

The Ingredients
cooking spray
corn tortillas (approximately 6 to 8)
8 large eggs
2 cups fat-free milk
2 cups shredded Mexican-blend cheese
1 (7-ounce) can green chiles, drained
1 red bell pepper, seeded and diced
1 tiny onion, diced
1 cup corn
1 cup sliced mushrooms (optional)
3/4 teaspoon kosher salt
1/2 teaspoon black pepper

The Directions
Use a 4-quart slow cooker. Spray the inside of your stoneware with cooking spray. Put a layer of corn tortillas on the bottom—you may have to tear some to make them fit nicely. In a very large mixing bowl, combine all of the other ingredients, and whisk together. Pour about one-half of the mixture into the stoneware, on top of the tortillas. Put in another layer of tortillas, and top with the remaining egg mixture. Top with another layer of corn tortillas. Cover and cook on low for 6 to 7 hours, or on high for 4 to 5 hours. If your slow cooker seals well (my 4-quart has a plastic lid, and a lot of condensation builds up), uncover 15 to 20 minutes before serving and cook on high to release condensation and to firm up the top a bit. You know your breakfast is done when the eggs are fully cooked and the edges have begun to brown, and the cheese gets a bit crispy on the sides.

The Verdict

I loved this. *Loved* it. The chiles were not spicy in the slightest, and Adam added salsa to his bowl. The kids picked out the "green stuff" but ate the rest just fine. I served this for dinner, and ate left-overs for breakfast and lunch for the next two days. If you have sausage or other meat you'd like to add, go for it, but omit the salt, and season to taste at the table. If you don't have corn tortillas in the house, or would prefer to go another way, you can pour the egg mixture on top of a bag of frozen hash browns (see p. 51).

OVERNIGHT BREAKFAST CASSEROLE

serves 6 to 8

The Ingredients

1 cup diced vegetables (optional)
1 cup potato, diced
1 cup diced sausage (I used chicken and apple)
6 large eggs
1 cup milk (2 percent or lower in fat content)
1½ cups shredded Mexican-blend cheese

The Directions

Use a 4-quart slow cooker. Put vegetables, if using, and diced potato (I didn't peel them) into the stoneware. Add the sausage. In a separate bowl, beat the eggs, milk, and cheese together, and pour on top of the other ingredients. Cover and cook on low for 8 hours, or on high for 4 hours. The casserole is finished when the eggs are fully cooked and the edges have begun to brown.

The Verdict

This tastes good, and cooks perfectly, but please note that eggs lose a bit of color when slow cooked. This is an easy meal to serve at an early morning breakfast, or to have available for overnight guests to serve themselves.

OVERNIGHT BREAKFAST POTATOES AND SAUSAGE

serves 8

The Ingredients

4 pounds red potatoes, cut in chunks
1 yellow onion, diced
2 tablespoons olive oil
$1/4$ teaspoon kosher salt
$1/4$ teaspoon black pepper
1 pound breakfast sausage (I used maple chicken sausage)

The Directions

Use a 4-quart slow cooker. Put the potatoes, onion, olive oil, salt, and pepper into your stoneware. Toss well to coat evenly. Lay the breakfast sausage on top. If you are using precooked sausage, feel free to slice it. Cover and cook on low for 6 to 8 hours.

The Verdict

I really like this breakfast. I don't peel the potatoes, so the skin comes off a bit, and creates a very rustic breakfast that feels like it should be eaten outdoors on a snow-capped mountain. I have served this at family brunches, and everyone enjoys the meal.

OVERNIGHT GRITS

serves 4

The Ingredients
  1 cup grits (not instant)
  5 cups water
  4 tablespoons (¹/₂ stick) butter
  ¹/₂ teaspoon kosher salt

The Directions
Use a 4-quart slow cooker. Combine all the ingredients. No need to melt the butter, just plop it in; it floats! Cover and cook on low for 6 to 8 hours. It takes 7 hours in my slow cooker. Stir well and top with desired toppings. (See below.)

The Verdict
These are wonderful—rich and creamy. The kids and I put a bit of shredded cheese on top, but my mom likes to stir in jam. Before trying this recipe, my knowledge of grits came from *My Cousin Vinny*. I now really like grits: they are good for you, supereasy to make, and are naturally gluten-free.

PANCAKES

serves 4 to 6

The Ingredients

    pancake mix (I used an 18-ounce gluten-free package)
    the rest of the ingredients needed to make the pancakes listed on the back of the package (I
        used a pancake and waffle mix, and needed to add 2 large eggs, soy milk, and canola oil. I used
        the whole package.)
    butter

The Directions

Use a 4-quart slow cooker. Mix the batter according to package directions, and pour it into the buttered stoneware. Cover completely, and cook on high for 2 hours, or until the pancake has browned on top, a knife comes out clean, and the edges have pulled away from the sides of the stoneware. Slice into wedges and remove with a spatula. Serve with butter, maple syrup, and jam.

The Verdict

This was an experiment—and it worked! My three-year-old had been begging me to make pancakes in the slow cooker and I put her off for months. (5$1/2$ months, actually. Oops.)

The one large pancake has the consistency of a scone, and tastes marvelous with melted butter and lots of syrup. I was happily surprised with how high it rose.

STRAWBERRY JAM

makes approximately 3 quarts

The Ingredients

    4 pounds fresh strawberries
    3 cups sugar
    2 (1.75-ounce) boxes pectin

The Directions

Use a 6-quart slow cooker. Keep a container of hand wipes nearby when making jam—the sticki-ness seems to spread throughout the house, especially if you cook with children. Wash all of the strawberries, and discard the stems. Quarter the berries and throw them into your stoneware. Use a potato masher to squish the strawberries and to create some liquid. We don't have a potato masher, so my three-year-old kitchen helper used the attachments from the hand mixer. Add the sugar and pectin and smash some more. Cover and cook on low for a hundred million years (10 to 12 hours). Let cool to room temperature, then pour into plastic or glass containers to store in the fridge or freezer.

YOGURT

serves 12

The Ingredients

8 cups (half-gallon) of whole milk (pasteurized and homogenized is fine, but do not use ultra-pasteurized)

1/2 cup store-bought natural, live/active culture plain yogurt

thick bath towel

1 (0.3-ounce) packet unflavored gelatin (optional)

1/2 cup nonfat dry milk (optional)

2 coffee filters

colander

frozen/fresh fruit for flavoring (optional)

1 (1.4-ounce) box instant pudding mix (optional)

The Directions

Use a 4-quart slow cooker. This takes a while, so make the yogurt on a day when you are home to monitor. Plug in your slow cooker and turn it to low. Add the milk. Cover and cook on low for 2½ hours. Unplug the cooker, leave the cover on, and let the yogurt sit for 3 hours.

When the time has passed, scoop out 2 cups of the warmish milk and put it in a bowl. Whisk in 1/2 cup of store-bought live/active culture yogurt. If desired, stir a packet of unflavored gelatin or some nonfat dry milk into your yogurt to help it thicken. Then dump the contents of the bowl back into the stoneware. Stir to combine. Put the lid back on the slow cooker. Keep it unplugged, and wrap a heavy bath towel all the way around the cooker for insulation. Go to bed, or let it sit for 8 hours.

In the morning, the yogurt will have thickened—it's not as thick as store-bought yogurt, but has the consistency of lowfat plain yogurt. Line colander with coffee filters, and pour in yogurt.

(C O N T I N U E D)

After a few hours, the whey will have separated (save the whey to use in other recipes!) and you'll be left with lovely yogurt. Stir in fresh or frozen fruit, if desired, or a packet of pudding mix.

Chill in a plastic container in the refrigerator. Your fresh yogurt will last 7 to 10 days. Save 1/2 cup as a starter to make a new batch.

The Verdict

Wowsers! This is awesome! I was completely astonished the next morning that the yogurt had thickened. I was so excited to feel the drag on the spoon—I scared the kids with my squealing. This recipe has been tried hundreds of times by readers of my Web site, and many like the thickness provided by the gelatin and/or nonfat dry milk. If your house gets rather chilly at nighttime, your yogurt will not set as well. My house was about 65°F.

BAKING

I was not aware of the ease of baking with the slow cooker before this challenge, and am annoyed at myself for not figuring it out earlier. I love that I can throw together a coffee cake or banana bread and leave for an hour or two to run errands instead of baby-sitting the oven. Although things can still burn in a slow cooker, the amount of wiggle room is much larger. It's okay to take a shower, answer the phone, or attend to a leaky diaper without worrying that your baked goods will be charred by the time you return to the kitchen. Do not try to bake on the low setting—stick to high.

FIVE-LAYER BROWNIES

serves 6

The Ingredients

4 tablespoons ($\frac{1}{2}$ stick) butter, melted

$\frac{1}{4}$ cup water

1 large egg

1 (16-ounce) package brownie mix (I used a gluten-free mix)

1 (14-ounce) can sweetened condensed milk

$\frac{1}{4}$ cup rolled (not instant) oats (make sure oats are certified gluten-free)

$\frac{1}{4}$ cup sweetened flaked coconut

$\frac{1}{4}$ cup chopped walnuts

The Directions

Use a 2-quart slow cooker. Put the melted butter into your crock, and add water, egg, and the package of brownie mix. Mix until none of the brownie powder is left dry; the batter will be quite thick. Pour the can of sweetened condensed milk over the top. Add the oats, then the coconut, then the walnuts. Cover, but prop the lid open with a chopstick or skewer, and cook on high for 2 to 4 hours. After 2 hours, test with a knife, and continue to check every 30 minutes until a knife inserted in the center comes out clean. Let stand with the lid off for 10 minutes before cutting.

The Verdict

This is one rich, satisfying, amazing dessert. And in our case, a rather tasty breakfast, too. I strongly recommend sticking with a small-size slow cooker, or your brownies will burn on the edges but remain gooey in the center.

BANANA BREAD

serves 8

The Ingredients

1½ cups all-purpose flour (I used a gluten-free baking mix)

1½ teaspoons baking powder (omit if baking mix includes it already)

¼ teaspoon baking soda

¼ teaspoon ground cinnamon

1 large egg, at room temperature

1 cup smashed bananas (about 2 large)

½ cup granulated sugar

¼ cup brown sugar, firmly packed

¼ cup canola oil

½ cup chopped walnuts (or chocolate chips!)

cooking spray

The Directions

Use an oval 6-quart slow cooker and a 9×5×3-inch metal or glass loaf pan. Combine all ingredients into a batter in a bowl with a handheld or stand mixer. Spray the loaf pan with the cooking spray, and pour in the batter. Place the pan inside your slow cooker. Do not add water. Put on the lid, but prop open with a chopstick or wooden spoon. Cook on high for 4 hours, or until a toothpick inserted in the center of the bread comes out clean. Carefully remove the hot pan from the stoneware and let cool before inverting, unmolding, and slicing the bread.

BLUEBERRY COFFEE CAKE

serves 8

The Ingredients

butter or cooking spray
2 cups biscuit mix (I used a gluten-free baking mix)
½ cup granulated sugar
½ cup brown sugar, firmly packed
1 teaspoon vanilla extract
10 tablespoons (⅔ cup) butter, melted
2 large eggs
1 cup sour cream
1 teaspoon ground cinnamon
½ cup frozen blueberries

The Directions

Use a 4-quart slow cooker. Butter the inside of your removable stoneware, or use cooking spray. Mix the biscuit mix, sugars, vanilla, butter, eggs, sour cream, and cinnamon in a bowl and carefully fold in the blueberries. Pour the batter into the slow cooker. Use a chopstick or wooden skewer to hold the lid ajar, and cook on high for 2 to 4 hours, or until a toothpick inserted in the center comes out clean.

COCONUT CAKE

serves 8

The Ingredients

1 box vanilla cake mix (Gluten-free cake mixes make a 1 layer cake. If you want a thicker, more
    traditional cake, use 2 boxes.)
ingredients the packaged cake mix tells you to use (butter, oil, eggs, etc.)
1 (14-ounce) can coconut milk
1 teaspoon coconut extract
cooking spray
2 tablespoons confectioners' sugar
$1/2$ cup sweetened shredded coconut
cream cheese frosting (optional)

The Directions

Use a 4-quart round slow cooker. Pour the dry cake mix into a mixing bowl. Follow the directions on
the box for the amount of eggs, butter, and oil to use. Instead of using milk or water for the required liquid, use the same amount of coconut milk. Make sure to shake the coconut milk can well
before opening. Add coconut milk and save the rest of the can; you'll need it later. Add the coconut
extract to the batter. Spray the stoneware with cooking spray, and pour in the batter. Cover and
cook on high for 2 to 4 hours, or until a toothpick inserted in the center comes out clean. I did not
vent the lid with a chopstick for this recipe, because I was interested in seeing if it would cook
without being vented. Our cake cooked perfectly in $2^{1/2}$ hours on high. If you see a lot of condensation on the lid, or if you'd prefer to vent, go for it. Your cake will take longer to cook, however.

    When fully cooked, mix $1/2$ cup of the reserved coconut milk with 2 tablespoons confectioners'
sugar. Poke holes in the hot cake with a skewer, and pour the sweetened coconut milk over the top
of the cake. If you are not going to frost the cake, sprinkle it with shredded coconut. If you are going

(CONTINUED)

to frost it, save the coconut for later. Let the cake cool to room temperature, then refrigerate for about an hour, or for as long as you can stand it. If you are going to frost the cake, do so now, and cover the top with shredded coconut. Serve the chilled cake right out of the stoneware.

The Verdict

I'm excited about this cake—it's now one of our family favorites. I made it on a busy weekend when we entertained houseguests. Everyone loved it. Cooking cake (especially a gluten-free cake) in the crock ensures a moist cake every time. I used a store-bought cake mix to save valuable flour mixing time, but if you have a favorite secret cake recipe, go ahead and use it.

CORNBREAD

serves 8

The Ingredients

1¼ cups all-purpose flour (I used a gluten-free baking mix)

¾ cup cornmeal

¼ cup sugar

2 teaspoons baking powder (do not use if your baking mix already has some included)

½ teaspoon kosher salt

1 cup milk (I used soy milk)

1 large egg, beaten

4 tablespoons (½ stick) butter, melted

cooking spray

The Directions

Use a 4-quart slow cooker. In a mixing bowl, combine the dry ingredients, and stir in the milk, egg, and butter. Coat your removable stoneware with cooking spray, and pour in the batter. Cover and cook on high for 2 to 4 hours, or until a toothpick inserted in the center comes out clean.

HONEY CAKE

serves 8

The Ingredients

cooking spray or butter

2½ cups all-purpose flour (I used a gluten-free baking mix, and *did* add the additional baking powder and soda, and would recommend you do so)

2 teaspoons baking powder

2 teaspoons ground cinnamon

½ teaspoon baking soda

½ teaspoon kosher salt

½ teaspoon ground cloves

1 cup sugar

3 large eggs, at room temperature

1 cup honey

1 cup canola oil

½ cup brewed coffee

¼ cup water

The Directions

Use a 4-quart round slow cooker. Coat the inside of your removable stoneware with cooking spray, or grease with butter, then flour (I used a bit of gluten-free baking mix). In a large mixing bowl, combine all of the dry ingredients, and then add the wet. Mix on high speed with a handheld or stand mixer for 2 minutes. Pour the batter into your prepared stoneware. Cover the cooker, but vent with a chopstick or the end of a wooden spoon. Cook on high for 2 hours, then check. When the cake begins to pull away from the sides of the crock, uncover and continue to cook on high, checking every 20 minutes. The cake will be moist, but a toothpick inserted in the center should come out clean.

The Verdict

This is delicious, but I burned it. It was cooking perfectly and had begun to pull from the sides, but I made the mistake of leaving to take the kids to swim lessons, and came home 45 minutes later to a horrible burning smell. The top and middle were okay, but the bottom and edges were not. Learn from my mistake, and don't wander off near the end of baking time.

PEANUT BUTTER BROWNIES

serves 8

The Ingredients

cooking spray
1 cup natural peanut butter
5 tablespoons butter, melted
1/2 cup sugar
1/2 cup all-purpose flour (I used a gluten-free baking mix)
1/4 teaspoon baking powder (do not add if mix already has some included)
2 large eggs
1 teaspoon vanilla extract
1/2 cup milk chocolate chips
1/2 cup white chocolate chips

The Directions

Use a 4-quart slow cooker. Spray the inside of your removable stoneware with cooking spray. In a mixing bowl, combine all the ingredients and mix with a handheld or stand mixer until a batter forms. Scrape the batter into the slow cooker. Cover with the lid, but prop open with a chopstick to release steam, or you'll end up with soggy brownies. Cook on high for 2 to 4 hours, or until the edges have browned and a knife inserted in the center comes out clean. My brownies looked finished at 2 hours, but I pushed it to 2 3/4 hours to see if the center would brown. It won't. Don't try.

PERFECT GLUTEN-FREE BREAD

serves 8

The Ingredients
cooking spray
1 box gluten-free bread mix (I like the 365 brand from Whole Foods)
the ingredients the box tells you to use: water, butter, eggs, enclosed yeast packet

The Directions
Use a 6-quart slow cooker and a 9×5×3-inch metal or glass loaf pan, or a 4-quart slow cooker, sprayed with cooking spray. Prepare the dough according to the instructions on the box for the oven method. Put the dough into the prepared loaf pan, or shape into a round ball directly into prepared 4-quart stoneware. Cover, but prop the lid ajar with a chopstick or wooden spoon. Cook on high for 2 to 5 hours. My loaves take about 3¾ hours. Remove from pan, and let cool before slicing.

The Verdict
If you aren't gluten-free, this might not mean as much to you as it does to me. When you go gluten-free, you miss bread—a lot. I've spent too much time and money trying to make gluten-free bread that doesn't stink, and I'm so pleased to have found the answer. The humidity of the slow cooker creates a perfect environment for the dough to rise slowly and bake evenly. If you are not gluten-free, you can bake frozen or homemade bread dough in the crock with similar results.

POUND CAKE

serves 12

The Ingredients

8 tablespoons (2 sticks) butter, melted
6 large eggs
1½ teaspoons vanilla extract
2 cups all-purpose flour (I used a gluten-free baking mix)
½ teaspoon cream of tartar
¼ teaspoon kosher salt
1 cup sugar
1 teaspoon ground nutmeg
cooking spray or butter

The Directions

Use a 2-quart slow cooker, or a large slow cooker with an oven-safe dish or 9×5×3-inch metal or glass loaf pan. Pour melted butter into a large mixing bowl. Whisk in the eggs and vanilla. Add the dry ingredients and mix with a handheld or stand mixer until the ingredients are well incorporated. Pour the batter into a greased 1- to 2-quart crock, or similar-sized oven-safe dish or pan.

Cover the cooker, but prop the lid open with a chopstick or wooden spoon, and cook on high for 2 to 4 hours, or until a toothpick inserted in the center comes out clean.

The Verdict

I ate all of this. Every last crumb. I have no idea what came over me, but I just kept "evening out" the edges until it was all gone. I really shouldn't make this unless we're having company—it's just way too good.

SIDE DISHES

RICE

I would not be able to entertain easily for holiday meals or dinner parties without my slow cookers. Or at least I would not be able to entertain without completely losing my mind. I love being able to line up two or three slow cookers on the countertop while Adam attends to the main course in the oven or outside on the barbecue. Having the side dishes taken care of allows me to visit with guests, rather than fussing in the kitchen.

ACORN SQUASH

BAKED POTATOES

BAKED SWEET POTATOES WITH CHILI, CUMIN, AND LIME

BROCCOLI CASSEROLE

BROCCOLI WITH TOASTED GARLIC AND HAZELNUTS

CANDIED SWEET POTATOES

COMPANY'S COMING POTATOES AU GRATIN

CORN ON THE COB

CORNBREAD STUFFING

CORN RISOTTO

CRANBERRY SAUCE

CREAMED SPINACH

CREAMY VEGETABLES

GARLIC BAKED POTATOES

GREEN BEAN CASSEROLE

HONEY AND CINNAMON GLAZED CARROTS

HONEY LENTILS

HORSERADISH SCALLOPED POTATOES

JALAPEÑO CORN PUDDING

MASHED POTATOES WITH SOUR CREAM AND CREAM CHEESE

PECAN-TOPPED BAKED SWEET POTATOES

RANCH VEGETABLES

RICE

RISOTTO

ROASTED CABBAGE AND POTATOES

ROASTED WINTER ROOT VEGETABLES

SEASONED POTATO WEDGES

SOUTHWESTERN SWEET POTATO AND CORN MEDLEY

STEWED TOMATOES

STUFFED ARTICHOKES

TRADITIONAL STUFFING

SWEET-AND-SOUR CARAMELIZED ONIONS

TOMATO CURRIED POTATOES

WALNUT AND SAGE POTATOES AU GRATIN

ACORN SQUASH

serves 2

The Ingredients

    1 acorn squash
    2 tablespoons butter
    2 tablespoons brown sugar
    2 teaspoons ground cinnamon
    4 pinches kosher salt

The Directions

Use a 4-quart slow cooker. Cut the squash in quarters, and scoop out the seeds and stringy pulp. Put 1/2 tablespoon butter and 1/2 tablespoon brown sugar into each quarter. Sprinkle 1/2 teaspoon cinnamon onto each brown sugar pile. Add a small pinch of salt to each quarter. Place the squash into your slow cooker. Cover and cook on low for 3 to 4 hours, or on high for about 2 hours. The squash is finished when it is fork-tender and peels away from the skin easily.

BAKED POTATOES
10 to 12 baked potatoes

The Ingredients
    10 to 12 baking potatoes
    aluminum foil

The Directions
Use a 6-quart slow cooker (10 to 12 potatoes should fit in a 6-quart cooker). Wash potatoes well, and dry. Use a fork to prick the skin of each potato. Wrap each individually in aluminum foil. Put the foil-wrapped potatoes into your stoneware. Do not add water. Cover and cook on low for about 10 hours, or on high for about 6. The potatoes are done when a knife inserts easily and the potato pulp is fluffy.

The Verdict
Prior to this challenge, I didn't know how to bake potatoes in a slow cooker, and was completely blown away at the simplicity and how incredible the potatoes tasted. They tasted more "potatoey" somehow, and were a huge hit. If you prefer to cook without aluminum foil, note that potato skin will be slightly more moist. I was able to fit 11 potatoes in a 6-quart oval slow cooker.

BAKED SWEET POTATOES WITH CHILI, CUMIN, AND LIME

The Ingredients

4 large sweet potatoes, scrubbed
1 teaspoon ground cumin
1 teaspoon chili powder
1 teaspoon kosher salt
aluminum foil
2 to 4 limes

The Directions

Use a 6-quart slow cooker. Scrub the potatoes with a vegetable brush under cold running water. Pat dry. Use a fork to prick the skin of each potato. In a small bowl, combine the dry spices and salt. Lay out a length of foil large enough to wrap 1 sweet potato. Put the potato in the middle of it, and rub one fourth of the spice mixture on the potato skin (it's okay if some falls off). Wrap the foil all around the potato. Repeat for each of your potatoes. Put them all into the slow cooker and cover. Do not add water. Cook on high for 6 to 8 hours. The potatoes are done when a knife inserts easily and the potato flesh is fluffy. Squeeze lime juice on each before serving.

BROCCOLI CASSEROLE
serves 6

The Ingredients
$1/3$ cup flour (I used a gluten-free baking mix)
$1/4$ teaspoon kosher salt
$1/4$ teaspoon black pepper
$1/2$ teaspoon dry mustard
2 pounds fresh broccoli florets
1 cup shredded "fancy" white cheese (fontina, provolone, Swiss, or Gouda)
1 cup low-fat or fat-free milk
1 cup chicken or vegetable broth
$1/2$ cup shredded Parmesan cheese

The Directions
Use a 4-quart slow cooker. In a large mixing bowl, combine the flour, salt, pepper, and dry mustard. Toss the broccoli in the mixture. Dump everything into your slow cooker. Cover with 1 cup shredded cheese. Add the milk and broth. Top with Parmesan cheese. Cover and cook on low for about 4 to 6 hours, or on high for 2 to 4 hours. The casserole is done when the broccoli reaches the desired tenderness and begins to brown a bit around the edges.

The Verdict
My kids loved this, they just *loved* it. They both ate 3 little plastic bowls for dinner and had more the next day for lunch.

BROCCOLI WITH TOASTED GARLIC
AND HAZELNUTS

serves 8

The Ingredients

2 pounds broccoli florets
1 head garlic, cloves peeled (about 12 cloves)
$\frac{1}{2}$ teaspoon kosher salt
$\frac{1}{2}$ teaspoon black pepper
1 cup large raw hazelnuts
2 tablespoons olive oil
juice of 2 lemons

The Directions

Use a 4-quart slow cooker. Wash and trim broccoli, and add to the stoneware. Add the garlic, salt, and pepper. Add the hazelnuts, olive oil, and lemon juice. Toss with two wooden spoons. Cover and cook on high for 2 hours, or on low for about 4 hours. This is done when the broccoli has reached the desired tenderness. The broccoli tastes quite lemony, while the garlic adds a great depth of flavor, and the hazelnuts provide a nutty burst.

CANDIED SWEET POTATOES

serves 12

The Ingredients

1 tablespoon butter

7 to 8 sweet potatoes or yams, peeled and sliced $1/2$-inch thick

$1/2$ cup orange juice

2 teaspoons vanilla extract

1 teaspoon ground cinnamon

$1/2$ cup brown sugar, firmly packed

$1/4$ teaspoon kosher salt

$1/2$ cup mini marshmallows

The Directions

Use a 4-quart slow cooker. Rub butter on the inside bottom and sides of your removable stoneware. Put the sweet potatoes inside. Add the orange juice, vanilla, cinnamon, brown sugar, and salt. Toss to coat. Cover and cook on low for 6 to 7 hours, or on high for 3 to 4 hours. When the sweet potatoes have reached the desired tenderness, scoop into an oven-safe serving dish, and top with the marshmallows. Broil in the oven for 3 to 5 minutes, or until the marshmallows have begun to brown.

COMPANY'S COMING POTATOES AU GRATIN

serves 10 to 12

The Ingredients

6 brown potatoes, such as Idaho or Russet, peeled and sliced in $1/4$-inch-thick pieces
2 parsnips (they look like big white carrots)
1 white onion, diced
12 tablespoons ($1^{1}/_{2}$ sticks) butter
6 tablespoons flour (I used a gluten-free baking mix)
$3^{1}/_{2}$ cups heavy cream
2 teaspoons dried thyme
4 teaspoons dry mustard
2 teaspoons kosher salt
1 teaspoon black pepper
2 cups shredded cheddar cheese
1 green onion (optional garnish)

The Directions

Use a 6-quart slow cooker. Put the potatoes, parsnips, and onion into your slow cooker, and set aside. Melt the butter in a saucepan over medium heat and add flour to create a roux. Stir continuously while slowly adding cream and thyme, mustard, salt, and pepper. Pour the cream and butter mixture over the potatoes, parsnips, and onion. Toss gently with a large spoon. Cook on low for 8 to 9 hours, or on high for 4 to 5 hours. My potatoes were still a bit crunchy at 4 hours. Before serving, stir in the cheddar cheese until it disappears. Garnish with green onion if you are feeling fancy.

The Verdict

This would be an excellent take-along for potlucks, or holiday dinners when you want to bring something but aren't sure exactly what. These potatoes would make Paula Deen proud—they're full of cream and butter and all that's good and yummy.

CORN ON THE COB

serves 6

The Ingredients

6 ears fresh corn, shucked and cleaned
aluminum foil

The Directions

Use a 6-quart oval slow cooker. Wrap each ear of corn completely in a piece of aluminum foil, twisting the ends to seal. Pile the corn into the crock. Do not add water. Cover and cook on high for 2 hours, or until corn is tender. I prefer my corn to have a nice crunch, and 2 hours was perfect in my cooker.

The Verdict

Slow-cooked corn on the cob is super easy, and doesn't take long to cook. I prefer cooking corn this way, because it doesn't heat up the kitchen or leave it steamy. The corn steams in its own juices and is cooked to absolute perfection.

CORNBREAD STUFFING

serves 10

The Ingredients

8×8-inch pan of baked cornbread (I used a gluten-free cornbread mix)

4 slices of toasted bread (I used brown rice bread)

2 cups chopped celery

1 large yellow onion, diced

1 tablespoon poultry seasoning

1/2 teaspoon kosher salt

1/2 teaspoon black pepper

4 tablespoons (1/2 stick) butter, melted

3 large eggs, beaten

2 cups chicken or vegetable broth, plus additional 1/4 cup, if needed

The Directions

Use a 6-quart slow cooker. Bake the cornbread according to package directions. Cut cornbread and sliced bread into cubes and bake at 300°F for 20 to 30 minutes, or until toasty.

While the breads are toasting, put the celery and onion into the stoneware. Add the poultry seasoning, salt, and pepper. Mix the melted butter together with the eggs. Stir into veggies and seasonings. Toss cubes of bread well with the ingredients in the stoneware. Pour in broth, and stir gently to combine. Cook on high for 2 hours. This can be on warm successfully for another 2 hours. If you'd like a more moist dressing, add up to 1/4 cup of broth before serving.

CORN RISOTTO

serves 4

The Ingredients

1 tablespoon olive oil

1¼ cups Arborio rice

1 teaspoon onion flakes

4 garlic cloves, chopped

1 teaspoon kosher salt

¼ to ½ teaspoon cayenne pepper, depending on taste

1 (16-ounce) package frozen corn

4 cups chicken or vegetable broth

1 tablespoon butter

¼ cup heavy cream

½ cup shredded Parmesan cheese

The Directions

Use a 4-quart slow cooker. Put the olive oil into the stoneware, and swirl the rice and the onion flakes around in it. Add the chopped garlic, salt, and cayenne. Stir in the frozen corn and broth. Drop in the butter. Cover and cook on high for about 2 hours, checking every 45 minutes or so. Your risotto is done when the liquid has been absorbed and the rice is tender. Unplug the cooker, and add the cream and Parmesan. Cover for 5 minutes, or until the cheese melts completely. Serve immediately.

The Verdict

Creamy and delicious. Making risotto is usually quite a pain (or so I've been told—I haven't actually made any on the stovetop because after reading the directions, I needed a nap), but it's quite easy in the slow cooker. You plug it in and turn it on. The kids said it was like corn oatmeal, and they're right—it kind of is.

CRANBERRY SAUCE

serves 12

The Ingredients

    12 ounces cranberries (fresh or frozen)
    ½ cup freshly squeezed orange juice
    ½ cup water
    ½ cup brown sugar, firmly packed
    ½ cup granulated sugar
    ¼ teaspoon ground cinnamon

The Directions

Use a 2-quart slow cooker. Rinse the cranberries and put them into your stoneware. Add the orange juice, water, sugars, and cinnamon. Stir. (There will be an awful lot of liquid, the cranberries will float, and you'll wonder how on earth this could possibly turn into cranberry sauce.) Cover and cook on high for 3 hours, stirring every hour.

When the skin on the cranberries has softened, the cranberries will "pop" when pushed with a spoon against the side of the crock. Smoosh all cranberries and stir well. Continue to heat enough for it to be warm throughout. Take the lid off and heat on high for another 30 to 45 minutes (your house will smell wonderful!). Serve or store in the refrigerator. This can be made up to 2 days in advance.

The Verdict

I've made cranberry sauce exactly once before, for a kindergarten class. We followed the directions on the bag, and it came out quite bitter. No one (except one little boy who enjoyed shocking his classmates with odd behavior) would eat it. But this? I liked this! It's way better than the canned stuff.

CREAMED SPINACH

serves 4

The Ingredients

1 cup milk (use 2 percent or lower to prevent curdling)
1/2 cup cream cheese
1/4 cup shredded mozzarella cheese
1/4 cup shredded Parmesan cheese
2 tablespoons butter
1/2 teaspoon ground nutmeg
2 (6-ounce) bags baby spinach

The Directions

Use a 4-quart slow cooker. Put the milk, cream cheese, shredded cheeses, butter, and nutmeg into the stoneware. Cover and cook on low 3 to 4 hours, stirring a few times to keep the cheeses from clumping. When everything is hot and melted, add baby spinach. You'll need to push it down to make it fit. Cover again and cook on high for 30 minutes. Stir. The spinach will wilt and incorporate into the sauce.

CREAMY VEGETABLES
serves 8

The Ingredients
12 ounces broccoli
16 ounces green beans
¼ cup sour cream
½ cup shredded cheddar cheese
¼ cup shredded Parmesan cheese
2 tablespoons butter
½ teaspoon black pepper
½ teaspoon garam masala (my new favorite spice!)
2 tablespoons water
2 whole jalapeño peppers (don't chop them up, just place them nicely on top)

The Directions
Use a 6-quart slow cooker. Wash and trim vegetables, and dump them into the crock. Add the sour cream, cheeses, butter, spices, and water. Lay the jalapeño peppers on top. Do not stir. Cover and cook on low for 3 to 4 hours, or until vegetables have reached the desired tenderness.

The Verdict
We shared these vegetables with friends, and all of the adults really enjoyed them—the kids weren't interested. I was happy that the sauce was creamy and flavorful without needing to make a roux beforehand. The jalapeño peppers provide a nice smoky heat without being overwhelming.

GARLIC BAKED POTATOES

serves 4

The Ingredients

4 big brown baking potatoes, such as Idaho
8 garlic cloves, thinly sliced
$1/4$ teaspoon kosher salt
$1/4$ teaspoon black pepper
2 tablespoons melted butter
2 tablespoons olive oil
sour cream, for garnish

The Directions

Use a 6-quart slow cooker. Wash the potatoes and pat dry. Do not peel. Carefully slice each potato crosswise every $1/2$ inch, almost but not all the way through. The potato should start to separate a bit like an accordion. Shove as many garlic slices as you can into each potato slit. Nestle the potatoes into your crock. I used an oval 6-quart, and the potatoes didn't fit all the way down to the bottom—they were kind of nestled against each other. It doesn't seem to matter. Sprinkle with salt and pepper. Combine the melted butter with olive oil and drizzle over the top of each potato, trying to get it into the garlic-filled slits, if you can. Cover and cook on low for about 6 hours, or on high for 2 to 4 hours. The potatoes are done when a knife inserts easily and the potato pulp is fluffy. Top with sour cream.

GREEN BEAN CASSEROLE

serves 6

The Ingredients

1 pound green beans

1 (10.75-ounce) can cream of mushroom soup, or 2 cups of homemade (see page 191)

1 teaspoon gluten-free soy sauce

1/2 cup skim milk (omit if using homemade soup)

1/3 cup shredded Parmesan cheese

1 cup French-fried onions, or 2 cups General Mills Gluten-Free Rice Chex Cereal, smashed and mixed with 1/2 teaspoon onion powder

The Directions

Use a 4-quart slow cooker. Wash and trim green beans in even lengths, and put into the cooker. Add the soup, soy sauce, and milk (if using). Toss the beans gently to coat. Sprinkle on the Parmesan cheese, and add the French-fried onions or homemade topping. Cover and cook on low for 4 to 6 hours, high for 2 to 3 hours, or until the green beans have reached the desired tenderness.

The Verdict

I don't like canned green beans. My grandma makes a three-bean salad that uses canned green beans, and I like that. But that's it. I liked this much better than the traditional canned green bean casserole—the green beans still had a crunch, even after being slow cooked. The topping wasn't as crisp as it would have been if I had used the French-fried onions, but the flavor was there, and the cheese added a nice salty touch. The homemade cream of mushroom rocks, and was quite flavorful.

HONEY AND CINNAMON GLAZED CARROTS

serves 6 to 8

The Ingredients

4 cups baby carrots
1/2 cup freshly squeezed orange juice
2 tablespoons honey
1 tablespoon butter
1/4 teaspoon ground ginger
1/2 teaspoon ground cinnamon
1/4 teaspoon kosher salt
1/4 teaspoon black pepper

The Directions

Use a 4-quart slow cooker. Throw everything together in your cooker, and stir to distribute the juice, honey, and spices. Cover and cook on low for 6 hours, or on high for about 4 hours. These carrots are sweet without being *too* sweet, and will please young children.

HONEY LENTILS

serves 6

The Ingredients

1½ cups brown lentils

3 cups water

½ red onion, diced

½ cup shredded carrot

1 (15-ounce) can garbanzo beans, drained and rinsed

1 teaspoon dry mustard

1 teaspoon kosher salt

¼ teaspoon ground ginger

2 tablespoons gluten-free soy sauce

⅓ cup honey (plus 1 tablespoon if needed)

1 dried bay leaf, or 2 fresh

The Directions

Use a 4-quart slow cooker. Rinse the lentils until the water runs clear, and put into the stoneware. Add the water, onion, and carrot. Pour in the garbanzo beans and stir in the dry mustard, salt, and ginger. Add the soy sauce and honey. Stir again to combine. Float the bay leaf (or leaves) on top. Cover and cook on low for 6 to 8 hours, or on high for 3 to 5 hours. Taste. If desired, stir in the extra tablespoon of honey. Serve with white or brown rice if you're a vegetarian, or a rib-eye steak if you're not.

HORSERADISH SCALLOPED POTATOES

serves 6

The Ingredients

3 pounds red potatoes, such as Red Bliss, washed and sliced (no need to peel, yay!)
cooking spray
2 cups heavy cream
3 tablespoons prepared horseradish (regular, not the creamy kind; I went with extra hot)
$1/4$ teaspoon ground nutmeg
1 teaspoon kosher salt
$1/2$ teaspoon black pepper
$1/2$ cup shredded Parmesan cheese (optional)

The Directions

Use a 4-quart slow cooker. Scrub the potatoes well and cut into $1/4$-inch slices. Layer into a removable stoneware you've sprayed with cooking spray. In a mixing bowl, combine the heavy cream, horseradish, nutmeg, salt, and pepper. Pour over the top of potatoes. Stir. Cover and cook on low for 6 to 8 hours, high for 4 hours, or until the potatoes are fork-tender. Garnish with shredded Parmesan.

The Verdict

Delicious! The kids surprised me and each had two bowls. The horseradish provides a bit of fun flavor that is not spicy as much as it is different and interesting. These are heavy; I'd say that this could serve 6 grownups as a side dish, yet Adam and I ate them as a main course—and then we went for a run.

JALAPEÑO CORN PUDDING

serves 6

The Ingredients

cooking spray
2 tablespoons unsalted butter, melted
1 cup milk (2 percent or lower)
2 large eggs
½ teaspoon kosher salt
2 tablespoons sugar
2 tablespoons flour (I used a gluten-free baking mix)
1 teaspoon baking powder (omit if using baking mix that has it included)
2 cups frozen or fresh corn kernels (I used frozen: 1 cup regular corn and 1 cup roasted)
½ cup shredded sharp cheddar cheese
2 tablespoons jalapeño pepper slices, chopped

The Directions

Use a 4-quart slow cooker. Spray the inside of your stoneware with cooking spray. Add the butter, milk, eggs, salt, sugar, flour, and baking powder. Whisk ingredients together. Stir in corn kernels, cheese, and chopped jalapeños. Cover and cook on low for 3 to 5 hours. The corn pudding is done when the edges brown and begin to pull from the sides, and the center is set. Remove the lid for 20 to 30 minutes when the pudding is set, and continue to cook on low to get rid of any condensation. This dish would be a welcome addition to a holiday dinner or potluck supper.

MASHED POTATOES WITH
SOUR CREAM AND CREAM CHEESE

serves 8

The Ingredients

5 pounds red potatoes, such as Red Bliss

1/2 cup water, reserved from boiling the potatoes

1 chicken bouillon cube

1 (8-ounce) block cream cheese, at room temperature (I used light)

1 cup sour cream (I used light)

1 tablespoon dried parsley

1 teaspoon garlic powder

The Directions

Use a 6-quart slow cooker. Wash and peel potatoes, leaving the skin on some if desired. Cut the potatoes into quarters to speed up the boiling time. Put the potatoes into a large pot and cover completely with water. Bring to a rapid boil on the stovetop for 10 to 20 minutes, or until the potatoes are fork-tender.

Scoop out 1/2 cup of the water from the pot; add the bouillon cube to the reserved water. Drain the potatoes, and return them to the pot.

Put cream cheese into the pot with the hot potatoes. Add the sour cream. Pour in bouillon-water along with the parsley flakes and garlic powder. Mash with a potato masher.

After mashing well, scoop the potatoes out of the pot and place into your slow cooker. Cook on high for 2 hours, or on low for 4. These can be kept on warm indefinitely.

(CONTINUED)

The Verdict

Psst. Make these potatoes. You won't be sorry. My kids seemed to have thought that they were spicy (makes no sense whatsoever) and weren't thrilled with the bits of skin I left on (I like a bit of skin, but apparently the kids find it highly offensive). I proudly served these potatoes on Thanksgiving, and everyone loved them. Although I only used the slow cooker to keep the potatoes warm, readers on my Web site felt strongly that I should include this recipe; the potatoes are delicious.

PECAN-TOPPED BAKED SWEET POTATOES

serves 6

The Ingredients

4 sweet potatoes, peeled and cut into 1/4-inch slices
3/4 cup brown sugar, firmly packed
1 (16-ounce) can whole-berry cranberry sauce
1 teaspoon vanilla extract
1 cup nonfat evaporated milk
4 tablespoons (1/2 stick) butter, cubed
1 cup chopped pecans
1/4 teaspoon kosher salt

The Directions

Use a 4-quart slow cooker. Stagger-stack sweet potatoes in your slow cooker. Cover with the brown sugar. Squish the cranberry sauce all over the top. Mix the vanilla with the milk, and pour on top. Dot with the butter. Sprinkle with the chopped pecans and salt. Cover and cook on low for 5 to 6 hours, or on high for 3 to 4 hours. This is done when the sweet potatoes have reached the desired tenderness. We like ours pretty squishy. Unplug the cooker and uncover. Let sit for 15 minutes before cutting. This is a wonderful addition to the holiday table.

RANCH VEGETABLES

serves 6

The Ingredients

5 cups fresh vegetables (I used broccoli, bell peppers, and tomatoes, and wished we had carrots and squash on hand)

1 to 2 (0.4-ounce) packets dry ranch dressing mix

3 tablespoons water

The Directions

Use a 4-quart slow cooker. Wash and trim all the vegetables, and add to the crock. Sprinkle in the ranch dressing packet(s). Toss the vegetables to coat. Add the water. Cover and cook on low 2 to 5 hours, or until the vegetables have reached the desired tenderness.

The Verdict

This is a simple way to have steamed, flavorful vegetables as an accompaniment to your main dish. My kids both really like broccoli, and they like ranch dressing. The taste is mild, it isn't dripping in flavor. If you prefer to mask the vegetables completely, you might want 2 packets of dressing mix.

RICE

serves 4

The Ingredients

1 tablespoon butter
1 cup white basmati rice (that's what I use, but I've heard other varieties work well, too)
2 cups water
pinch of kosher salt

The Directions

Use a 4-quart slow cooker. Rub the butter on the inside of the stoneware. Pour in the rice. Stir in the water and salt. Cover and cook on high for 2 to 3 hours, checking every 45 minutes or so. My rice cooked in 2 hours, 15 minutes.

The Verdict

I wanted to see if I could use the slow cooker as a rice cooker. Now I know I can. The end result was fluffy, lovely rice we had with some takeout—I felt like we needed some takeout.

RISOTTO

serves 6

The Ingredients

5 garlic cloves, chopped

1/4 cup olive oil

1 1/4 cup raw Arborio rice

1 teaspoon dried onion flakes

1 teaspoon kosher salt

1/4 teaspoon black pepper

3 3/4 cups chicken or vegetable broth

1/4 cup dry white wine

2/3 cup shredded Parmesan cheese

The Directions

Use a 4-quart slow cooker. Sauté the garlic with the olive oil in a saucepan over medium heat until the garlic softens. If you skip this step, the garlic will remain crunchy in your risotto. Scrape the garlic and remaining oil into your slow cooker.

Add the uncooked Arborio rice and toss. Add the seasonings, and pour in the broth and white wine. Stir to combine. Cover and cook on high for 2 to 4 hours, or until rice is tender. It took 2 1/2 hours for my rice to be completely tender.

Stir in shredded Parmesan cheese, and let the risotto stand with the lid off for 15 minutes before serving. The finished texture will be creamy and porridge-like.

The Verdict

This is such an easy way to make risotto, and it tastes delicious. The garlic was too much for the kids, but Adam and I couldn't get enough. I love that risotto works so well when slow cooked and doesn't need to be babysat.

ROASTED CABBAGE AND POTATOES

serves 12

The Ingredients

    2 pounds tri-colored potatoes, cut in chunks
    1 small head cabbage
    10 to 12 whole garlic cloves (about 1 head)
    1/4 cup olive oil
    1 teaspoon kosher salt
    1/2 teaspoon black pepper
    2 tablespoons balsamic vinegar

The Directions

Use a 6-quart slow cooker. Put the chunked (I didn't peel them) potatoes into the stoneware. Cut the cabbage into wedges—no need to separate the leaves. Peel the garlic, and add the whole cloves. Toss the vegetables with the olive oil, salt, pepper, and balsamic vinegar. Cover and cook on low for 4 to 6 hours, or on high for 3 hours. The vegetables are done when the potatoes reach the desired tenderness. The cabbage on the edge of the stoneware will caramelize and get a bit crispy. This is a good thing.

The Verdict

It's no secret to my family that I don't like corned beef. I also don't like boiled vegetables. I tolerate them out of respect to whomever prepared the meal, but it's just not my thing. I happily ate three platefuls of these slow-cooked vegetables for St. Patrick's Day. They were perfect—not soggy—and didn't taste like salty meat.

ROASTED WINTER ROOT VEGETABLES

serves 12

The Ingredients

2 pounds carrots
2 pounds rutabagas
2 pounds parsnips
1/2 cup chopped fresh parsley
3 tablespoons olive oil
1 teaspoon dried basil
1 teaspoon kosher salt
1 teaspoon black pepper

The Directions

Use a 6-quart slow cooker. Peel the vegetables, and cut them into 2-inch chunks. I'm usually a huge fan of the baby carrot (because of laziness), but wanted a more rugged look for this dish. If you would like to use baby carrots, go for it, but don't cut them. Put all the vegetables into your stoneware, and add the parsley, olive oil, basil, salt, and pepper. Toss with your hands to fully coat. Cover and cook on low for 8 hours, or on high for 4 to 5 hours. The vegetables are done when they have reached the desired tenderness.

The Verdict

I love the ease of roasting vegetables in the slow cooker. Not only do they taste marvelous, I would have needed to make quite a few batches in the oven for this much food and would have risked burning them (I am no good with the oven!), but in this case, I put the veggies on in the morning and was out for most of the day. The kids picked out a few carrots, but found them to be spicy.

SEASONED POTATO WEDGES

serves 8

The Ingredients

12 brown baking potatoes, such as Idaho or Russet
1 tablespoon seasoned salt
1 teaspoon dried basil
1/4 to 1/2 teaspoon chipotle chili powder
cooking spray

The Directions

Use a 6-quart slow cooker. Scrub the potatoes well with a vegetable brush (this is a great job for children) under cold running water. Slice the potatoes into long wedges; no need to peel. In a large bowl, toss the potatoes with the seasoned salt, basil, and chipotle chili powder to taste. Spray the inside of your stoneware with cooking spray, and add the seasoned potatoes. Cook on high for 4 to 6 hours, discarding accumulated liquid after 2 hours. Drain again before serving. The potatoes are done when they have reached the desired tenderness.

The Verdict

This was our contribution to a family barbecue. These are remarkably similar to oven-baked French fries. The wedges weren't overly moist, and the ones on the side of the crock even got a bit of a crust on the skin—an unexpected happy bonus. I was happy not to have to heat up the oven on an unseasonably warm day, and I was able to fit more food into the slow cooker than would have fit on baking sheets.

SOUTHWESTERN SWEET POTATO AND CORN MEDLEY

serves 6

The Ingredients

3 medium sweet potatoes, peeled and chopped in 1-inch chunks
1/4 cup diced onion
1 (15-ounce) can corn, drained
3 tablespoons chopped fresh basil leaves
1 teaspoon chili powder
1/2 teaspoon kosher salt
juice of 2 limes

The Directions

Use a 4-quart slow cooker. Plop the sweet potato into the stoneware. Add the onion, corn, and basil. Sprinkle in the chili powder and salt. Add the lime juice, and then toss everything so the seasoning is dispersed somewhat evenly. Cover and cook on low for 5 hours, or on high for 3 to 4 hours. The medley is done when the potatoes have reached the desired tenderness.

The Verdict

This is a great side dish. The flavors dance in your mouth—which is a saying I never, ever thought I'd ever say (or type), but there you go. That's what they do. This is simple to put together, but looks great on a buffet table.

STEWED TOMATOES

serves 6

The Ingredients
2 (28-ounce) cans whole plum tomatoes (I used the kind seasoned with basil)
1/4 teaspoon black pepper
1 1/2 cups shredded Parmesan cheese
5 tablespoons butter, sliced

The Directions
Use a 4-quart slow cooker. Drain the tomatoes—use a strainer, you don't want any liquid. Plop the tomatoes into your stoneware. Sprinkle on the black pepper, and add the Parmesan cheese. Slice the butter into thin squares, and dot them over the top. Cover and cook on high for 4 hours, or until the cheese bubbles and begins to brown.

The Verdict
These tomatoes are delicious. They are warm, flavorful, and a bit spicy. Stewed tomatoes get a really bad rap, probably because they look like baby animal hearts, but I promise they taste amazing.

STUFFED ARTICHOKES

serves 2

The Ingredients

2 large fresh artichokes
1 tablespoon olive oil
$1/3$ cup shredded Parmesan cheese
$1/4$ cup bread crumbs (I used crumbs from a loaf of brown rice bread)
juice of 1 lemon
$1/2$ cup water

The Directions

Use a 6-quart slow cooker, so the 'chokes can sit side-by-side. Peel and chop up the stem from the artichokes (be careful—I cut myself) and mix the stem pieces with the other ingredients in a small bowl; the mixture should be moist and gooey. Use a knife to cut off the top of each artichoke, and use kitchen shears to cut off the pointy leaf tips. Spread the leaves slightly and fill the spaces with the breading mixture. Nestle the artichokes into the slow cooker, and add $1/2$ cup of water. Cover and cook on low for 4 to 5 hours, or on high for 2 to 4 hours. My artichokes took 4 hours to cook on high. This is a much fancier way to eat artichokes than the traditional way of dipping leaves into mayonnaise.

TRADITIONAL STUFFING

serves 8

The Ingredients

1 large yellow onion, diced
1/4 cup chopped fresh parsley
1 cup diced celery
1 cup tart apple, peeled and diced
1 tablespoon ground sage
1 teaspoon ground marjoram
1/2 teaspoon dried savory
1/2 teaspoon dried thyme
1 teaspoon kosher salt
1 teaspoon black pepper
4 tablespoons (1/2 stick) butter, melted
1 loaf bread, cubed and lightly toasted in the oven (I used brown rice bread)
1 1/2 cups chicken or vegetable broth, plus additional 1/4 cup, if needed

The Directions

Use a 6-quart slow cooker. Put the onion, parsley, celery, and apple into the stoneware. Add the seasonings, and the melted butter. Stir well. Add the bread cubes, and toss to combine. When the bread is coated nicely, pour in the broth. Cover and cook on high for 2 hours. When done, the bread will have browned a bit on the top and around the edges, and it will be hot throughout. Your stuffing can stay on warm for up to 2 hours before serving. Stir. If you'd like more moisture, add up to 1/4 cup of additional broth.

The Verdict

I am so excited I can hardly stop squirming. This tastes amazing and is absolutely wonderful—it tastes just like a store-bought mix. I'm thrilled with this recipe.

SWEET-AND-SOUR CARAMELIZED ONIONS

serves 8

The Ingredients

2 pounds tiny onions (sometimes called boiling or pearl onions)
2 tablespoons balsamic vinegar
1/4 teaspoon kosher salt
1/4 teaspoon black pepper
1 tablespoon sugar
1 tablespoon butter
1/2 cup raisins
1/4 cup pine nuts

The Directions

Use a 4-quart slow cooker. Cut the tops and bottoms off all the onions and peel away the papery skin. It takes a while to peel the onions, so make sure you're in a good mood. Put the onions into the stoneware and toss with the balsamic vinegar, salt, pepper, and sugar. Add the pat of butter and raisins. Toss in the pine nuts. Cover and cook on high for 2 to 4 hours, stirring approximately every 45 minutes. I cooked ours for a bit more than 3 hours, and stirred 3 times. You want the onions to get brown and caramelized. The raisins plump and take on the vinegar flavor while slow cooked, and the pine nuts add a bit of crunch and a smoky flavor.

TOMATO CURRIED POTATOES
serves 6

The Ingredients
7 red potatoes, such as Red Bliss
1 tablespoon olive oil
2 teaspoons paprika
2 teaspoons curry powder
2 teaspoons chili powder
2 teaspoons sugar
1/2 teaspoon kosher salt
1 (14.5-ounce) can diced tomatoes, drained

The Directions
Use a 4-quart slow cooker. The night before cooking, wash and chop the potatoes in 1-inch chunks (I didn't peel them), and put into a ziplock freezer bag. Add the olive oil, paprika, curry, chili powder, sugar, and salt. Shake well. Add the drained tomatoes, and toss again. Refrigerate overnight.

In the morning, pour the contents of the bag into the slow cooker, and turn it on. Cover and cook on low for 6 to 7 hours, or on high for about 4 hours. The potatoes are done when they are fork-tender.

The Verdict
These smelled delicious while they were cooking, and cooked beautifully in the slow cooker. The potatoes were tender and the skin browned nicely. The first time I made these potatoes, I didn't add enough spice, nor did I refrigerate them overnight. If you have the time, marinating overnight is really the way to go for maximum flavor.

WALNUT AND SAGE POTATOES AU GRATIN

serves 12

The Ingredients

cooking spray

6 medium brown potatoes (such as Idaho or Russet), peeled and sliced 1/4 inch thick

1/2 yellow onion, diced

1/4 cup flour (I used a gluten-free baking mix)

4 tablespoons (1/2 stick) butter, melted

2 1/2 cups heavy cream or half-and-half

1 teaspoon kosher salt

1/4 teaspoon black pepper

1 teaspoon dried sage

1 1/2 cups shredded Gruyère cheese

1 1/2 cups walnut halves

The Directions

Use a 4-quart slow cooker. Spray the inside of the removable stoneware with cooking spray. Put the sliced potatoes and onion into the stoneware. In a mixing bowl, whisk the flour into the melted butter. Add the cream and salt, pepper, and sage to the bowl, mixing well. Pour the cream mixture into the slow cooker, and toss with the potatoes and onion. Sprinkle the shredded Gruyère and the walnut halves on the top. Cover and cook on high for 3 to 5 hours, or until potatoes are tender.

The Verdict

Adam made this because I was recovering from the flu, and he wasn't. It's quite annoying how he never gets sick. I barked orders from a fetal position on the couch. I never got to eat any, but sent it off with my parents for Easter dinner, and everybody reported back "thumbs up."

BEANS

The awesome thing about beans (actually, there are a few awesome things) is that they are cheap, full of fiber, and supereasy to prepare in the slow cooker. Dried beans can be purchased in bulk, cooked ahead, and frozen (Dried Beans, page 126) for all recipes that call for canned beans.

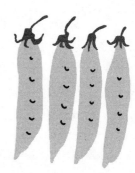

SIXTEEN-BEAN SOUP

serves 10

The Ingredients

1 (16-ounce) bag Sixteen-Bean Soup Mix (discard flavor packet)
water
1 onion, chopped
3 garlic cloves, minced
2 teaspoons of your favorite spice blend (I used McCormick's roasting rub)
1 (14-ounce) can Italian-style diced tomatoes with their liquid
kosher salt
shredded Parmesan cheese (optional garnish)

The Directions

Use a 6-quart slow cooker. Sort and rinse beans, and add to the stoneware. Add enough water to completely cover the beans, plus an additional 3 inches or so. If you want more broth, use more water. If you want it thick and beany, use less. Add the onion, garlic, spice blend, and the entire can of tomatoes. Cover and cook on low 8 to 10 hours, or until the beans are tender; soup tastes better the longer you cook it. Add salt to taste. Since water was used instead of broth, your soup will require quite a bit. Garnish with Parmesan cheese, if desired. For additional bulk, you can add some sliced sausage. My family ate this for lunch for a good week.

BAKED BEANS WITH APPLES AND JALAPEÑO

serves 6

The Ingredients

1 pound bacon (I used turkey bacon)
2 (15-ounce) cans white kidney beans, drained and rinsed
1 or 2 canned jalapeño peppers, diced
1/2 yellow onion, diced
2 Granny Smith apples, cored and diced (no need to peel)
3 garlic cloves, minced
1 teaspoon dry mustard
1/2 teaspoon kosher salt
1 tablespoon brown sugar
1/4 cup ketchup
2 tablespoons molasses
1/3 cup apple juice

The Directions

Use a 4-quart slow cooker. Put 2 pieces of bacon into the bottom of your stoneware. Layer in the beans, jalapeño, onion, apples, and garlic. Sprinkle the mustard, salt, and sugar on top. Add ketchup, molasses, and apple juice. Stir gently to combine. Add 2 more pieces of bacon. Cover and cook on low for 6 to 8 hours, or on high for 4 hours. Cook the remaining slices of bacon on the stovetop and crumble over the top before serving.

BARBECUE BEANS AND WEENIES

serves 8 to 10

The Ingredients

    4 (15-ounce) cans kidney beans, drained and rinsed
    4 cups barbecue sauce
    2 (16-ounce) packages Lil' Smokies, or cut-up hot dogs

The Directions

Use a 6-quart slow cooker. Pour the canned beans into the stoneware, and add the barbecue sauce. Toss in the Lil' Smokies and stir to combine. Cover and cook on low for 4 to 5 hours, or high for 2 to 3 hours.

The Verdict

This is a kid crowd-pleaser. If you want to use dried kidney beans, it's important to soak the beans for at least 5 hours in fresh water, then parboil them on the stove for 10 to 15 minutes. Then cook in fresh water in the slow cooker until the beans are soft and squishy. Add barbecue sauce and Lil' Smokies. Kidney and red beans have the potential to be toxic if not thoroughly cooked.

BASIC CHILI
serves 6 to 8

The Ingredients
    1 pound ground meat, browned and drained
    4 (15-ounce) cans kidney beans, drained and rinsed
    1 onion, diced
    8 garlic cloves, minced
    1 large (29-ounce) can diced tomatoes, drained
    1 (15-ounce) can tomato sauce
    1 tablespoon Tabasco sauce
    3 tablespoons chili powder
    2 teaspoons ground cumin
    1 teaspoon kosher salt
    1 teaspoon black pepper
    2 whole jalapeño peppers

The Directions
Use a 6-quart slow cooker. Put the browned meat into your cooker. Add the beans, onion, garlic, tomatoes, tomato sauce, Tabasco, chili powder, cumin, and salt and pepper. Stir to combine. Do not cut the jalapeños, but instead place them on top of the beans and meat for a nice mellow smoky heat. Cover and cook on low for 8 to 10 hours, or on high for 4 to 6 hours.

The Verdict
This is a nice basic chili recipe. It has a kick, but isn't too spicy for (my) kids. If you prefer to use dried beans, please soak overnight and parboil them for 10 to 15 minutes and cook in fresh water. When soft, drain liquid and add chili ingredients. Kidney beans can carry a toxin if they aren't thoroughly cooked.

BEAN STEW

serves 8

The Ingredients

1 potato, chopped
1 yellow bell pepper, seeded and chopped
4 green onions, chopped
3 vine-ripened tomatoes, chopped
1 cup baby carrots
handful of broccoli (or other veggies you have lying around)
1 (15-ounce) can kidney beans, drained and rinsed
1 (15-ounce) can black beans, drained and rinsed
2 cups dried split peas
6 cups chicken or vegetable broth
1 teaspoon dried dill
1 teaspoon kosher salt
$1/2$ teaspoon black pepper
$1^1/_2$ teaspoons paprika

The Directions

Use a 6-quart slow cooker. Put the chopped vegetables into the stoneware, and add the beans. Pour in the split peas. Cover with the broth, and stir in the dill, salt, pepper, and paprika. Cook on low for 7 to 9 hours, or on high for 4 to 5 hours; soup tastes better the longer it cooks.

The Verdict

I had read somewhere that dill enhanced soups and stews and it was an under-utilized spice, so I threw some in. I think the dill works. It tastes too strong if the broth isn't salty enough, so make sure to add salt and pepper to taste.

BEANS AND RICE

serves 4 to 6

The Ingredients

1 tablespoon olive oil
1 cup raw rice
1 (15-ounce) can pinto beans, drained
1 (15-ounce) can black beans, drained
1 (14.5-ounce) can diced tomatoes, liquid reserved
1/2 tablespoon dried onion flakes, or 1/2 cup diced fresh onion
1/2 teaspoon kosher salt
1 teaspoon Italian seasoning
water

The Directions

Use a 4-quart slow cooker. Put the olive oil into the stoneware, and add the rice. Swirl the rice around to coat it nicely with the oil. Add the beans. Drain the tomatoes, but reserve the liquid in a 2-cup measuring cup. Add the tomatoes, onion, salt, and Italian seasoning. Add water to the tomato liquid to make a full 2 cups. Pour the liquid into the slow cooker. Stir. Cover and cook on low for 6 hours, or on high for 3 to 4 hours. Your dinner is complete when the rice is tender. Brown or wild rice will take longer to soften than white rice.

The Verdict

I made this on a day I had two extra kids in the house, and couldn't go to the store. I pulled stuff from the pantry to make a "free" meal for dinner. Slow cooking rocks for pulling together dinner when you don't have a meal planned. Some of my best soups and meat dishes have come from dumping in a can of this, or adding some herb that I had never before used. We all enjoyed our dinner.

BLACK BEAN SOUP

Serves 6

The Ingredients

1½ cups chopped vegetables (I used carrots, celery, broccoli, cauliflower)

3 (15-ounce) cans black beans (opt for low sodium if available)

1 (15-ounce) can Italian stewed tomatoes

2 cups chicken or vegetable broth

2 tablespoons taco sauce (great use for those fast food packets!)

shredded cheese, sour cream, avocado slices (optional garnishes)

The Directions

Use a 4-quart slow cooker. Finely chop vegetables with a food processor or blender and put into your slow cooker. Put contents of all cans on top, no need to drain. Add broth and taco sauce. Mix. Cover and cook on low for 8 to 10 hours, or on high for 5 to 6 hours; the longer the better. Before serving, use a handheld immersion blender to soupify. Serve with shredded cheese, a dollop of sour cream, and some sliced avocado, if desired. I loved this and ate it daily for lunch for six days in a row.

BLACK-EYED PEA SOUP

serves 8

The Ingredients

1 pound dried black-eyed peas, soaked overnight
1 yellow onion, diced
1 cup diced carrots
1 cup diced celery
1 pound spicy sausage, sliced
6 cups chicken broth
4 garlic cloves, chopped
1/2 teaspoon Italian seasoning
1 teaspoon kosher salt
1/2 teaspoon black pepper
Tabasco sauce

The Directions

Use a 6-quart slow cooker. Put the drained beans into the stoneware with the vegetables and the sliced sausage. Pour in the broth, and stir in the garlic, Italian seasoning, salt, and pepper. Cover and cook on low for 8 hours, or on high for about 6 hours. Before serving, use a handheld immersion blender to smoosh up some of the beans. Don't blend too much—just enough to get the broth thicker and creamy-looking. Ladle the soup into bowls, and add Tabasco sauce to taste.

The Verdict

This tastes amazing. I am so glad I made this; my first rendezvous with black-eyed peas didn't go so well, and I was scared. They are earthier than other beans and make a fantastic soup base. My brother and sister-in-law liked this soup a lot, too. Eating black-eyed peas on New Year's Day is said to bring prosperity and good luck—two things everyone can use.

BOSTON BAKED BEANS

serves 8 as a side dish

The Ingredients

3 (15-ounce) cans kidney beans
2 medium onions, finely chopped
½ cup brown sugar, firmly packed
¼ cup molasses
⅓ cup ketchup
1 teaspoon kosher salt
1½ teaspoons dry mustard
¼ teaspoon black pepper
½ pound of bacon, or equivalent (I used chicken and apple sausage)

The Directions

Use a 2-quart slow cooker. Drain and rinse the beans, and put into the stoneware. Add the onion and the brown sugar. Pour in the molasses and ketchup. Add the salt, mustard, and pepper. Stir to combine. Lay slices of uncooked bacon over the top of the beans, or slice chicken and apple sausage and lay it over the top. Cover and cook on low for 5 to 7 hours, or on high for about 4 hours. Remove the bacon, dice it, and return it to the pot, or stir in the sliced chicken and apple sausage.

CLEAN-OUT-THE-PANTRY CHILI

serves 6

The Ingredients

3 (15-ounce) cans beans, drained and rinsed (I used garbanzo, white kidney, and black beans)
2 (6-ounce) cans tomato paste
1 tablespoon Italian seasoning
1 yellow onion, chopped
2 garlic cloves, chopped
2 cups chicken broth
2 tablespoons sliced jalapeño peppers from a jar or can

The Directions

Use a 6-quart slow cooker. Dump beans into the crock. Add all the rest of the stuff—there aren't any rules here (except to recycle the cans). Cook on low for 8 to 10 hours.

The Verdict

One of the reasons I love slow cooking so much is that you don't really need to follow a recipe—many times I just start opening cans and clean out the fridge and create a delicious meal without trying. This is one of those meals. We had too much food in the house for me to feel comfortable buying more, so I dug through what we had on hand, threw it in the pot, held my breath, and hoped for the best. I was quite happy with the results.

DRIED BEANS, A TUTORIAL

yields approximately 45 ounces, or the same as 3 (15-ounce) cans

The Ingredients

1 pound dried beans

water

The Directions

Use a 6-quart or larger slow cooker. Pour the bag of dried beans into a colander and rinse under cold running water. If you see any beans that have broken in half, or skins that float to the surface, get rid of them. Also pick out any beans that look shriveled or weird. Dump all the beans into your slow cooker, and add enough water to cover the beans completely by an additional 2 inches. Cover. Do not turn on the cooker. Let the beans soak for at least 6 hours, or overnight. If you live in a very warm area, and the slow cooker won't be in a room that is climate-controlled, put the stoneware in the fridge. You don't want bacteria to have the opportunity to grow.

In the morning, drain the beans in a colander, discard the soaking water, and rinse the beans. The water will be bean-colored. If you are using kidney or red beans, you must boil the beans in fresh water on the stovetop for at least 10 minutes. Kidney and red beans can harbor a toxin and are unsafe if undercooked.

Put the beans back into your slow cooker and cover with enough fresh water to completely cover the beans by an extra 2 or 3 inches. Cover and cook on low for 8 to 10 hours, or until bite-tender. Don't worry if the water hasn't all been absorbed. Drain the beans.

When cool, put 1²/₃ cups of beans into storage containers or freezer bags (you're adding this amount because you aren't adding filler-liquid like cans have). The beans will store nicely in the refrigerator for 1 week, or in the freezer for 6 months. Use as you would canned beans in your favorite recipe.

The Verdict

One bag of dried black beans costs $1.89 at our fancy-pants grocery store, and $.89 at our local produce stand. One can of organic black beans at Trader Joe's costs $.99. One pound dried beans = 3 (15-ounce) cans of beans. This means that even if you buy expensive dried beans, you will save some money making them at home yourself. I like knowing what is in my food, and I like the idea that we can save money and reduce garbage by using dried beans.

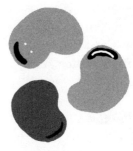

LIMA BEAN CASSEROLE CASSOULET

serves 8

The Ingredients

1 pound dried lima beans, soaked overnight

1 cup water

2 cups diced ham, or turkey ham

1 (28-ounce) can diced tomatoes, with their juices

1 medium yellow onion, chopped

3 garlic cloves, smashed and chopped

$1/2$ teaspoon black pepper

1 tablespoon dry mustard

The Directions

Use a 4-quart slow cooker. Soak the lima beans overnight in a generous amount of cold water. They will expand, so use enough water to cover them by at least 4 inches. In the morning, drain and rinse the beans, and pour into your slow cooker. Add a fresh cup of water. Dice up the ham and strew over the top. Add the tomatoes, onion, and garlic. Stir in the pepper and mustard. Cover and cook on low for 6 to 8 hours.

The Verdict

I "Googled" casserole versus cassoulet and didn't get a very good answer, which is why this recipe is named twice.

I really was astonished at how much I liked these lima beans. I'm pretty sure I annoyed Adam by going on and on (and on some more) about how amazing it was that lima beans could taste so good. Don't be scared to try lima beans; I got the kids to try them, and my parents both had two bowls.

MOROCCAN LENTIL SOUP

serves 8

The Ingredients

1/2 cup chopped celery

1/2 cup chopped carrots

1 onion, chopped

1 (15-ounce) can garbanzo beans, drained and rinsed

1 (15-ounce) can pinto beans, drained and rinsed

1 cup dried lentils

1 (1-inch) piece fresh ginger, peeled and grated

2 garlic cloves, smashed and chopped

1 1/2 teaspoons garam masala

1/2 teaspoon cayenne pepper

1/2 teaspoon ground cumin

1/4 teaspoon ground nutmeg

1/4 teaspoon ground cinnamon

4 cups vegetable broth

1 (28-ounce) can diced tomatoes and their juices

The Directions

Use a 6-quart slow cooker. Chop the vegetables and add to the stoneware. If you are rushed in the morning, consider chopping the vegetables the night before—it took me longer than I wanted it to.

Drain and rinse the beans and add to the mix. Add the dried lentils. Add the ginger, garlic, and spices. Stir in the vegetable broth and the entire can of tomatoes. Cover and cook on low for 8 to 10 hours.

(CONTINUED)

Before serving, use a handheld immersion blender and pulse to blend some of the vegetables and beans together. This isn't necessary, but it really improves the texture of the soup and melds the flavors nicely. This makes a lot of food, but freezes and reheats well. I've discovered soups, stews, and chili dishes sometimes taste better as leftovers than they do on cooking day.

PRESIDENTIAL CHILI

serves 6 to 8

The Ingredients

1 pound lean ground meat (I used ground chicken)

5 to 6 medium tomatoes, chopped (include seeds and all)

4 garlic cloves, chopped

1 large onion, chopped

1 green bell pepper, chopped

1 (15-ounce) can kidney beans (and goop!)

1 teaspoon ground cumin

1 teaspoon dried oregano

1 teaspoon dried basil

1 teaspoon ground turmeric

1 to 2 teaspoons chili powder (start with 1, add more to taste before serving)

1 teaspoon kosher salt

3 tablespoons red wine vinegar

The Directions

Use a 6-quart slow cooker. I used ground chicken and opted not to brown the meat. If you use a fattier type of meat, or enjoy browning meat, go ahead and do so. Otherwise, crumble the meat directly into your stoneware. Add the tomatoes, garlic, onion, and bell pepper. Add the beans. Stir in all of the herbs and spices, the salt, and the red wine vinegar. Cover and cook on low for 7 to 9 hours, or on high for 4 to 5 hours. Season to taste with a bit more salt and chili powder, if desired. President Obama serves his chili over rice.

(CONTINUED)

The Verdict

Good Morning America posted Barack Obama's "secret family recipe" on their Web site during the 2008 presidential campaign, and I was eager to modify it for the slow cooker.

This chili isn't hot and spicy, which makes it suitable for all ages. The kids gladly ate this, and not once complained about spice—a complaint that is quite common at our dinner table.

REFRIED BEANS

serves 10

The Ingredients

 2 cups of dried pinto beans, sorted
 2 teaspoons ground cumin
 1 teaspoon ground coriander
 1½ yellow onions
 1½ red onions
 10 whole garlic cloves
 butter, olive oil, or lard (optional)

The Directions

Use a 4-quart slow cooker. You need to soak the beans overnight to soften them, and to help release gas. Rinse the beans well in a colander, and pour into your slow cooker. Add enough water so that the beans are fully immersed, with an additional 2 to 3 inches of water on top. Put the lid on the slow cooker. Do not turn on the cooker.

In the morning, drain and rinse the beans under cold running water. Put them back in the crock with enough clean water to cover the beans with about 1 inch of water. Stir in the cumin and coriander. Peel and cut the onions in half, and put them in, too. Peel all of the garlic and toss it in whole. Cover and cook on low for 8 to 10 hours, or until the beans are tender.

Fish out the onions and garlic cloves. If you want to keep some of the garlic in for flavor, you may; it's your choice. If the beans are soft and you still have a bit of liquid left, carefully drain, saving a little liquid to help with the smooshing and for added flavor. Use a potato masher, or handheld mixer, to mash the beans.

(CONTINUED)

Now you have two options. You can just start using the beans (the way I did, because I'm pretty darn lazy), or you can scoop hunks of smooshed beans out of the crock and fry them on the stovetop with a bit of butter, olive oil, or lard. No salt was added, so you'll need to season to taste. I was able to make four freezer containers to pull out for lunches and snacks. This is a very cost-effective way to make refried beans.

TACO SOUP

serves 12

The Ingredients

1 pound ground turkey or beef, browned and drained

1 medium onion, chopped

2 (15-ounce) cans kidney beans

2 (15-ounce) cans pinto beans

2 (15-ounce) cans corn with their juices

1 (28-ounce) can diced tomatoes with their juices

1 (14-ounce) can tomatoes with chiles (Rotel), with their juices

1 packet taco seasoning

1 packet ranch dressing mix

sour cream and cheddar cheese, for garnish

The Directions

Use at least a 6-quart slow cooker. There are a lot of cans here; recycle and make Al Gore happy.

Put the meat and onion into the slow cooker. Drain and rinse beans, and add to the cooker. Add the corn and tomatoes. Stir in contents of the seasoning packets. Cover and cook on low for 8 hours, or on high for 4 hours. Ladle into bowls.

Add a handful of cheddar cheese and a dollop of sour cream to each bowl before eating.

The Verdict

This is the dish that made me fall in love with my slow cooker a hundred million years ago. I can't estimate how often I've made this, but each time I'm thrilled with the ease in preparation and the finished result. I've proudly served this soup at birthday parties and potlucks. The leftovers make fantastic burrito filling.

WHITE CHILI

serves 6

The Ingredients

1 (16-ounce) bag frozen white corn
2 (15-ounce) cans white beans
1 (4-ounce) can green chiles
1/2 white onion, chopped
2 garlic cloves, minced
1 cup vegetable or chicken broth
juice of 1 lemon
1 1/2 teaspoons ground cumin
1/2 teaspoon Italian seasoning
salt and pepper
shredded mozzarella cheese (optional)

The Directions

Use a 6-quart slow cooker. Dump everything in. Seriously—you need to chop the onion and garlic, but the rest of the stuff can just go right in. You don't need to drain the beans or the chiles. Cover and cook on low for 8 to 9 hours, or on high for 4 to 6 hours.

Ladle the chili into bowls, garnish with shredded mozzarella if desired, and serve with corn-bread. This is more soup-y than chili-y, and since the corn floats while the beans sink, you need to dig to the bottom of the bowl to make sure you get beans in each bite.

WHITE BEAN AND APPLE CHILI

serves 6 to 8

The Ingredients

3 tablespoons butter

2 (15-ounce) cans of white beans, drained and rinsed

1 onion, chopped

2 green apples, cut in tiny chunks (no need to peel)

3 garlic cloves, minced

2 teaspoons chili powder

1/2 teaspoon dried thyme

1 teaspoon ground cumin

1/4 teaspoon kosher salt

1/4 teaspoon black pepper

3 cups chicken or vegetable broth

1/2 cup plain nonfat yogurt

1/2 cup shredded sharp cheddar cheese (optional)

The Directions

Use a 5-quart slow cooker. Put the butter into the stoneware. Dump in the beans. Add the onion and apple. Add the garlic, chili powder, thyme, cumin, salt, and pepper, and pour in broth. Stir in the yogurt. Cover and cook on low for 8 hours, or on high for 4 to 5 hours. The chili is done when the onion has softened and the flavors have melded. Stir in cheddar cheese before serving, if using. These beans pair wonderfully with cornbread.

The Verdict

This is a creamy, lightish chili that doesn't taste at all like there is fruit in it, but it isn't so light that you walk away from the table hungry. You might want to sprinkle some Tabasco on top, or add more chili powder to the grown-up portions. This was mild enough for the kids to eat.

WHITE BEAN AND SAUSAGE SOUP

serves 6

The Ingredients

1 (15-ounce) can white kidney beans, drained
1 (15-ounce) can garbanzo beans, drained
2 cups chopped fresh vegetables (I had broccoli, carrots, asparagus on hand)
1/2 yellow onion, chopped
2 to 4 spicy chicken or turkey sausages
1 teaspoon dried thyme
1/4 cup raw long-grain rice
4 cups chicken broth
Parmesan cheese (optional garnish)

The Directions

Use a 6-quart slow cooker. Pour the drained beans into the stoneware, and add the vegetables. Slice the sausage, and add. I chose to use two spicy turkey sausages—if you would like your soup to have a kick, use more than two. Two just kind of gives flavor without spice. Add the thyme, rice, and broth. Cook on low for 6 to 9 hours, or on high for 4 to 5 hours. The soup is done when it's heated through and the vegetables are tender, but it's not going to hurt anything to cook it longer and give the flavors more time to meld. Garnish with Parmesan cheese, if desired, before serving.

PASTA & CASSEROLES

$\mathcal{G}$etting the proportions right to cook rice or pasta to perfection in the slow cooker is tricky. The following meals are those which "made the cut"—and have become not only family favorites, but favorites on my Web site. Making casseroles is a fantastic way to use up leftover food in your refrigerator or pantry, and is a great way to stretch meat from a previously slow-cooked roast or chicken.

AUTUMN SAUSAGE CASSEROLE

serves 4

The Ingredients

3 cups cooked long-grain rice (I used white basmati)
1 pound sausage, sliced (I used chicken with artichoke and garlic)
1 yellow onion, chopped
1 large or 2 small apples, chopped (no need to peel)
1/2 cup chopped carrots
1/2 cup raisins
1 tablespoon brown sugar
1 tablespoon dried parsley flakes
1/2 teaspoon ground allspice
1/2 teaspoon ground cinnamon
1/8 to 1/4 teaspoon black pepper
1/3 cup chicken broth or water (I used water)

The Directions

Use a 4-quart slow cooker. Put the rice into the stoneware crock, and add the sliced sausage. If you are going to use uncooked sausage, I'd recommend browning it on the stovetop, and then draining excess fat before adding it to the slow cooker. Add the onion, apple, carrots, raisins, brown sugar, parsley, allspice, cinnamon, and pepper. Pour in the broth or water. Stir to combine. Cover and cook on low for 5 to 7 hours, or on high for 3 to 4 hours. You're really only heating it through, and allowing the vegetables to soften. This will not stick together like a gloppy casserole; it has the consistency of fried rice. Use bowls when serving rather than plates. We decided that eating this felt exactly like eating a bowl full of Fall. The spices are spot-on, and taste comforting and hearty.

BAKED SPINACH AND CHEESE NOODLES

serves 6

The Ingredients

2 tablespoons butter

$\frac{1}{3}$ cup flour (I used a gluten-free baking mix)

$2\frac{1}{2}$ cups milk (2 percent or lower in fat content)

1 (15-ounce) container ricotta cheese

1 (10-ounce) package frozen spinach (chopped or leaf, your choice), thawed and drained

1 red bell pepper, seeded and chopped

3 tablespoons Dijon mustard

$\frac{1}{4}$ teaspoon ground nutmeg

1 teaspoon kosher salt

$\frac{1}{2}$ teaspoon black pepper

1 (16-ounce) package of uncooked noodles (I used brown rice penne)

$\frac{1}{4}$ cup shredded Parmesan cheese

cooking spray

The Directions

Use a 4-quart slow cooker. Melt the butter in a large saucepan, and whisk in the flour. Add the milk, ricotta cheese, drained spinach, bell pepper, mustard, nutmeg, salt, and black pepper. Set aside.

Spray the inside of your crock with cooking spray, and dump in uncooked noodles. Pour in the milk and spinach mixture. Top with the Parmesan cheese. Cover and cook on high for 2 to 4 hours, or until the noodles are tender. I really like the hint of nutmeg in this meal.

BARBECUED CHICKEN AND CORNBREAD CASSEROLE

serves 6

The Ingredients

cooking spray

1 pound cooked chicken, cubed or shredded

1 small sweet potato, peeled and cut in 1-inch chunks

1 cup frozen or fresh corn

1 red onion, diced

1 (18-ounce) bottle of your favorite barbecue sauce

1/4 cup hot water

THE CORNBREAD TOPPING

3/4 cup cornmeal

1 1/4 cups of flour (I used a gluten-free baking mix)

1 cup milk

1/4 cup sugar

1 large egg

1 teaspoon baking powder (don't add if using a baking mix that has some already)

The Directions

Use a 4-quart slow cooker. Spray the inside of your stoneware with cooking spray. Add the chicken and sweet potato to the crock. Add the corn and onion. Empty the contents of the barbecue sauce bottle into the crock, then add 1/4 cup of hot water to the bottle, shake, and pour in. Mix well with a spoon.

In a mixing bowl, mix together cornbread topping with a fork. Spread onto the chicken mixture. Cover and cook on low for 6 to 8 hours, or until the cornbread has browned, and starts to pull away from the sides.

The Verdict

Barbecue and cornbread pair just as well as peanut butter and jelly. The cornbread cooked perfectly in the slow cooker, even though I didn't vent the lid at all. We all really enjoyed this meal.

BUFFALO CHICKEN LASAGNA

serves 8

The Ingredients

4 cooked boneless, skinless chicken breast halves, chopped
1 (26-ounce) jar pasta sauce
1 cup buffalo wing sauce
8 to 10 uncooked traditional lasagna noodles (I used gluten-free)
1 (15-ounce) container ricotta cheese
3 red, yellow, or orange bell peppers, chopped
2 cups shredded cheese (I used a mozzarella and cheddar blend)
½ cup blue cheese crumbles
¼ cup water

The Directions

Use a 6-quart slow cooker. In a mixing bowl, combine the chicken, pasta sauce, and buffalo wing sauce. Ladle a big spoonful of the sauce into the bottom of your stoneware. Cover with a layer of uncooked lasagna noodles. You'll have to break them to get a proper fit. Add a smear of ricotta cheese to the top of the noodles. Add a layer of bell pepper, and top with some shredded cheese. Repeat the layers until you run out of ingredients. Add the blue cheese crumbles. Put the water into your empty pasta sauce jar and shake. Pour the liquid over the top of the entire lasagna. Cover and cook on low for 6 to 7 hours, or on high for 4 to 5 hours. When the cooking time is complete, unplug the crock and take off the lid. Let the lasagna sit for 20 minutes before cutting.

The Verdict

Delicious. Quite tasty, with a mild buffalo tang that is noticeable, but not overwhelming. The kids picked out the chicken and ate crumbles of blue cheese. This is a dish that is in our regular meal rotation, and what I prepared on *Good Morning America*.

CABBAGE ROLLS

serves 6

The Ingredients

12 large cabbage leaves

1 pound lean ground turkey

$1/2$ cup raw brown rice

1 large egg

1 envelope onion soup mix

$1/3$ cup shredded Parmesan cheese

1 (8-ounce) can tomato sauce

3 cups tomato juice

The Directions

Use a 6-quart slow cooker. Separate 12 cabbage leaves from a head of cabbage. Steam lightly by placing them into a covered casserole dish with a few tablespoons of water. Cook on high for 2 minutes in the microwave. Set aside to cool slightly.

In a mixing bowl, combine the ground turkey, raw rice, egg, onion soup mix, cheese, and tomato sauce. Mix well—the mixture will be like a gloppy meatloaf. Scoop about one-third cup of the mixture into each cabbage leaf and roll or fold. Put the stuffed cabbage leaves into the bottom of your cooker, seam side down. Pour tomato juice over the top; it's okay if the cabbage rolls aren't fully submerged. Cover and cook on low for 6 to 8 hours, or until meat is cooked through and rice is tender.

The Verdict

Cabbage was invented for cabbage rolls. And for hiding babies. Or is it for growing babies? Or for growing dolls with huge heads? I honestly was not expecting to like cabbage rolls, but I really did. Adam and I both ate three, and happily gobbled the leftovers for lunch. The children had boxed macaroni and cheese, and then played dolls for hours.

CHICKEN AND BROWN RICE CASSEROLE

serves 6

The Ingredients

1½ cups chicken broth

1½ cups milk (stick with 2 percent or lower in fat content; I used soy milk)

¾ cup flour (I used a gluten-free baking mix)

cooking spray

1½ cups raw brown rice

½ teaspoon onion powder

¼ teaspoon black pepper

¼ teaspoon paprika

1 small yellow onion, diced

8 ounces sliced mushrooms

4 to 5 boneless, skinless chicken thighs

kosher salt

The Directions

Use a 4-quart slow cooker. Combine the chicken broth and ½ cup milk in a saucepan and heat over medium heat on the stovetop. In a separate bowl, whisk the remaining 1 cup of milk with ¾ cup flour. When the broth and milk have begun to boil (it will be quick; don't wander off!), reduce the heat, and slowly stir in the milk and flour mixture. When everything is fully incorporated, set the saucepan aside to cool.

Spray the inside of your stoneware with cooking spray. Add the rice and seasonings. Add the onion and mushrooms. Stir in the broth, flour, and milk mixture. The rice will turn a bit red from the paprika. Lay the chicken pieces on top. Cover and cook on high for 4 hours, or low for about 8 hours. When you take the lid off the slow cooker, stir the rice. If the rice is fully cooked and you have extra liquid, keep the lid off for about 15 minutes. The liquid will absorb quickly. Season with salt to taste.

The Verdict

I was happy with the way that this turned out—chicken and rice casserole was one of the first things I learned how to cook as a newlywed, yet I always managed to burn the edges.

The brown rice held up nicely in the slow cooker, and had good flavor. The kids ate their chicken separate from the rice.

CHICKEN POTPIE

serves 4 to 6

The Ingredients

THE FILLING

cooking spray

2 uncooked skinless chicken thighs or breast halves, chopped in bite-size chunks

1/2 cup chopped carrots

1/2 cup frozen corn

1/2 cup frozen peas

1/2 teaspoon dried marjoram

1/2 teaspoon dried thyme

1/2 teaspoon celery seed

1 teaspoon onion powder

1 (10.75-ounce) can cream-of-something soup (or see homemade alternatives, pages 191 and 248)

2 tablespoons low-fat milk (omit if using homemade soup alternative)

THE BISCUIT TOPPING

2 cups biscuit mix (I used a gluten-free baking mix)

1/2 tablespoon granulated sugar

8 tablespoons melted butter (that's a whole stick)

3/4 cup milk (stick with 2 percent or lower cow's milk; I used soy milk)

The Directions

Use a 4-quart slow cooker. Spray the stoneware with cooking spray, and add the chicken. Add the vegetables and seasonings. Stir in the cream-of-something soup and add 2 tablespoons of milk to the can; swish it around to get all the good stuff out of the can, and pour it into the crock. Stir well. In a mixing bowl, make the biscuit topping. The dough will be pretty "play-doughy," and I pretty much mixed it with my hands. Spread the dough on top of the chicken and veggie mixture. Cover and cook on low for 6 to 7 hours, or on high for 3 to 4 hours. The potpie is done when the biscuit topping is golden brown, and is hard to the touch in the middle. If you find that your slow cooker seals really well and you have a lot of condensation building up, you can prop open the lid with a wooden spoon or chopstick.

The Verdict

This was neat to try, and I'm glad that I did it. I like that you can use whatever vegetables and meat you have on hand, and throw it in under the biscuit topping. My brother really likes potpies, and next time I make this, I'm going to have him over. The filling is really good, and the flavor reminded Adam of stuffing.

CREAMY BEEF OVER NOODLES

serves 6

The Ingredients

2 pounds stew meat

2 tablespoons butter

¼ cup soy milk (or 2 percent or lower in fat content cow's milk)

1 tablespoon gluten-free Worcestershire sauce

2 tablespoons dried minced onion, or 1 fresh, diced

¼ cup beef broth

½ teaspoon kosher salt

1 tablespoon black pepper

1 teaspoon herbes de Provence

4 ounces cream cheese

The Directions

Use a 4-quart slow cooker. Put meat into crock; frozen is fine. Add the butter, milk, Worcestershire sauce, onion, broth, salt, pepper, and herbes de Provence. Cook on low 10 to 12 hours, or until the meat is tender. Stir in the cream cheese. Serve over hot buttered noodles.

The Verdict

I completely made this up using ingredients on hand, and did a happy dance when I tasted the end result. Usually we blow money on the weekends on takeout or dinners out, but instead we came home from a very busy Saturday filled with errands, swim lessons, and birthday parties to a wonderful smell and a hot meal.

CREAMY CORN AND SPINACH ENCHILADA CASSEROLE

serves 6

The Ingredients

1 cup shredded cooked meat (I used chicken)

1 (14.5-ounce) can creamed corn

1/4 cup finely chopped fresh cilantro leaves

1 cup baby spinach leaves

2 tablespoons chopped sliced jalapeños

2 cups shredded cheese (I used a packaged Mexican blend)

8 to 10 corn tortillas

2 cups green enchilada sauce

2/3 cup sour cream

The Directions

Use a 4-quart slow cooker. In a large mixing bowl, combine the shredded meat, creamed corn, cilantro, spinach leaves, jalapeños, and 1½ cups shredded cheese. Mix. You may need to use your hands to get the spinach leaves really wilty and coated with the creamed corn. This is your filling.

Place a corn tortilla into the bottom of your stoneware. Add a hearty spoonful of filling. Top with another corn tortilla. Repeat the layers until your crock is full. In a mixing bowl, combine the green enchilada sauce with the sour cream, and pour on top. Add the remaining ½ cup shredded cheese. Cover and cook on low for 5 to 7 hours, or on high for 2 to 4 hours. Let stand with the lid off for 20 minutes before cutting.

ENCHILADA CASSEROLE

serves 6

The Ingredients

    2 cups cooked and diced chicken
    1 (28-ounce) can enchilada sauce
    6 corn tortillas
    1 orange bell pepper, seeded and chopped
    1 yellow bell pepper, seeded and chopped
    1 (15-ounce) can black beans, drained and rinsed
    1 (6-ounce) can pitted, sliced black olives
    $2^{1}/_{2}$ cups shredded cheddar cheese
    1 tablespoon water
    Sour cream, avocado slices (optional garnishes)

The Directions

Use a 4-quart slow cooker. Combine chicken with enchilada sauce, and set aside. Starting with a corn tortilla (or 2 if needed), layer ingredients into stoneware: tortillas, chicken and sauce, chopped bell pepper, black beans, olives, cheese. Repeat layers. Finish with a handful of cheese and 1 tablespoon of water that you swirl around in the bowl that held the chicken and enchilada sauce. Cover and cook on low for 4 to 6 hours. Serve with a dollop of sour cream and a slice of avocado, if desired.

JAMBALAYA

serves 6

The Ingredients

2 cups chicken broth
1/2 cup dry white wine
1 cup raw brown rice
3 celery stalks, sliced
1/2 onion, diced
1 green bell pepper, seeded and chopped
1 red bell pepper, seeded and chopped
1 cup frozen white corn
1 cup canned black beans, drained and rinsed
1 (14-ounce) can Italian stewed tomatoes
6 garlic cloves, minced
5 sausages: 2 spicy, and 3 not so spicy
2 cups cooked frozen shelled shrimp

The Directions

Use a 6-quart slow cooker. Combine the broth, wine, and uncooked rice in your stoneware. Add the vegetables, frozen corn, black beans, canned tomatoes, and garlic. Add the sausage. I promise it's enough liquid. Cook on low for 8 hours, or on high for about 6 hours.

Before eating, stir in the frozen shrimp and turn to high until the shrimp are pink and slightly curled, about 30 minutes.

The Verdict

We ate this on Super Duper Tuesday—the very first time Super Tuesday collided with Fat Tuesday—and truly enjoyed our meal. The heat comes from whatever sausages you happen to use. I used 2 Louisiana Hot Links, and 3 garlic-artichoke turkey sausages. It was a great combination.

LASAGNA

serves 6

The Ingredients

1 pound ground beef or turkey, browned and drained

1 (25-ounce) jar pasta sauce

10 dry lasagna noodles (traditional, not the no-cook kind; I used brown rice noodles)

1 (15-ounce) container ricotta cheese

1 pound sliced mushrooms

2 handfuls baby spinach leaves (optional)

3 hard-boiled eggs, sliced (optional)

8 slices mozzarella cheese

2 cups shredded Italian-style cheese

1/4 cup water

The Directions

Use a 6-quart slow cooker. Brown the ground meat on the stovetop, and drain well. Add the jar of pasta sauce to the meat. Save the jar, you'll need it later.

Spoon some of the meat and sauce mixture into the bottom of your slow cooker. Cover with a layer of uncooked lasagna noodles. Smear some ricotta cheese on the noodles, and add some mushrooms, a handful of spinach, and some egg slices, if using. Put a few slices of mozzarella on top, and 1/2 cup or so of the shredded cheese. Add another spoonful of the meat and sauce mixture, and repeat the layers until you run out of ingredients, or the crock is full.

Put water into the empty pasta jar and shake. Pour the contents over the assembled ingredients. Cover and cook on low for 6 to 8 hours, or on high for 3 to 4 hours. Check about an hour before serving, and push down the top noodles into the liquid, if they are getting too brown and crispy. The lasagna is done when the pasta has reached the desired tenderness and the cheese has melted completely and has begun to brown on the edges.

The Verdict

Lasagna is a family favorite around here, and I usually make it about once a month. I really appreciate the slow-cooked version, because I can assemble everything in the morning when I'm still fully awake. I like to sneak extra diced vegetables like zucchini and broccoli into my lasagnas. As long as there is enough cheese to hide the stowaways, my kids gladly eat it up.

MACARONI AND CHEESE

serves 6 to 8

The Ingredients

cooking spray
1 large egg, whisked
4 cups of milk (2 percent or lower in fat content)
1/2 teaspoon kosher salt
1/2 teaspoon black pepper
1 teaspoon dry mustard
4 cups shredded cheese (I used all cheddar; many of my readers prefer American)
1/2 pound uncooked macaroni or hearty pasta (I used brown rice fusilli)

The Directions

Use a 4-quart slow cooker. This is one of those dishes you need to keep an eye on. It will cook quickly, and you will need to stir every so often. Spray the crock well with cooking spray. In a mixing bowl, whisk egg and milk together. Stir in the seasonings. Add the cheese and noodles, and stir well to combine. Pour the mixture into the slow cooker. It will be very liquidy. Cover and cook on low for 2 to 5 hours, or on high for 1 to 3 hours, stirring every 30 to 45 minutes. Don't wander too far away—I was quite surprised at how quickly our pasta got fork-tender.

The Verdict

We all really liked this. The cheese on top was bubbly and brown and had the neat texture it gets when baked in the oven. The pasta swelled and completely filled my round 4-quart cooker, even though I only used 8 ounces. There are over 80 reviews of this recipe listed at crockpot365.blog spot.com—I'd recommend reading them before making this dish. It's rather "advanced" for a slow-cooked meal, and you might find the reader suggestions helpful.

QUINOA CASSEROLE

serves 6

The Ingredients

1½ cups uncooked quinoa
1 tablespoon olive oil
3 cups chicken broth
½ teaspoon kosher salt
½ teaspoon ground cinnamon
¼ cup sliced or chopped almonds
⅓ cup dried unsweetened cranberries

1 cup cherry tomatoes, halved or quartered depending on size
½ cup crumbled feta cheese
handful of baby spinach

The Directions

Use a 4-quart slow cooker. Rinse the quinoa in a fine-mesh strainer under cold running water until the water runs clear. Dump the quinoa into the crock. Add the olive oil and mix around. Pour in the chicken broth, and add the salt and cinnamon. Stir in the almonds and cranberries. Cover and cook on low for 4 to 6 hours, or on high for 2 to 4 hours. The quinoa is done when you can fluff it with a fork and it is tender. The liquid should be pretty well absorbed, similar to when rice is done. Fluff the quinoa with a fork, and add the tomatoes and feta cheese. Stir gingerly to mix. Add a large handful of baby spinach to the top of the crock, and close lid. Cook on high for about 20 minutes, or until the spinach has wilted. Stir again to distribute the spinach. The tomatoes, spinach, and feta provided a great "fresh" aspect not usually present in casseroles.

SHEPHERD'S PIE

serves 6

The Ingredients

1 pound ground turkey or beef
1 medium onion, chopped finely
½ teaspoon seasoned salt
½ teaspoon onion powder
¼ teaspoon black pepper
¼ teaspoon paprika plus a wee bit more for garnish
2 garlic cloves, chopped
cooking spray
2 cups frozen vegetables (I used roasted corn and peas)
1 cup water
2 cups shredded cheddar cheese
3 cups leftover mashed potatoes

The Directions

Use a 4-quart slow cooker. Brown the ground meat and onion on the stovetop, and drain any excess fat. Stir the salt, spices, and garlic into the meat. Spray the inside of your stoneware with cooking spray. Put the meat into the slow cooker and stir in the frozen vegetables, and a cup of water. Add 2 cups of cheese on top. Press the mashed potatoes down on top of the cheese and meat. Sprinkle with a bit of paprika. Cover and cook on low for 6 hours or high for about 3 hours, then remove the lid and cook on high for 30 minutes to release the condensation and allow the potatoes to brown a bit on top. Everything is cooked already, so you're really just allowing the flavors to meld and the potatoes to brown.

SPANISH RICE

serves 4

The Ingredients

    1 pound ground meat (I used turkey)
    1 tablespoon dried minced onion (or one cup diced fresh onion)
    1 teaspoon Italian seasoning
    2 garlic cloves, minced
    1 cup long-grain brown rice
    1 (14-ounce) can diced tomatoes
    shredded cheese, salsa, sour cream, sliced avocado (optional toppings)

The Directions

Use a 4-quart slow cooker. Brown meat in a skillet on the stovetop with the dried onion, Italian seasoning, and garlic. Drain. Put browned meat in your crock and add rice. Open the can of tomatoes, and drain the juice into a measuring cup. Add enough water to measure 2 cups of liquid. Add to the crock. Toss in the tomatoes. Cover and cook on low for 2 to 4 hours, or until rice is cooked and tender. This is best eaten as soon as the rice has finished cooking.

SUN-DRIED TOMATO AND CAPER PASTA SAUCE

serves 4

The Ingredients

5 fresh tomatoes, chopped
8 garlic cloves, chopped
1 medium onion, minced
1 tablespoon Italian seasoning
1/2 cup sun-dried tomatoes in oil, drained and rinsed
2 tablespoons capers, drained
1/2 cup frozen peas (optional)
1 pound cooked pasta (I used Trader Joe's brown rice penne)
fresh Parmesan cheese (optional)

The Directions

Use a 6-quart slow cooker. Put the tomatoes, garlic, and onion into your stoneware. Add the Italian seasoning. Add 1/4 cup whole sun-dried tomatoes to the crock. Chop up the remaining 1/4 cup, and add. Stir in capers. Cover and cook on low for 6 to 8 hours. Stir in frozen peas, if using, 20 minutes before serving. Toss with hot cooked pasta, and garnish with shredded Parmesan cheese, if desired.

The Verdict

This is a wonderful recipe to use if you have a tomato surplus in your garden, and are looking to make something other than the traditional marinara. I didn't happen to use tomatoes I grew, since I've never successfully grown anything except for the children. The tart bite from the sun-dried tomatoes and capers turned a boring pasta dinner into a pretty exciting meal.

SUPEREASY SPAGHETTI SAUCE

makes approximately 9 cups

The Ingredients

   1 pound superlean ground turkey meat
   1 (28-ounce) can whole peeled tomatoes
   1 (15-ounce) can tomato sauce
   1 (12.5-ounce) can Italian diced tomatoes
   1 tablespoon Italian seasoning, plus more to taste
   1 pound mushrooms, sliced

The Directions

Use a 6-quart slow cooker. Add the ground turkey meat to the crock. Dump in the cans of tomatoes with their liquid, and break up the ground meat with a large spoon. Stir in the Italian seasoning and mushrooms. Cover and cook on low for 8 to 10 hours. When the cooking time has elapsed, break the ground meat up a bit more and season to taste with the Italian seasoning.

Bottled pasta sauce is awfully salty; I didn't add any salt, but your tongue might desperately want you to. Serve right away, or package for freezing. If you decide to use a different type of meat, you can chill the sauce, and scrape off the collected fat before freezing or using.

The Verdict

There aren't any rules when it comes to making spaghetti sauce. Use tomatoes from your garden, what's on sale at the supermarket, and feel free to add lots and lots of garlic.

TAMALE PIE

serves 6

The Ingredients

FOR THE FILLING

cooking spray

1 (15-ounce) can black beans, drained and rinsed

1 (15-ounce) can fire-roasted diced tomatoes

1 (15-ounce) can corn, drained

1 tablespoon chili powder

1 teaspoon ground cumin

1/2 teaspoon paprika

1/4 cup diced onion

1/2 cup shredded cheddar cheese

CORNBREAD TOPPING

3/4 cup cornmeal

1 1/4 cups flour (I used a gluten-free baking mix)

1 teaspoon baking powder (omit if using a gluten-free baking mix that already has baking powder added)

1 cup milk

1/4 cup sugar

1 large egg

The Directions

Use a 4-quart slow cooker. Spray the inside of your stoneware with cooking spray. Dump in the filling ingredients (cheese too!) and stir well to distribute the spices. You will not be able to stir this again, so please check to see that the spices aren't clumpy. In a separate bowl, mix together the cornbread topping. When combined, pour the batter evenly over the filling, spreading it with a spatula, if needed. Cover and cook on low for 4 to 7 hours or on high for 2 to 4 hours.

The Verdict

I was shocked at how quickly this cooked. I set it on low and expected it to take about 8 hours, but it was all brown and golden and perfectly crispy at the 6-hour mark. So we ate it for lunch!

ZITI

serves 4

The Ingredients

cooking spray
1 (16-ounce) bag pasta (I used brown rice penne)
2 cups shredded Italian cheese
1 (25-ounce) jar pasta sauce
1 cup sliced mushrooms
1/4 cup hot water

The Directions

Use a 4-quart slow cooker. Spray the sides and bottom of the stoneware with cooking spray. Rinse the pasta in a colander to add a bit of moisture to the noodles, and put into the slow cooker. Add 1 cup shredded cheese, and the jar of pasta sauce. Stir in the sliced mushrooms. Put the rest of the cheese on top. Add the water to the empty pasta sauce jar, and shake to release any remaining sauce. Pour evenly over the top of the pasta. Cover and cook on low for 3 to 4 hours, or until pasta has reached the desired tenderness. If you find that your noodles are getting crispy on top, you can push them down a bit more into the sauce an hour before serving to ensure proper tenderness.

SOUPS & STEWS

*U*sing your slow cooker for soups and stews is a no-brainer, and I certainly made quite a few during my one-year slow-cooking challenge. I enjoy making a big batch of soup or stew on the weekend to package in single-serving containers for lunch throughout the week or to freeze for use later. I also appreciate how I can sneak extra vegetables into soups and stews for added nutrients and fiber.

ALBONDIGAS SOUP

AZOREAN SPICED BEEF STEW

BEEF STOCK

BORSCHT

BROCCOLI AND THREE-CHEESE SOUP

BUFFALO WING SOUP

BUTTERNUT SQUASH SOUP

CABBAGE SOUP

CHEESEBURGER SOUP

CHICKEN AND DUMPLINGS SOUP

CHICKEN AND RICE SOUP

CHICKEN BROTH

CLEAN-OUT-THE-PANTRY MINESTRONE SOUP

CORN CHOWDER

COWBOY STEW

CREAM OF ASPARAGUS SOUP

CREAM OF MUSHROOM SOUP

FRENCH ONION SOUP

GUMBO

HARVEST STEW

HEARTY OXTAIL STEW

JAMAICAN PUMPKIN SOUP

LAMB, OLIVE, AND ONION TAGINE

PASTA E FAGIOLI

PIZZA SOUP

POTATO-LEEK SOUP

ROASTED CAULIFLOWER SOUP WITH CURRY AND HONEY

SALSA CHICKEN AND BLACK BEAN SOUP

SMOKY REFRIED BEAN SOUP

SPLIT PEA SOUP

SWEET POTATO SOUP

TORTILLA SOUP

TRADITIONAL BEEF STEW

TURKEY AND WILD RICE SOUP

ALBONDIGAS SOUP

serves 4

The Ingredients

    4 cups chicken broth
    ³/₄ cup cherry tomatoes, quartered
    1 cup baby carrots, diced
    3 celery stalks, diced
    ¹/₂ cup frozen corn
    ¹/₄ cup prepared pasta sauce
    ¹/₂ teaspoon dried mint
    15 to 18 frozen meatballs, Italian or similar flavored (Coleman Natural say gluten-free right on
        the label)
    1 cup frozen peas
    shredded cheese (optional garnish)

The Directions

Use a 6-quart slow cooker. Put the broth, vegetables, pasta sauce, and mint into your slow cooker. Stir in the frozen meatballs. Cover and cook on low for 8 to 9 hours. The seasoning from the meatballs is what is going to flavor your soup. The longer and slower you cook the soup, the more flavor the broth will have. Stir in frozen peas 20 minutes or so before serving. Garnish with a bit of shredded cheese before serving.

The Verdict

The mint is what differentiates Albondigas (meatballs in Spanish) from other soups and provides a unique flavor. I was happily surprised by the subtle mint, and how it provided a cooling sensation on my tongue. If you'd like a punch of heat, you can add some hot sauce or crushed red pepper flakes at the table.

AZOREAN SPICED BEEF STEW

serves 6

The Ingredients

1 pound beef stew meat

3 cups beef stock

2 potatoes, chopped in 1-inch chunks

1 cup cherry tomatoes, cut in quarters, or 2 large chopped tomatoes

1 cup baby carrots

3 green onions, chopped

5 to 6 garlic cloves, smashed and chopped

1 to 2 tablespoons kosher salt (start with 1, then salt to taste)

1/2 tablespoon crushed red pepper flakes

1 teaspoon ground allspice

1 teaspoon ground cumin

1 bay leaf

2 cinnamon sticks

The Directions

Use a 6-quart slow cooker. Put the meat into your stoneware; frozen is fine. Add the stock. Add the potatoes, tomatoes (ha, that rhymed!), carrots, green onions, and garlic. Stir in the salt, red pepper flakes, allspice, and cumin. Float the bay leaf on top and add the cinnamon sticks. Cover and cook on low for 8 to 10 hours, or on high for about 6 hours.

The Verdict

This is a very good stew. It has a fantastic cinnamon-y flavor, but it isn't sickly sweet or weird. It's just good. A big thank you to Sean Timberlake and DPaul Brown for this great recipe.

BEEF STOCK

makes 3 quarts

The Ingredients

4 pounds oxtail, soup bones from a butcher, or bones/meat you've been saving for broth
1 cup baby carrots
1 onion, chopped
1 bunch celery, chopped
8 garlic cloves, whole or chopped
1 tablespoon Italian seasoning
1 teaspoon kosher salt
1 teaspoon black pepper
1 tablespoon apple cider vinegar
water

The Directions

Use a 6-quart slow cooker. This will take 2 days. Prepare yourself. Roast whatever meat and bones you are going to use on a high-sided baking sheet in the oven at 400°F for 30 minutes.

While the meat is roasting and releasing flavor, wash and coarsely chop the vegetables and put into the cooker. They do not need to look pretty.

When the meat is done, let it cool a bit, then scrape it into your stoneware. Include any juices. Add the seasonings and vinegar, and enough water to fill the remainder of the stoneware, minus 2 inches. Cover and cook on low for 10 to 12 hours. Let your slow cooker cool down on the countertop, then place the removable stoneware into the refrigerator overnight.

In the morning the fat will have floated to the top. It's quite gross. Skim off and discard the fat, and drain the broth through a colander into a large pot or bowl. Discard the bones and vegetables. Your stock is now ready to be used in your favorite soup or stew, and can be frozen for later use.

The Verdict

Although time-consuming, homemade broth provides a flavorful punch to any recipe, without excess salt or chemicals. Kalyn Denny, who writes kalynskitchen.blogspot.com, recommends saving meat scraps and bones for a few months in the freezer to use for broth, and using past-prime vegetables. This saves a lot of money.

BORSCHT

serves 6

The Ingredients

8 beets, peeled and sliced (wear old clothes, beets stain!)
1 yellow onion, chopped
1½ cups sliced mushrooms
1½ cups chopped celery
½ cup chopped carrot
1 cup chopped parsnip
1 potato, peeled and chopped
2½ cups shredded red cabbage
3 garlic cloves, minced
1 teaspoon kosher salt
¼ teaspoon black pepper
1 tablespoon dill
1 (6-ounce) can tomato paste
2 teaspoons sugar
2 tablespoons apple cider vinegar
½ cup beer (Redbridge is gluten-free)
5 cups water
sour cream (at least 2 tablespoons per family member)

The Directions

Use a 6-quart slow cooker. Put the vegetables into the stoneware. Don't fuss too much when chopping the vegetables; the soup will be blended. Add the salt, pepper, dill, tomato paste, sugar, vinegar, beer, and water. Cover and cook on low for 6 to 8 hours, or on high for 4 to 6. You want the vegetables fully smooshy so you can blend them easily. Carefully (and wearing *old* clothes) use a handheld immersion blender to soupify. Ladle the soup into bowls and top with a generous dollop of sour cream.

The Verdict

Borscht is good, and healthy. It is also red. Very, very red. It looked like raspberry jam to me, but it doesn't taste like it at all. It tastes like vegetable soup made with beets. Adam and I enjoyed our meals, but the kids didn't have any. The guinea pigs were thrilled to eat the beet stems.

BROCCOLI AND THREE-CHEESE SOUP

serves 6

The Ingredients

½ white onion, diced

2 cups milk (2 percent or lower in fat content)

1 quart chicken broth

½ teaspoon black pepper

½ teaspoon kosher salt

½ teaspoon ground nutmeg

2 (10-ounce) bags of frozen broccoli florets

1 cup each of three different shredded cheeses (I used Jarlsberg, Gruyère, and cheddar)

The Directions

Use a 6-quart slow cooker. Dice the onion into really small pieces (I used a handheld chopper), and put it into the cooker. The onions are going to soften in the milk and broth, and need to be quite small so you don't crunch on onion pieces. Pour in the milk and broth, and add the pepper, salt, and nutmeg. Stir in the frozen broccoli. Cook on low for 7 to 9 hours, or on high for 4 to 6 hours. The broth is done when the onion is soft and translucent. Stir in the shredded cheese 20 minutes before serving. The cheese will be stringy and stick to the broccoli florets. This didn't bother me or my family, but many of my readers opted to use an immersion blender to make the soup look pretty. Serve with your favorite rolls or drop biscuits.

The Verdict

This is the best broccoli and cheese soup I have ever had. That sounds like a big stretch or an exaggeration, but this really beats the canned soup, or the stuff I've had at restaurants. My children both had three helpings! I read about six different recipes before deciding to make this one. I didn't like the idea of making a roux with butter and flour and stirring it in to thicken the broth; it seemed like an unnecessary step. The broth is thin, but very buttery in flavor. If you opt to use the immersion blender, your soup will thicken through emulsification and have a creamier texture.

BUFFALO WING SOUP

serves 4 to 6

The Ingredients

4 tablespoons ($\frac{1}{2}$ stick) unsalted butter

$\frac{1}{4}$ cup flour (I used rice flour)

$\frac{1}{2}$ yellow onion, chopped

3 celery stalks, chopped

2 cups cooked and cubed chicken

$\frac{3}{4}$ cup chicken broth

2 cups milk (no higher fat content than 2 percent, or it will curdle; soy milk is okay)

$\frac{1}{2}$ teaspoon celery salt

$\frac{1}{2}$ teaspoon garlic salt

$\frac{1}{2}$ cup hot wing sauce

4 ounces Velveeta cheese

The Directions

Use a 4-quart slow cooker. Make a roux with the butter and flour in a saucepan on the stovetop. Set aside. Put the onion and celery into the stoneware. Add the chicken. Pour in the broth and milk. Add the celery salt and garlic salt. (This is saltier than I am used to. If you are on a low-sodium diet, omit the salt altogether. You can always season to taste after cooking.) Stir in the flour and butter mixture. Add the hot sauce. Cover and cook on low for 6 to 8 hours, or on high for 3 to 4 hours. The soup is done when the celery and onion reach the desired tenderness and the flavors have melded. Add cubed Velveeta 20 minutes before serving.

BUTTERNUT SQUASH SOUP

serves 8

The Ingredients

1 butternut squash
2 tablespoons olive oil
4 cups chicken or vegetable broth
2 small onions, diced
2 small apples, peeled and cubed
1½ teaspoons kosher salt
¼ teaspoon black pepper
¼ teaspoon ground nutmeg
¼ teaspoon ground cloves
¼ teaspoon ground coriander
¼ teaspoon ground cinnamon

The Directions

Use a 6-quart slow cooker. Cut the squash in half lengthwise. This is terribly hard to do, but if you microwave the entire squash for 2 to 5 minutes on high, the skin will soften a bit. Scoop out the seeds and stringy pulp. Brush the olive oil on the inside of the squash and roast in the oven cut side up at 400°F for 15 minutes, or until the skin peels away from the flesh.

Plug in the slow cooker and turn to high. Add the broth, onions, and apples. Stir in the salt, pepper, and spices. Cover to let heat. When the squash has finished roasting, add it to the pot. Cover and cook on low for 6 to 8 hours, or on high for about 4 hours. Carefully blend with a handheld immersion blender.

The Verdict

This is my comfort soup. I like to curl up with a mug and watch TV. My mom, grandma, and I all like squash soup. It's so creamy and full of flavor that it tastes like it has a bunch of butter and cream in it even though there isn't any.

CABBAGE SOUP

serves 1 for lunch for 2 weeks

The Ingredients

　　1 small head cabbage
　　1 cup baby carrots
　　1 bunch celery
　　1 red bell pepper
　　2 green onions
　　4 cups vegetable or chicken broth
　　4 cups water
　　3 garlic cloves, minced
　　1 teaspoon seasoning blend (Italian, herbes de Provence, etc.)
　　1/4 teaspoon crushed red pepper flakes
　　Tabasco sauce (optional)

The Directions

Use a 6-quart slow cooker. Chop all vegetables into bite-size chunks and plop into cooker. Pour in the liquid. Stir in the garlic, seasoning blend, and pepper flakes. Cover and cook on low for 8 to 10 hours. Season with a bit of Tabasco sauce, if desired.

The Verdict

I've never followed the Cabbage Soup diet fully (my friend Amie lost 45 pounds!), but evidently cabbage is supposed to help with water retention. That's enough of a reason for me to make this every once in a while when I'm feeling terribly vain.

CHEESEBURGER SOUP

serves 6

The Ingredients

1/2 pound lean ground beef

4 cups chicken broth

1 tablespoon dried onion flakes

2 small garlic cloves, minced

1 red bell pepper, seeded and chopped

2 potatoes, cut in 1-inch cubes

1 cup cow's milk

12 ounces Velveeta cheese, cubed

Tabasco sauce (optional)

crumbled bacon (optional)

The Directions

Use a 4-quart slow cooker. Brown the meat on the stovetop, and drain excess fat. Set aside to cool for a bit. Pour the chicken broth into the stoneware, and stir in the onion flakes and minced garlic. Add the bell pepper and potatoes (I didn't peel them). Stir in the browned meat. Cover and cook on low for 4 to 6 hours, or until potatoes are tender. Stir in milk and Velveeta 20 to 30 minutes before serving. Garnish with Tabasco sauce and crumbled bacon, if desired.

CHICKEN AND DUMPLINGS SOUP

serves 6

The Ingredients

    3 pounds boneless, skinless chicken (I used frozen thighs)
    1 yellow onion, chopped
    1 cup mushrooms, chopped
    16 ounces frozen vegetables (I used corn, peas, and carrots)
    2 (10.5-ounce) cans cream-of-something soup, or alternative (see below)
    1 (10-ounce) can refrigerated biscuits, or one batch biscuits (I used a gluten-free baking mix,
       and used the drop-biscuit recipe listed on the back of the bag)

The Directions

Use a 4-quart slow cooker. Put the chicken and vegetables into the bottom of the stoneware insert. Add the cream-of soups, or your homemade substitute (see below). Cover and cook on low for 6 to 8 hours, or on high for 4 to 5 hours.

An hour before serving, shred the chicken with two large forks, and drop in the biscuit dough. Cover and cook on high for another hour. The dumplings are done when a knife is easily inserted and comes out clean. The dumplings will be spongy, and will brown a bit on the sides and top. Serve in bowls, with a dumpling or two per person.

ALTERNATIVE SOUP

    4 tablespoons butter
    6 tablespoons flour (I used a gluten-free baking mix)
    1 cup milk (I used soy)

1 cup chicken broth
$1/2$ teaspoon salt
$1/4$ teaspoon black pepper
1 teaspoon poultry seasoning

The Directions
Combine the ingredients in a saucepan.

CHICKEN AND RICE SOUP

serves 10

The Ingredients

2 cups blended vegetables (I used celery, carrots, broccoli, cauliflower, a red bell pepper, and green onion)
1 cup cooked, shredded chicken
2 quarts (8 cups) chicken broth
1 cup water
1 cup raw brown rice
1 teaspoon herbes de Provence
kosher salt
black pepper

The Directions

Use a 6-quart slow cooker. Wash and trim the vegetables, and put in a blender or food processor to purée. Place into slow cooker. Add the chicken, broth, water, brown rice, herbes de Provence, salt, and pepper. Cover and cook on low for 8 to 10 hours.

The Verdict

Chicken and rice is the gluten-free family's chicken noodle soup. Everything is right with the world when you have a steamy bowl of home-cooked goodness. This is a fantastic way to clean out the produce drawer of your refrigerator—it's perfectly fine to use vegetables that are a bit past their prime.

CHICKEN BROTH

makes approximately 9 cups

The Ingredients

    1 rotisserie chicken carcass
    1 onion, chopped
    1 cup celery, coarsely chopped
    2 cups carrots, coarsely chopped
    5 green onions, chopped
    1 head garlic, cloves peeled
    3 bay leaves
    1 tablespoon Italian seasoning
    6 cups water

The Directions

Use at least a 6-quart slow cooker. This is a 2-day process, so plan accordingly.

Put the chicken carcass into your slow cooker. Nestle the chopped vegetables in with the chicken bones. Add the peeled garlic cloves, bay leaves, seasoning, and water. Cover and cook on low for 8 to 10 hours.

Remove the stoneware from the heating element and let cool completely. Wash your hands well, and find all the little chicken bones. Peel off any remaining chicken and discard the bones and bay leaves. This is a good exercise in finding your inner nine-year-old self.

Scoop the soupy liquid and vegetables into your blender to brothicize. When finished, pour the broth into freezer bags in manageable portions. I chose to use 1-cup servings. Place the bags on a baking sheet and freeze. Once the bags are frozen, they can be tucked in nooks around your freezer.

(CONTINUED)

The Verdict

I'm not a purist, but I do like to use my own broth when I have it on hand. Knowing exactly what is going into your family is important if you have allergies, health problems that call for low-sodium diets, or sensitivities to preservatives. This broth has no added salt, but has a bunch more flavor than store-bought. When using your homemade broth, add salt to taste.

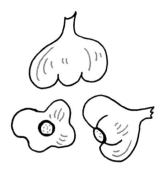

CLEAN-OUT-THE-PANTRY MINESTRONE SOUP

serves 6

The Ingredients

2 (15-ounce) cans canned beans (your choice), drained
1 (15-ounce) can tomatoes and their juice
1 (15-ounce) can corn and its juice
2 cups chopped vegetables (fresh or frozen)
3 cups chicken or vegetable broth
kosher salt
black pepper

The Directions

Use a 4-quart or larger slow cooker. Open the cans and dump the contents into the stoneware. I drained the bean goop only, and kept the tomato and corn juices. Add the chopped vegetables. This is a good recipe to use when you've got a mishmash of past-prime vegetables in your crisper drawer. Slightly wilted celery or browned cauliflower is fine to toss in. Pour in the broth. Cover and cook on low for 8 to 10 hours, or on high for 4 to 5 hours. Season to taste with salt and pepper.

The Verdict

This is a super easy and budget-friendly soup, using pantry staples and leftover vegetables. I have made it completely vegetarian, and have also added leftover diced meat with great results. My children like some shredded cheese added to the top, and when I serve it with cornbread.

CORN CHOWDER

serves 8

The Ingredients

1 yellow onion, diced
1 cup chopped carrots
1 red bell pepper, seeded and chopped
6 small white potatoes, peeled and diced
2 (16-ounce) bags frozen roasted corn
2 quarts chicken broth
kosher salt
black pepper

The Directions

Use a 6-quart slow cooker. Put chopped onion, carrots, bell pepper, and potatoes into the stoneware. Add the frozen corn and chicken broth. Season with salt and pepper. Cover and cook on low for 8 to 9 hours, or on high for 4 to 5 hours. Before serving, use a handheld immersion blender and pulse until the contents have reached a chowder consistency.

The Verdict

The roasted corn makes this chowder. I didn't add any other seasonings, but did put salt and pepper on the table. The flavor was wonderful, and we all enjoyed it, including my parents, who were over for dinner.

COWBOY STEW

serves 8

The Ingredients

1 pound hamburger (you can use turkey)
2 garlic cloves, chopped
1 (15-ounce) can tomato sauce
1 (15-ounce) can diced Italian seasoned tomatoes
1 (15-ounce) can corn, drained
2 (15-ounce) cans whole baby potatoes, drained
1 (10.5-ounce) can tomatoes with green chiles (Rotel)
1 (16-ounce) can ranch-style beans (usually with the baked beans in the grocery store)
1 cup water
sliced jalapeño peppers (optional garnish)

The Directions

Use a 6-quart slow cooker. Brown the hamburger with the garlic on the stovetop, and drain the fat. Let sit for a bit to cool. Put the canned ingredients into the crock. Add the browned meat and a cup of water. Stir with a spoon to mix a bit. Cover and cook on low for 8 to 10 hours, or on high for 4 to 5 hours. Soup and stew tastes better the longer you cook it, so opt for the longer cooking time if you can. Garnish with sliced jalapeño peppers, if desired. Recycle your cans!

The Verdict

I had never before bought canned potatoes, or the ranch beans, which intrigued me about this recipe. The kids really liked how the canned potatoes stayed perfectly oval and looked like baby dinosaur eggs. The taste was fantastic—a bit tangy and spicy. Thanks to headlessfamily5.blogspot.com for this new favorite!

CREAM OF ASPARAGUS SOUP

serves 6

The Ingredients

1½ pounds asparagus

½ white onion, chopped

2 tiny red potatoes (or one medium white potato), chopped

4 cups vegetable broth

½ teaspoon seasoned salt

½ teaspoon black pepper

½ cup half-and-half (optional; to add at the end of cooking time)

kosher salt

The Directions

Use a 6-quart slow cooker. Wash and trim the woody ends of the asparagus, and cut the rest into 2-inch lengths. Add them to the crock, along with onion and potatoes; no need to peel. Pour in the broth and add the seasoned salt and black pepper. Cover and cook on low for 7 to 9 hours, or on high for 3 to 5 hours. The soup is ready when the potatoes are tender. *Carefully* use a handheld immersion blender to soupify. If you don't have an immersion blender, you can blend the soup in batches in your traditional blender. Return the soup to the crock, stir in the half-and-half, if desired, and heat through. Season with salt and pepper to taste.

The Verdict

This is a good soup; very asparagus-y and creamy. I liked it both ways: with and without the half-and-half. The no-cream kind is just as rich, but doesn't leave a velvety film on your tongue the way the other does. The color is also more forest green instead of light green.

CREAM OF MUSHROOM SOUP

makes 10 to 12 cups

The Ingredients

2 pounds mushrooms
1/2 teaspoon kosher salt
1/2 teaspoon black pepper
1 tablespoon dried minced onion
2 tablespoons Italian seasoning
juice of 1 lemon
4 cups vegetable broth
2 cups water
1 quart milk (to add later; I used fat-free cow's milk)

The Directions

Use a 6-quart slow cooker. Wash the mushrooms well and cut into quarters. Put into the stoneware and add the salt, pepper, onion, seasoning, and lemon juice. Pour in the vegetable broth and water. Cover and cook on low for 8 hours. Carefully blend with a handheld immersion blender until soupy. If you don't have an immersion blender, carefully blend in batches in a traditional blender. Stir in the milk. You can use any fat percentage you'd like—even heavy cream.

Let cool on the counter for a few hours, then pour into freezer bags or plastic containers in 2-cup portions, and freeze. You can use this soup for cooking in lieu of canned cream of mushroom soup.

The Verdict

I'm impressed with the way this tastes, and how it behaves when used in recipes instead of canned soup. It's thinner, and is brown instead of white, but packs a flavorful punch.

I'm not a food purist by any stretch of the imagination, but I like having a homemade substitute on hand in the freezer to use in favorite recipes.

FRENCH ONION SOUP

serves 2

The Ingredients

3 tablespoons butter

2 yellow onions, sliced into rings

2 (15-ounce) cans beef broth

½ tablespoon sugar

½ teaspoon kosher salt (or more to taste if you're using unsalted butter)

¼ cup dry sherry (dry white wine would probably work)

2 to 4 slices of bread (brown rice bread or French bread), toasted

2 to 4 slices Gruyère cheese, or Swiss cheese

The Directions

Use a 2-quart slow cooker. Heat your slow cooker to high, and plop in the butter to start melting. Add the onion rings. Break the rings up with your fingers and rub them around in the melted butter. Add the broth, sugar, salt, and sherry. Cook on low for 8 to 10 hours, or on high for 4 to 6. This is finished when the onions are translucent and pliable.

Before serving, remove the stoneware from the heating element, and float toasted bread with cheese slices on top of the soup. Broil in the oven for a minute, or until cheese has melted.

The Verdict

There is nothing better than French onion soup. Nothing! This is ridiculously easy to make, and tastes like it belongs in a fancy restaurant—except I used brown rice bread so it was completely gluten-free (toast brown rice bread twice to get desired crunch). This is a good dish to simmer all day long while you are at work or while out and about saving the world.

GUMBO

serves 6

The Ingredients

1 cup frozen okra

½ cup frozen white corn

1 cup chopped onion

1 green bell pepper, chopped

5 flavored sausages (I used 3 chicken with garlic and artichokes, and 2 Cajun chicken)

1 (14-ounce) can diced tomatoes with their juice

1 cup raw brown rice

4 cups chicken broth

1½ cups fully cooked frozen shrimp

The Directions

Use a 6-quart slow cooker. Add the frozen and fresh vegetables to the stoneware. Slice the sausage in rounds, and add to the crock. Pour in the tomatoes, brown rice, and chicken broth. Because I used Cajun-seasoned sausage, I didn't need to add any additional spices. If you are using milder sausage, add ½ teaspoon or so Cajun seasoning. Cover and cook on low 8 hours, or on high 4 to 6 hours. Add the frozen shrimp and turn the cooker to high 30 minutes before serving. Serve with some crusty bread or corn muffins.

The Verdict

I've never been to New Orleans (I'm pretty sure the part in Disneyland doesn't count), so I've never had traditional gumbo. I have ordered it in restaurants, though, and have always been quite impressed with the medley of flavors. I enjoyed this, as did the rest of the family.

HARVEST STEW

serves 6

The Ingredients

1 yellow onion, chopped
3 garlic cloves, chopped
1 sweet potato, peeled and chopped
3 red potatoes, peeled and chopped
1 acorn squash, peeled and chopped
1 pound lean ground turkey or chicken
1 (15-ounce) can kidney beans, rinsed
1 (10-ounce) can tomatoes and chiles (Rotel)
4 cups chicken broth
¼ teaspoon ground cloves
¼ teaspoon ground allspice
kosher salt
black pepper

The Directions

Use a 6-quart slow cooker. Guess what? I didn't brown the meat. If you are using extra lean ground turkey or chicken, there really isn't a need. The only worry about using beef or pork is the fat content. If you prefer one of those types of meat, or already have it on hand, brown it on the stovetop and drain before adding to the stew. Peel and chop all of the vegetables, and add them to the cooker. Break up ground meat and add. Add the kidney beans and the whole can of tomatoes and chiles. Pour in the broth and seasonings. Stir well. It will look like there isn't enough liquid, but more will be made from the vegetables and meat, I promise. Cover and cook on low for 7 to 9 hours.

The Verdict

This is a cozy stew certain to warm you after a day of pumpkin-picking. Or after a day of spending $5 a pop for a corn maze, hay ride, pumpkin cannon, inflatable bouncer, pony ride, or kid-size tractor. Or after a day watching *other* people pay $5 a pop for those things, and then deciding to get your pumpkins in front of the grocery store. This stew has lovely flavors, and makes wonderful leftovers.

HEARTY OXTAIL STEW

serves 8

The Ingredients

½ tablespoon olive oil

3 pounds oxtails

½ teaspoon Italian seasoning

½ teaspoon ground ginger

½ teaspoon ground cumin

1 (28-ounce) can tomatoes, with their juices

1 cup beef broth

1 cup dry white wine

2 green onions, chopped

1 cup frozen roasted corn

5 small red potatoes, cut in chunks

1 cup celery, sliced

1 cup carrots, sliced

4 whole garlic cloves

1 ounce semisweet baking chocolate (optional)

The Directions

Use a 6-quart slow cooker. This recipe takes 2 days—you need to cook it a bit the first day to release fat from the oxtails, then cook low and slow the next day to soften the meat and create flavor. Rub olive oil onto the bottom of your stoneware. Plop in oxtails, and cover with Italian seasoning and spices. Add the tomatoes, broth, wine, vegetables, and garlic. Drop in the baking chocolate square, if desired.

Cook on high 5 to 6 hours the first day, then refrigerate overnight. Scrape off the congealed fat. Allow the removable stoneware to reach room temperature before putting it back into the heating element. Cook on low for 8 to 10 hours. Serve in bowls.

The Verdict

This is a rich, flavorful, and hearty stew. We all gladly ate it up, and while it's probably more polite to cut the meat off the bones, it's oddly satisfying to gnaw on them like a wild animal.

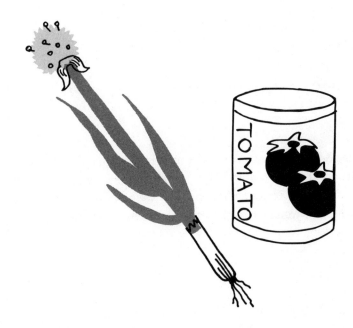

JAMAICAN PUMPKIN SOUP

serves 6

The Ingredients

1 (15-ounce) can pure pumpkin
1 red onion, chopped
2 celery stalks, chopped
2 yams, peeled and chopped
3 garlic cloves, chopped
1 (1-inch) piece fresh ginger, peeled and grated
2 teaspoons kosher salt
1 teaspoon ground turmeric
1/4 teaspoon ground allspice
1/4 teaspoon ground nutmeg
1 tablespoon sugar
4 cups vegetable broth
2 cups water
heavy (whipping) cream, 1 tablespoon per family member (optional)

The Directions

Use a 6-quart slow cooker. Put canned pumpkin into stoneware, and add chopped vegetables. Add spices and sugar. Pour in vegetable broth and water, stirring well. Cover and cook on low for 8 hours. Carefully use a handheld blender to soupify about three-quarters of the soup. If you have little ones in the house with texture issues, feel free to blend it all. Serve with a bit of cream to stir in.

The Verdict

The flavors in this are rich and distinguished. It's completely fat-free until you add the cream, which is optional. To cut back on cream consumption, I measured out 1 tablespoon per family member and we stirred it in ourselves at the table. This is a gorgeous soup. The kids enjoyed it (they liked it better when it turned yellow with the cream), and Adam and I liked it an awful lot. I'd most definitely serve this to guests.

LAMB, OLIVE, AND ONION TAGINE

serves 6

The Ingredients

- 2 yellow onions, sliced in rings
- 1 head garlic cloves, peeled (about 8 to 10 cloves)
- 2 pounds lamb stew meat or leg of lamb, cut in chunks
- 2 teaspoons ground cumin
- 1 teaspoon ground coriander
- 1 (1-inch) piece fresh ginger, peeled and grated
- 2 (6-ounce) cans pitted black olives, drained
- 2 tablespoons capers
- 1 (750ml) bottle red wine

The Directions

Use a 6-quart slow cooker. Put the onions and garlic into the stoneware. Drop in the lamb, and sprinkle in the dried spices and fresh ginger. Add the olives, capers, and wine. Cover and cook on low for 8 to 12 hours. Serve with mashed potatoes, polenta, or quinoa.

PASTA E FAGIOLI

serves 6

The Ingredients

1 pound lean ground beef, browned, and drained of excess fat

1 cup carrots, chopped

1/2 large red onion, chopped

2 celery stalks, sliced

1 (15-ounce) can kidney beans, drained and rinsed

1 (15-ounce) can white beans, drained and rinsed

2 (14.5-ounce) cans diced tomatoes with their juice

1 (16.5-ounce) jar pasta sauce

4 cups beef broth

1/2 teaspoon kosher salt

1/4 teaspoon black pepper

2 teaspoons dried oregano

1 tablespoon Tabasco sauce

1/2 cup dry pasta (I used brown rice fusilli)

Parmesan cheese (optional garnish)

The Directions

Use a 6-quart slow cooker. Put the meat into the stoneware. Add the chopped carrots, onion, and celery. Add the beans, tomatoes, and pasta sauce. Pour in the beef broth. Season with salt, black pepper, oregano, and Tabasco sauce. Stir to combine. Cover and cook on low for 8 hours, or on high for 4 hours. When the vegetables are tender, stir in 1/2 cup of dry pasta. Cover and cook for another hour on low, or until the pasta is al dente. It will swell quite a bit. Garnish with Parmesan cheese.

(CONTINUED)

The Verdict

This soup is based upon Olive Garden's Pasta e Fagioli soup, which I haven't had, but it sounded good. So I made it, in the slow cooker. This is a crowd-pleasing soup. There's nothing odd in it, and it has a fun kick that isn't spicy as much as it is noticeable.

PIZZA SOUP

serves 4 to 6

The Ingredients

1 green bell pepper, seeded and chopped

1/2 red onion, chopped

1 cup sliced mushrooms

1 cup cherry tomatoes, cut in quarters (or 1 (15-ounce) can diced tomatoes, drained)

2 Italian sausages (I used Italian-style chicken sausage)

1 cup sliced pepperoni, cut into quarters

8 fresh basil leaves, chopped (or 1/2 tablespoon dried)

1 tablespoon dried oregano

1 (14-ounce) jar pizza sauce

3 sauce jars full of water

1/2 to 1/3 cup of dried pasta (If your pasta is tiny, use 1/3 cup; if it's big, use 1/2 cup)

shredded mozzarella cheese (optional garnish)

The Directions

Use a 6-quart slow cooker. Prepare the veggies. Dump them into the stoneware. Slice the sausage into small pieces and add, along with the pepperoni. Add the basil and oregano. Pour in the pizza sauce, and follow with three sauce jars of water. Cover and cook on low for 7 to 9 hours. Add the dry pasta 30 minutes before serving, and turn the cooker to high. My brown rice pasta only took 20 minutes to soften quite nicely. Garnish with shredded mozzarella cheese. This is a regular in our family meal plan.

POTATO-LEEK SOUP

serves 6

The Ingredients

3 large leeks (white part only), cleaned and diced
1 medium yellow onion, chopped
1 pound brown potatoes (weigh them—you'll only need 2 or 3), peeled and chopped
5 cups chicken or vegetable broth
1/2 teaspoon dried thyme
1/4 teaspoon black pepper
2 garlic cloves, chopped
1 cup heavy cream (optional, I didn't add any)

The Directions

Use a 6-quart slow cooker. Put the vegetables into your stoneware. Pour in the broth, thyme, pepper, and garlic. Stir. Cover and cook on low for 7 to 9 hours, or on high for about 4 hours. When the potatoes and onion are fully cooked and soft, use an immersion blender to soupify, or blend in small batches *carefully* in a traditional blender. Stir in heavy cream, if desired.

The Verdict

This couldn't have been easier to prepare, especially since I didn't lift a finger. I lucked out due to a possible jury duty stint, so Adam stayed home from work and did it all. This is a light, creamy soup that is perfect for a starter course, or for sipping out of a mug on the couch. The kids didn't try it, and thought it smelled gross. They were right—it does have an "earthy" aroma. I opened a window and turned on a fan while it cooked.

ROASTED CAULIFLOWER SOUP WITH CURRY AND HONEY

serves 6

The Ingredients

1 head cauliflower
3 tablespoons olive oil
1 teaspoon kosher salt
$1/2$ teaspoon black pepper
2 cups chicken or vegetable broth
2 cups warm water
1 yellow onion, chopped in chunks
$1/4$ to $1/2$ teaspoon cayenne pepper ($1/4$ teaspoon was enough for me)
$2^{1}/2$ teaspoons curry powder
1 to 2 tablespoons honey

The Directions

Use a 6-quart slow cooker. Cut the cauliflower into florets, toss with the olive oil, salt, and pepper, and roast in a 400°F oven for about 20 minutes, or until the cauliflower has begun to caramelize. While the cauliflower is roasting, plug in the slow cooker and turn it to high. Add the broth and water. Put in the onion, cayenne, and curry powder. Add the cauliflower to the broth. Cover and cook on low for 6 to 7 hours, or on high for 3 to 4 hours. The soup is done when the onion and cauliflower are fully tender. Carefully use an immersion blender to smash the cauliflower and onion.

Ladle into soup bowls and drizzle honey into each bowl at the table.

The Verdict

I found the flavor to be mysterious—it's not like anything I had ever had before. This would be fun to serve at a fancy dinner, where guests can squeeze on their own honey. I really like how rich and velvety it tastes without a drop of cream. The kids had bean burritos on brown rice tortillas.

SALSA CHICKEN AND BLACK BEAN SOUP

serves 6

The Ingredients

    1 cup dried black beans (or 2 cans, drained and rinsed)
    1 pound boneless, skinless chicken pieces
    4 cups chicken broth
    1 (16-ounce) jar prepared salsa
    1 cup frozen corn
    1 cup sliced mushrooms
    1½ teaspoons ground cumin
    ½ cup sour cream
    shredded cheddar cheese, avocado slices, fresh cilantro (optional garnishes)

The Directions

Use a 4-quart slow cooker. If you're using dry beans, soak them overnight. Drain and rinse the beans, and put into the stoneware. Add the chicken, broth, and salsa, then add the corn, mushrooms, and cumin. Cover and cook on low for 8 to 10 hours, or high for 5 to 6 hours. If you'd like to thicken the broth (I did), you can use an immersion blender (I love that thing!) to blend a bit of the beans and chicken. If you don't have one, scoop out 2 cups of the soup and carefully blend in a traditional blender. Stir the mixture back into the soup. Mix in the sour cream before serving, and garnish with shredded cheese, avocado slices, and cilantro if desired.

The Verdict

My kids both ate their weight in this soup. It smelled delicious while cooking, and tasted even better. The Internet crowd really likes this soup, too—it has received lots of positive reviews. I was worried that the salsa would be too spicy, but it isn't—it just adds a fun flavor with a tiny kick.

SMOKY REFRIED BEAN SOUP

serves 6

The Ingredients

1 (15-ounce) can refried beans
1 (15-ounce) can black beans
1 cup cherry tomatoes, quartered
1 cup diced carrots
1 cup frozen roasted corn
2 cups vegetable broth
1 tablespoon Tabasco sauce
3 garlic cloves, chopped
1 teaspoon ground cumin
1/2 teaspoon chipotle chili powder
1/4 teaspoon black pepper
1/4 teaspoon kosher salt

The Directions

Use a 4-quart slow cooker. Put the refried beans in the crock, and turn to high to begin melting the bean blob. Drain and rinse the black beans, and add to the crock. Add the tomatoes, carrots, and roasted corn. Pour in the vegetable broth. Stir in the Tabasco sauce garlic, spices, and salt. Cover and cook on high for 3 to 4 hours, or on low for 6 to 8 hours. The soup is done when the carrots have reached the desired tenderness.

The Verdict

This recipe comes from Susan Voisin, who writes at blog.fatfreevegan.com. That means that along with being delicious, this soup is both fat-free and vegan! It was a bit too spicy for the kids, but had a wonderful kick for Adam and me. I liked the thickness a lot, and how it cleared my sinuses nicely.

SPLIT PEA SOUP

serves 4

Ingredients

  1 (16-ounce) package dried split peas
  1/2 yellow onion, diced
  1 potato, peeled and diced
  1 cup diced carrot
  4 cups vegetable broth
  1 cup water
  1 teaspoon kosher salt
  1/2 teaspoon black pepper
  1 pound bacon (or ham hock)

The Directions

Use a 4-quart slow cooker. Put the peas, vegetables, broth, and water into the cooker. Mix in the salt and pepper. Add bacon, reserving 4 to 6 pieces for later use (or add ham hock). Cover and cook on low 8 to 10 hours, or on high 4 to 6 hours. If you are using the ham hock, scrape off any remaining meat and discard the bone. If you use bacon, remove the strips and discard. Use a handheld immersion blender to blend the soup to the desired consistency. Cook the reserved bacon on the stovetop or in the microwave, and crumble over the soup.

SWEET POTATO SOUP

serves 4

The Ingredients

3 sweet potatoes
2 cups broth (chicken or vegetable)
1 (15-ounce) can sliced mangoes, and their juices
¼ teaspoon ground allspice
½ cup heavy cream

The Directions

Use a 4-quart slow cooker. Peel and cube the sweet potatoes and add them to your slow cooker with the broth, mangoes, and allspice. Cover and cook on low for 8 hours, or high for 4 hours. When the potatoes are tender, blend with an immersion blender. Stir in the heavy cream.

TORTILLA SOUP

serves 8

The Ingredients

1½ cups cooked chicken
½ onion, chopped
1 cup frozen roasted corn
2 green onions, chopped
1 (28-ounce) can tomatoes with their juices
1 cup chopped fresh vegetables (I used celery, carrots, and some leftover roasted veggies)
4 garlic cloves, chopped
¼ teaspoon crushed red pepper flakes
½ teaspoon cayenne pepper
1 teaspoon ground cumin
kosher salt
3 cups chicken broth
tortilla chips, shredded cheese, sour cream, for garnish

The Directions

Use a 4-quart slow cooker. Add the chicken, all the vegetables, the garlic, spices, salt, and broth. Cover and cook on low for 8 hours, or on high for 4 hours. Your soup is done when vegetables have reached the desired tenderness, and the broth is fully heated, but you really can't overcook this one. Serve with tortilla chips, shredded cheese, and a dollop of sour cream.

The Verdict

I ate this for lunch for four days in a row. It was a bit spicy for the kids, which was totally fine with me. The liquid absorbed a bit, so it was more chowdery than soupy after the first day, but still amazingly good, and much healthier than Taco Bell for my Mexican food fix.

TRADITIONAL BEEF STEW

serves 8

The Ingredients

    1 yellow onion, sliced
    1 cup cherry tomatoes, quartered
    3 celery stalks, sliced
    1 cup sliced carrots
    2 cups green beans
    2 cups sliced mushrooms
    2 pounds beef stew meat
    1/2 cup flour (I used gluten-free baking mix)
    1/2 teaspoon kosher salt
    1 teaspoon black pepper
    1/2 teaspoon dried rosemary
    1 teaspoon garlic powder
    1 teaspoon gluten-free Worcestershire sauce
    1/4 cup dry red wine
    2 (15-ounce) cans beef broth

The Directions

Use a 6-quart slow cooker. Put all the vegetables into the cooker. Dredge the meat in flour, and add to the crock. Discard any remaining flour. Add the dry seasonings, Worcestershire sauce, wine, and beef broth. Cover and cook on low for 8 to 12 hours.

The Verdict

There are as many different variations of stew as there are missing Barbie shoes. Use what you have on hand in the crisper drawer and pantry. I don't think I've ever made the same beef stew twice. This is a great basic recipe; feel free to create your own variation.

TURKEY AND WILD RICE SOUP

serves 8 to 10

The Ingredients

turkey carcass (if you don't have one, you can use 2 cups of cooked turkey)

8 cups water (to make broth; if you don't have a carcass, use 8 cups chicken broth)

1 yellow onion, chopped

1 cup chopped celery

1 cup chopped carrots

²/₃ cup raw wild rice

1 teaspoon dried sage

1 chicken bouillon cube (only if you are using the carcass to make broth; don't use if you're using broth)

2 tablespoons balsamic vinegar

2 cups baby spinach leaves

The Directions

Use a 6-quart slow cooker. This is a 1½-day project. We are going to use the turkey bones to make broth. If you are using chicken broth and 2 cups of turkey, bypass this step.

Put the turkey carcass into the slow cooker and cover with 8 cups of water. My carcass was only from a tiny turkey, so if you need to break the bones down to fit in your slow cooker, do so. My turkey was still stuffed with a quartered onion and some apple, so I didn't bother to add any vegetables to season the water. You may certainly add some onion, celery, or anything else you'd like to season the broth with. The more meat and skin left on the bones, the more flavorful the broth.

Cover and cook on low overnight, or 8 to 10 hours. Drain the broth into a large pot (do not discard), pick off meat, and add it to the broth.

Rinse out your stoneware and put in the chopped vegetables. Return the broth and meat to the stoneware and add the wild rice, sage, bouillon cube, and balsamic vinegar. Stir. Add 2 heaping handfuls of baby spinach to the mix. It will look like a lot, but will wilt down nicely while cooking. Cover and cook on low for 8 to 10 hours, or on high for 4 to 6 hours. The soup is done when the vegetables have reached the desired tenderness.

The Verdict

Kalyn Denny, from kalynskitchen.blogspot.com, gave me the recipe for this soup. I love it. The wild rice exploded a bit, and actually resembled barley by the time we ate it. Adam proclaimed it the best turkey soup he's ever had, and the kids both ate two bowls. I may have wept.

SEAFOOD

Cooking fish and seafood in the slow cooker is sometimes thought of as off-limits, but I was thrilled to learn that slow-cooking seafood is terribly easy and doesn't leave a "fish smell" in the house—a huge bonus for me. I played around with placing foil packets in the slow cooker, and found them to work perfectly. Foil + fish = good fish. And foil + fish + slow cooker = a real, live American family eating fish. Seafood doesn't take long to cook; I recommend staying home to keep an eye on it.

BARBECUED SHRIMP

CEDAR PLANKED SALMON

CIOPPINO

FILLET OF SOLE WITH PESTO

FISH CHOWDER

JAMAICAN SALMON

LEMON AND DILL SALMON

LOBSTER BISQUE

MAHIMAHI WITH ASPARAGUS, BROCCOLI, AND
   SPINACH

PARMESAN TILAPIA

SEAFOOD ALFREDO

SWEET AND SPICY SALMON

BARBECUED SHRIMP

serves 8

The Ingredients

2 pounds fresh raw shell-on shrimp (ask the fish guy for shrimp in the 21 to 25 per pound size range)

8 tablespoons (1 stick) butter

¼ cup olive oil

¼ cup gluten-free Worcestershire sauce

1 to 2 tablespoons Tabasco sauce (I used 1½)

1 teaspoon kosher salt

1 teaspoon ground black pepper

juice of 3 lemons

1 tablespoon chopped fresh basil

The Directions

Use a 6-quart slow cooker. Rinse the shrimp, but don't soak them too much. Put the shrimp into the stoneware with the butter, olive oil, and Worcestershire sauce. Add the Tabasco, salt, and pepper, then add the lemon juice and basil. Toss just a bit with a big spoon to mingle the flavors. The butter will be in a big stick, but that's okay. Cover and cook on high for about 2 hours, checking every 30 minutes. You'll know the shrimp is done when it has turned pink, and can be peeled easily. I turned ours off at exactly 2 hours. It was perfect.

Serve with French bread to sop up the juice. If you are gluten-free, make a fresh loaf of your favorite bread to go along—the juice is amazing.

The Verdict

This recipe is adapted from Ree Drummond, who writes *The Pioneer Woman Cooks*, a fantastic blog and cooking resource. I brought this shrimp to my friend Nancy's house, where eight grownups and three kids gobbled it up. I was thrilled with the way the shrimp cooked in the slow cooker with very little attention.

CEDAR PLANKED SALMON

serves 2 to 3

The Ingredients

1 single-use untreated cedar plank, cut to size
1 teaspoon kosher salt
1 teaspoon ground cumin
1 teaspoon garlic powder
1 teaspoon dried rosemary
1 teaspoon onion powder
1 pound salmon
1 tablespoon honey
2 limes, sliced

The Directions

Use a 6-quart slow cooker. Have your amazing husband (or other handy-type person who is not afraid of saws) cut the cedar plank to size. Soak the plank in water for at least an hour.

While soaking, combine the salt and dried spices in a bowl. Coat the salmon on all sides with the spice rub, and drizzle on the honey. Top with the lime slices and slide it all into a plastic ziplock bag. Refrigerate the salmon while the board is soaking—at least 1 hour, but overnight in the refrigerator is fine.

When the appropriate time has elapsed, put the wet cedar plank into the bottom of your stoneware. Put the salmon (with the lime slices) directly on the board. If you are using a great-big-huge slow cooker, put a sheet of aluminum foil over the salmon and scrunch it down to create a smaller area for steam to collect. Cover and cook on low for 2 hours. Check the salmon—it should flake easily with a fork. If it doesn't, cook on low for an additional 30 minutes, and check again.

The Verdict

I found the cedar board in the grocery store near the charcoal briquettes. This is a fun way to cook fish in the slow cooker—it's different, and the cedar provides a hint of smoky and woodsy flavor to the fish. My kids love fish, and both ate a bunch, which provided the excuse to get frozen yogurt for dessert.

CIOPPINO

serves 6 to 8

The Ingredients

FOR THE STEW BASE

1 (28-ounce) can crushed tomatoes with their juices

1 (8-ounce) can tomato sauce

1 cup white wine

1/2 cup clam juice

1/2 cup chopped onion

6 garlic cloves, minced

1/2 cup parsley, chopped

1 green bell pepper, chopped

1 hot pepper, chopped (optional—I used a red jalapeño)

1 teaspoon dried thyme

2 teaspoons dried basil

1 teaspoon dried oregano

1/2 teaspoon paprika

1/2 teaspoon cayenne pepper

FOR THE SEAFOOD

1 deboned and cubed fillet of white fish (I used red snapper)

1 dozen prawns, shells on or off

1 dozen sea scallops

1 dozen mussels, cleaned

1 dozen clams, cleaned

1 cracked Dungeness crab

kosher salt

black pepper

The Directions

Use a 6-quart slow cooker. Place all the ingredients into the stoneware except for the seafood. Stir to mix well. Cover and cook 8 hours on low or 4 to 5 hours on high. Add the seafood 45 minutes before serving, and turn the heat up to high. Stir occasionally. Season with salt and pepper to taste.

The Verdict

There is nothing better than a big bowl of hot, spicy cioppino. It's a little messy, but oh so very good. Change into a red- or dark-colored shirt so the drips and spots don't show. The kids ate a bunch, along with my in-laws. This is an impressive meal to serve to company.

FILLET OF SOLE WITH PESTO

serves 4

The Ingredients

aluminum foil
2 pounds fillet of sole, cut into 4 pieces
3 tablespoons prepared pesto
¼ cup shredded Parmesan cheese

The Directions

Use a 6-quart slow cooker. Spread a layer of foil on the countertop large enough to wrap a piece of the fish. Put the fish on it, cover with a spoonful of pesto, and a sprinkle of cheese. Fold over the foil to create a little packet. Put the packet into the slow cooker. Continue to layer in the foil packets until you run out of fish. Do not add water. Cover and cook on low for 3 to 4 hours, checking after 3 hours. The fish is done when it is opaque white and flakes nicely with a fork.

FISH CHOWDER

serves 4 to 6

The Ingredients

8 to 10 baby white potatoes, diced
1 cup frozen roasted corn
1/2 white onion, chopped
1 handful baby carrots, chopped
3 celery stalks, chopped
3 cups chicken broth
3 to 4 garlic cloves, chopped
1/2 teaspoon black pepper
1/4 teaspoon Old Bay Seasoning (optional)
kosher salt
1 cup heavy whipping cream
1 pound white fish, cut into cubes (frozen okay)
2 cups frozen shelled fully cooked shrimp

The Directions

Use a 4-quart slow cooker. Put the vegetables into your stoneware. Cube fish, and add—it's okay if it's still frozen. Plop everything else on top except the cream and shrimp. Cover and cook on low for 8 hours, high for 4 hours, or until the potatoes are tender. Stir in the heavy cream and shrimp 20 minutes before serving, and turn the slow cooker to high.

The Verdict

The kids went through a phase of splitting a can of Progresso Clam Chowder every day for lunch. It was a very easy time for me. This tastes remarkably similar, and it was supereasy to throw together.

JAMAICAN SALMON

serves 2

The Ingredients

1/8 teaspoon dried thyme
1/8 teaspoon ground cloves
1/8 teaspoon ground ginger
1/8 teaspoon ground nutmeg
1 teaspoon onion powder
2 teaspoons granulated sugar
1/4 teaspoon chipotle chili powder
1/4 teaspoon black pepper
1/2 teaspoon ground cinnamon
1 teaspoon kosher salt
aluminum foil
1 pound salmon

The Directions

Use a 6-quart slow cooker. Combine all the herbs, spices, and salt in a bowl. Spread out a length of aluminum foil, and put the salmon in the middle. Rub both sides of the fish with the dry spice rub. Fold the foil over to make an enclosed packet, and crimp the ends. If it looks like there is a gap that might leak fish juice, wrap with another piece of foil, just in case. Put the foil packet into your slow cooker. Do not add any water. Cover and cook on low for 2 hours. Your salmon is done when it flakes easily with a fork. Serve with rice or pasta and vegetables.

The Verdict

I like it when sweet and spicy flavors commingle, so I was intrigued by the idea of making a Jamaican dry rub of my own to use on chicken or fish. That, and whenever I hear someone on TV name a dish "Jamaican Me Crazy" something or other, I simultaneously groan and laugh. Every. Single. Time. The fish cooked perfectly, the crock was a cinch to clean, and the house didn't smell fishy. What a wonderful meal.

LEMON AND DILL SALMON

serves 4

The Ingredients

1 (12-ounce) package fresh spinach
2 pounds salmon
³/₄ teaspoon kosher salt
¹/₂ teaspoon black pepper
2 teaspoons dried dill
2 lemons
¹/₄ cup white wine

The Directions

Use a 6-quart slow cooker. I didn't make foil packets for this fish. Wash spinach and put all of it into your stoneware. It will completely fill it, but shove the spinach down; it will wilt quite a bit while cooking. Place the fish onto the spinach bed, and sprinkle each side with salt, pepper, and dill. Slice the lemons and lay them on top of fish and on each side. Pour in the wine. Cook on low for 2 hours, or until fish flakes easily with a fork.

LOBSTER BISQUE

serves 4

The Ingredients

3 cups chicken broth
8 ounces clam juice
1 (14.5-ounce) can stewed tomatoes and their juices
1 onion, diced
8 ounces sliced mushrooms
1 large leek (just the white part!) diced
1 tablespoon dried parsley
2 teaspoons Old Bay Seasoning mix
1 teaspoon dried dill
2 lobster tails
1 cup heavy cream
lemon slices as garnish

The Directions

Use a 6-quart slow cooker. Combine the broth, clam juice, tomatoes, onion, mushrooms, leek, parsley, Old Bay, and dill. Cover and cook on low for 6 to 8 hours, or on high for 4 to 5 hours, or until the onions are translucent and the flavors have melded. Use a handheld immersion blender to blend into a chowdery broth. Add the lobster tails. Cover and cook on high for 30 to 45 minutes, or until the tails have turned pink and the meat is fork-tender. Remove the tails from the stoneware, and stir in the heavy cream. Ladle the bisque into dishes, and serve with lemon slices and the lobster meat. You can take the meat out of the tail, and mix it in the soup, or leave it intact and pick at the table.

(C O N T I N U E D)

The Verdict

Lobster . . . in the slow cooker . . . life is so very good. This was an incredible meal. It was fun to eat, and it felt quite fancy. My kids both liked the lobster, and thought the soup part was "yummy." But they also thought sucking on the lemon slices was the best part of their dinner. I don't have a reason for this.

MAHIMAHI WITH
ASPARAGUS, BROCCOLI, AND SPINACH

serves 2

The Ingredients

2 cups fresh broccoli florets

8 asparagus stalks

2 cups fresh spinach

1 tablespoon olive oil

1/4 teaspoon kosher salt

1/4 teaspoon black pepper

1/2 teaspoon crushed red pepper flakes

1/4 cup lemon juice

1 pound mahimahi

The Directions

Use a 6-quart slow cooker. Wash and trim all the veggies, and put them into the stoneware. In a small bowl, combine the olive oil, salt, pepper, red pepper flakes, and 1 tablespoon lemon juice. Using a pastry brush, paint the fish on all sides with the mixture, and place on top of vegetables. Add the remaining lemon juice. Cover and cook on low for approximately 2 to 3 hours. Mahimahi is pretty thick; if you opt to use a thinner fish (such as tilapia), check after 90 minutes. Your fish is done when it is opaque white and flakes easily with a fork.

(CONTINUED)

The Verdict

A moist, tender fish packed with flavor. The vegetables release quite a bit of liquid, which steams the mahimahi nicely. I was very happy that I made this and ate it for lunch. I forget about lunch a lot, and grab whatever is lying around, or pick at leftovers. I've also noticed the kids are more inclined to try new foods in the middle of the day, before the 4 o'clock crankies hit. My three-year-old ate this with me, and my six-year-old had it as an after-school snack. The stars must have been in proper alignment or something, because there wasn't any fuss about having fish and vegetables as a snack.

PARMESAN TILAPIA
serves 4

The Ingredients
1/4 cup mayonnaise
1/2 cup shredded Parmesan cheese
4 garlic cloves, minced
juice of 2 lemons
pinch of kosher salt
pinch of black pepper
aluminum foil
3 to 4 tilapia fillets

The Directions
Use a 6-quart slow cooker. In a bowl, combine the mayonnaise, Parmesan, garlic, lemon juice, salt, and pepper. Set the sauce aside. Lay out sheets of aluminum foil, and put a fillet or two in the center of each sheet. Rub the sauce mixture on both sides of the fish. Fold the foil over to make a little packet surrounding the fish, and crimp the ends. Put the foil packet into your slow cooker. Do not add water. Cover and cook on low for 3 to 4 hours; fish should flake easily with a fork when done. Please take care when opening foil packets—the steam will be quite hot. Remove fish from the foil, and serve with your favorite side dishes.

The Verdict
Even people who aren't crazy about fish will like this recipe. You've got cheese, mayonnaise, and lemon juice—a trifecta that can't be beat. This is my family's favorite fish recipe.

SEAFOOD ALFREDO

serves 4

The Ingredients

8 tablespoons (1 stick) butter
2 tablespoons flour (I used a gluten-free baking mix)
2 cups milk (2 percent or lower in fat content)
1 teaspoon herbes de provence
1/2 teaspoon kosher salt
3 garlic cloves, minced
3/4 cup shredded mozzarella cheese
3/4 cup shredded Parmesan cheese
1 pound frozen cooked shrimp or seafood medley
freshly cooked pasta, for serving

The Directions

Use a 4-quart slow cooker. Make a roux by melting butter in a saucepan on the stovetop and slowly stirring in flour until no lumps remain. Add to slow cooker. Pour in milk, add herbs, salt, garlic, and shredded cheeses. Cover and cook on low for 4 hours. Add frozen seafood, and stir well. Cover again and cook on high for 30 minutes, or until the seafood is heated through. Toss with freshly cooked pasta; I used brown rice spaghetti.

SWEET AND SPICY SALMON

serves 4

The Ingredients

1 teaspoon paprika
1 teaspoon ground cumin
1/2 teaspoon dried oregano
1/2 teaspoon crushed red pepper flakes
1/2 teaspoon kosher salt
2 garlic cloves, minced
2 tablespoons brown sugar
aluminum foil
1 pound salmon fillets

The Directions

Use a 4-quart or larger slow cooker. In a shallow dish, combine all the spices, salt, garlic, and brown sugar. Spread out a length of foil for each piece of salmon. Put a salmon fillet in the center of a foil sheet, and rub the spice and sugar mixture on all sides of the fish. Fold the foil over and crimp the sides to make a foil packet. Repeat with each piece of fish. Put the packets into a dry slow cooker. Cover and cook on low for 2 to 4 hours, or until fish flakes easily with a fork.

POULTRY

$\mathcal{W}$e eat a lot of chicken in our house. I grew up on boneless, skinless chicken, and we had it quite often. When I started cooking and shopping for my own family, I followed suit and made sure that we had plenty of chicken parts in the freezer. The problem with eating a lot of chicken is that you get bored. *Really* bored. And you start to hate chicken. And maybe you begin to kind of want to gouge your eyeballs out with a fork at the idea of another boring dry chicken meal. These aren't boring chicken (or turkey) meals. These chicken meals are moist and packed full of flavor.

20- TO 40-CLOVE GARLIC CHICKEN

ABSOLUTELY CRAZY TURKEY

APPLE, CHEDDAR, AND TURKEY MEATBALLS

APPLESAUCE CHICKEN

APRICOT CHICKEN

BACON AND CHEESE CHICKEN

BACON-WRAPPED CORNISH GAME HENS

BALSAMIC CHICKEN WITH SPRING VEGETABLES

BROWN SUGAR CHICKEN

CAJUN ROASTED TURKEY BREAST

CHICKEN ADOBO

CHICKEN CORDON BLEU

CHICKEN MASALA

CHICKEN NUGGETS

CHICKEN PARMESAN

CHICKEN TACOS

CHIPOTLE CHICKEN WITH SWEET POTATOES

COQ AU VIN

CREAM CHEESE CHICKEN

"FRIED CHICKEN"

HONEY AND APRICOT GLAZED DUCK

INDONESIAN PEANUT BUTTER CHICKEN

LAZY CHICKEN

LEMON-AND-HERB-ROASTED CHICKEN

MAPLE-DIJON CHICKEN

MARGARITA CHICKEN

MEDITERRANEAN CHICKEN

MOROCCAN CHICKEN

ROTISSERIE-STYLE CHICKEN

SALSA CHICKEN

SLOPPY JOES

SPANISH BRAISED CHICKEN

SWEET-AND-SOUR CHICKEN WITH MANGO LETTUCE WRAPS

STUFFED PEPPERS

TURKEY BREAST

TURKEY CUTLETS IN MANGO SALSA

WHOLE ENTIRE CHICKEN

20- TO 40-CLOVE GARLIC CHICKEN

serves 6

The Ingredients

    1 large yellow onion, sliced

    3 to 4 pounds chicken (I used drumsticks)

    1 tablespoon olive oil

    2 teaspoons kosher salt

    2 teaspoons paprika

    1 teaspoon pepper

    20 to 40 garlic cloves, peeled but intact

The Directions

Use a 6-quart oval slow cooker. Place onion slices on the bottom of the stoneware insert. In a large mixing bowl, toss chicken parts with olive oil, salt, paprika, pepper, and all of the garlic cloves. Pour into stoneware, on top of the onion. Do not add water. Cover and cook on low for 6 to 8 hours, or on high for 4 to 6. The longer you cook chicken on the bone, the more tender it will be. If you use drumsticks, the ones on the sides of the crock will brown, and may stick, burning a bit. If this bothers you, you can rearrange them with tongs an hour before serving. I cooked our chicken on low for 7 hours, then kept it on warm for another 2.

The Verdict

This is wonderful! I used thirty-three cloves, because that's how many I had in the house. The onion and garlic had a mild, nutty garlic flavor that was a bit sweet. Some of the larger cloves of garlic that were still intact were kind of strong—they itched my nose. The kids ate the chicken (no onions or garlic for them) dipped in barbecue sauce. Adam and I each ate three drumsticks that night, and I used the leftovers to make some amazing slow-cooked fried rice (see p. 359).

ABSOLUTELY CRAZY TURKEY

serves 4

The Ingredients

   6 slices of bacon (I used turkey bacon)
   1 (2-ounce) can anchovies, drained and rinsed
   1¼ pounds turkey breast cutlets
   1 (8.5-ounce) jar sun-dried tomatoes, drained and rinsed

The Directions

Use a 4-quart slow cooker. Spread the bacon slices on the bottom of your stoneware. Lay anchovies on top. Add the turkey cutlets; it's okay if they overlap. Sprinkle on the sun-dried tomatoes. Cover and cook on low for 6 to 8 hours.

The Verdict

I got adventurous with this dish, and was actually the only one in the house to give it a try—everyone else was scared. The combo of the smoky and slightly salty turkey with the acidity and tang of the sun-dried tomatoes was crazy-good. I didn't eat the bacon or the anchovies—I just used them for flavor.

APPLE, CHEDDAR, AND TURKEY MEATBALLS

serves 4

The Ingredients
1½ pounds extra-lean ground turkey
1 large egg
1 teaspoon kosher salt
1 teaspoon black pepper
1 teaspoon onion powder
1 green apple, peeled and shredded
½ cup shredded sharp cheddar
½ cup dried unsweetened cranberries

The Directions

Use a 4-quart slow cooker. In a large mixing bowl, mix the ground turkey with the egg, seasonings, apple, cheese, and cranberries. I used my hands. Make golf-ball size meatballs, and place into your stoneware, stagger-stacking. Cover and cook on low for 5 to 8 hours, or on high for 4 to 6 hours.

While they cook, juice will collect on the bottom of the crock, and the meatballs will begin to look bright white and slimy. Don't be alarmed—they will continue to cook and will brown. They (miraculously enough!) don't seem to stick together in a big blob; you'll be able to separate them.

The Verdict

We all really liked these a lot. They're moist, flavorful, and fun to pop in your mouth. I did need to fish the cranberries out of my three-year-old's portion, because evidently eating warm cranberries is "wrong."

APPLESAUCE CHICKEN

serves 4

The Ingredients

4 boneless, skinless chicken breast halves or thighs (I used 2 of each, and they were frozen)
1/2 yellow onion, chopped, or 1 tablespoon dried onion flakes
1 1/2 cups applesauce
1 tablespoon apple cider vinegar
2 garlic cloves, minced
1/4 teaspoon ground cinnamon
1/2 teaspoon black pepper
1/4 teaspoon crushed red pepper flakes (optional)

The Directions

Use a 4-quart slow cooker. Put the chicken pieces into your stoneware. Add the onion (if you are using the dried onion, wait and add it to the applesauce). In a small bowl, mix the applesauce, vinegar, garlic, and spices together. Pour on top of the chicken. Cover and cook on low for 5 to 7 hours, or on high for 3 to 4 hours. Serve with rice or quinoa.

The Verdict

This is a good chicken recipe. Don't be concerned by the name—the chicken doesn't turn into applesauce, it gets cooked in it, but still keeps its shape. The kids ate this! And liked it! And said I was the best mother ever and that I should make this every single night from now on. And it had nothing to do with the long lecture about wasting food and starving people. Nothing at all.

APRICOT CHICKEN

serves 4

The Ingredients

2 pounds boneless, skinless chicken thighs
1 (11-ounce) jar apricot preserves
1 teaspoon dried onion flakes
1 tablespoon Dijon mustard
1 tablespoon gluten-free soy sauce
$\frac{1}{4}$ teaspoon ground ginger
$\frac{1}{4}$ to $\frac{1}{2}$ teaspoon crushed red pepper flakes (optional)

The Directions

Use a 4-quart slow cooker. Put the chicken into the stoneware. In a small bowl, combine the other ingredients, and pour evenly over the chicken. Cover and cook on low for 6 to 8 hours, or on high for 3 to 4 hours. Serve with white or brown rice.

The Verdict

This tastes so good that everyone you serve will be astonished that it was cooked in a slow cooker. That is a compliment.

BACON AND CHEESE CHICKEN

serves 4

The Ingredients

2 tablespoons olive oil

4 to 6 chicken breast halves, or equivalent bird pieces (I used 8 breast tenders)

¼ cup teriyaki sauce (I used a gluten-free variety)

½ cup ranch salad dressing

1 cup shredded cheddar cheese

12 pieces cooked bacon, crumbled (I used beef bacon, but any kind is fine)

The Directions

Use a 4-quart slow cooker. Pour the olive oil into the bottom of your crock and spread it around. If you are using thighs, or a fattier cut of meat, this step is not needed. Place chicken pieces on top of the oil.

In a small bowl, combine the teriyaki sauce with the ranch dressing. (I kept tasting this—the flavor is so bizarre and tasty; I've never had anything like it.) Pour the sauce over the top of the chicken. Add the shredded cheese and the crumbled bacon to the crock, distributing it between the chicken pieces, if you can. Cover and cook on low for 6 to 8 hours, or on high for 3 to 4 hours. The cooking time will depend on how thick your chicken pieces are, and if they are fresh or frozen.

BACON-WRAPPED CORNISH GAME HENS

serves 4

The Ingredients

    2 Cornish game hens, skin removed
    1 teaspoon kosher salt
    1 teaspoon dried thyme
    1 teaspoon dried rosemary
    6 slices of bacon (I used beef bacon, but any kind is fine)

The Directions

Use a 6-quart slow cooker. Remove as much skin from the birds as you can with poultry shears. In a small bowl, mix together the salt, thyme, and rosemary. Rub the mixture all over the birds, inside and out. Place birds into stoneware. Wrap the bacon strips around each, 2 strips one way, and 1 strip the other, tucking the ends into the cavities. Cover and cook on low for 6 to 8 hours, or on high for 4 to 5 hours. I cooked ours on low for 4 hours, and then switched it to high for the last hour. Serve with rice and roasted veggies.

The Verdict

Oooh, boy. I like Cornish game hens. The meat is moist and rich—maybe a bit gamey for some, but quite full of flavor. The kids ate all the little drumsticks and a lot of the breast meat. The rosemary and thyme were perfect, and the bacon provided a neat smoky flavor.

BALSAMIC CHICKEN WITH SPRING VEGETABLES

serves 6

The Ingredients

6 boneless, skinless chicken thighs (mine were frozen)

2 zucchinis, sliced into rounds

2 yellow squash, sliced into rounds

1 orange bell pepper, chopped

1 yellow bell pepper, chopped

1 red onion, chopped

1 head garlic, cloves peeled

1/4 cup balsamic vinegar

2 teaspooons gluten-free Worcestershire sauce

kosher salt

black pepper

The Directions

Use a 6-quart slow cooker. Place the chicken into the stoneware. Put all the vegetables into a large mixing bowl with the peeled garlic cloves. Toss the vegetables with the balsamic vinegar and Worcestershire sauce, add salt and pepper to taste, and pour on top of chicken. Cover and cook on low for 6 to 8 hours, or on high for 4 to 6 hours. Serve with brown rice or quinoa.

BROWN SUGAR CHICKEN

serves 6

The Ingredients

12 boneless, skinless chicken thighs, or 6 boneless, skinless chicken breast halves
1 cup brown sugar, firmly packed
1 teaspoon black pepper
3 garlic cloves, minced
2 tablespoons gluten-free soy sauce
²/₃ cup white wine vinegar
¼ cup lemon-lime soda

The Directions

Use a 4-quart slow cooker. Plop the chicken into your crock. Cover with the brown sugar, black pepper, chopped garlic, and soy sauce. Add the vinegar, and pour in the soda. It will bubble! Cover and cook on low for 6 to 9 hours, or on high for 4 to 5 hours. The chicken is done when it is cooked through and has reached the desired tenderness. The longer you cook it on low, the more tender your chicken will be. Serve over a bowl of white rice with a ladle full of the broth.

The Verdict

It should be noted that this chicken has been named "Candy Chicken" in our house. I don't think my kids have ever eaten so much chicken in their lives. If you are tired of dried out, boring chicken, you must try this. You simply must. Go. *Now.* Go to the store and buy the ingredients.

CAJUN ROASTED TURKEY BREAST

serves 4

The Ingredients

3- to 4-pound turkey breast
1/2 teaspoon black pepper
1 teaspoon kosher salt
1/2 teaspoon cayenne pepper
1 tablespoon onion powder
1/2 teaspoon paprika
1/2 teaspoon dried thyme
1/4 teaspoon ground nutmeg
3 to 4 sprigs of fresh rosemary, or 1/2 teaspoon dried
1 cup chicken broth

The Directions

Use a 5- to 6-quart slow cooker. If desired, remove the skin from the turkey breast (I always do). In a small bowl, combine the pepper, salt, cayenne, onion powder, paprika, thyme, nutmeg, and rosemary. Rub the mixture all over the turkey. Place the turkey into the slow cooker. If you have any extra mixture remaining in the bowl, sprinkle it on top. Add the chicken broth. Cover and cook on low for 6 to 8 hours, or on high for 4 to 5 hours.

The Verdict

You can rub whatever herbs and spices you like on the turkey breast, but I was in a Cajun mood, and was pleased with this combination. I like turkey, but don't like the dryness and blandness that sometimes (read: lots of times) comes along for the ride when making turkey. This isn't possible when slow cooked. We ate this for dinner, then had cold sandwiches the next day.

CHICKEN ADOBO

serves 6

The Ingredients

3 to 5 pounds boneless, skinless chicken
1/2 teaspoon salt
1 teaspoon black pepper
1/4 cup gluten-free soy sauce
4 garlic cloves, chopped
1/2 cup apple cider vinegar
4 bay leaves
1 yellow onion, sliced in rings
1 1/2 cups shredded carrots

The Directions

Use a 4-quart slow cooker. It's best to marinate the chicken overnight in a large plastic ziplock bag with salt, black pepper, soy sauce, garlic, vinegar, and bay leaves. In the morning, put the onion and carrots into your slow cooker, and pour the contents of the plastic bag on top. Cook on low for 7 to 8 hours, or on high for 4 to 5 hours. Serve with rice.

CHICKEN CORDON BLEU

serves 4

The Ingredients

cooking spray
4 chicken breast halves, pounded thin
4 to 8 slices ham
4 to 8 slices Swiss cheese
1 (10-ounce) can cream-of-something soup, or alternative (see next page)
2 tablespoons low-fat milk

The Directions

Use a 4-quart slow cooker. Spray crock with cooking spray. Pound chicken breasts flat (put them in a plastic zippered bag before you pound so chicken juice doesn't spray all over the kitchen) and put a slice of ham and one of Swiss on the top of each chicken breast and roll it up. Place into slow cooker, seam side down. If desired, top with another piece of ham and one of cheese. Continue with the other pieces. It's okay to stagger-stack the chicken. It will still cook nicely for you.

Open a can of cream-of-something soup. Pour into the crock. Put the 2 tablespoons of low-fat milk into the empty soup can and swirl it around to get the remaining stuck-on good stuff. Pour that in, too. Cover and cook on low for 6 to 8 hours, or on high for 4 to 5 hours. This is done when the chicken is cooked through and has begun to brown on top.

(CONTINUED)

ALTERNATIVE SPECIAL SOUP

The Ingredients

    1 tablespoon butter
    3 tablespoons flour (I used a gluten-free baking mix)
    1/2 cup low-fat milk (I used soy milk)
    1/2 cup chicken broth
    1/4 teaspoon salt
    1/4 teaspoon black pepper

The Directions

If you are a crazy Californian like me, and prefer not to use canned soup, make your own "special soup." Make a roux on the stovetop with the butter and flour, and whisk in the milk, broth, salt, and pepper. Pour on top of the chicken. No need to add extra milk.

The Verdict

I liked that this chicken wasn't breaded—I've ordered Cordon Bleu in restaurants before and the breading on it reminded me of a frozen chicken patty and it grossed me out. This was tender and quite flavorful. Adam was excited to take leftovers for lunch.

CHICKEN MASALA

serves 4

The Ingredients

6 boneless, skinless chicken thighs

1 cup diced onion

1 (15-ounce) can diced tomatoes, drained

2 garlic cloves, minced

$1/2$ teaspoon ground ginger

$1/2$ teaspoon ground coriander

$1/4$ teaspoon cayenne pepper

1 teaspoon garam masala

$1/2$ cup plain nonfat yogurt

The Directions

Use a 4-quart slow cooker. Put the chicken and onion into the stoneware. In a small bowl, combine the tomatoes with the garlic and all the spices, reserving $1/2$ teaspoon of garam masala for use later. Pour the tomato mixture on top of the chicken. Cover and cook on low for 8 hours, or on high for 4 hours. Shred the chicken with two forks, and stir in the yogurt. Add the remaining $1/2$ teaspoon garam masala, or more to taste. There is no salt added, so salt at the table to taste.

CHICKEN NUGGETS

serves 6

The Ingredients

4 to 6 boneless, skinless chicken breast halves

4 tablespoons (½ stick) butter, melted

4 large eggs

1 cup bread crumbs, or a mixture of cracker, cereal, tortilla chip, etc. crumbs

½ teaspoon seasoned salt

½ teaspoon garlic powder

1 tablespoon flaxseed meal (optional—I threw it in; they'll never know.)

cooking spray

aluminum foil

The Directions

Use a 6-quart slow cooker. Make sure the chicken is fully thawed. Cut the chicken into child-size pieces (about 2-inch squares). I found the smaller pieces cooked better than the larger ones. The larger ones also didn't get crispy on top, so stick to 2-inch pieces.

In a bowl, mix the melted butter with the eggs. Mix together cracker and cereal crumbs with seasoned salt and garlic powder as well as the flaxseed meal, if using.

Spray your stoneware with cooking spray. Dip each piece of chicken in the egg mixture, and then toss in the crumbs. Put a layer of battered chicken pieces into the bottom of the crock. When the bottom is full, add a piece of aluminum foil. Poke tiny holes in the foil with a fork to allow steam to escape. I found that the layer with the most holes worked the best, and the layer with fewer holes resulted in a soggy topping, so the holes are important. I made 4 layers with 6 cut-up chicken breast halves. Cover your slow cooker, but vent the lid with a wooden spoon or chopstick. Cook on high for 2 to 4 hours.

The Verdict

These were really good. A few in the middle got soggy so I ate them, and gave the kids the ones that were crunchier. I was impressed with the topping, and the kids didn't freak out, so they must have liked it too. My older daughter thought they were store bought—a pretty gracious compliment.

CHICKEN PARMESAN

serves 4

The Ingredients

1 tablespoon olive oil

1 large egg, beaten

½ cup bread crumbs (I use a food-processed loaf of brown rice bread)

½ teaspoon Italian seasoning

¼ teaspoon black pepper

¼ teaspoon kosher salt

¼ cup Parmesan cheese

4 boneless, skinless chicken breast halves

4 slices mozzarella cheese

1 (25-ounce) jar pasta sauce

The Directions

Use a 4-quart slow cooker. Smear the olive oil around the bottom of your slow cooker.

Beat the egg in a shallow bowl, and set aside. Combine the bread crumbs with the seasonings and Parmesan cheese in a flat dish.

Dip the chicken into the egg, then into bread-crumb mixture, coating both sides. Place the chicken breast pieces in the bottom of the slow cooker, staggering, if needed. Place a slice of mozzarella cheese on top of each chicken piece. Pour the jar of pasta sauce on top. Cover and cook on low for 6 to 7 hours, or on high for 4 hours. Serve with your favorite pasta. We chose brown rice penne.

The Verdict

Chicken Parmesan is my comfort meal. I love Italian food, and this is one of my favorite dinners. It translates very nicely to slow cooking, and gives the chef the opportunity to get out of the kitchen and house. This tasted great, was really easy, and presented well. It is definitely something you can serve to company without hesitation.

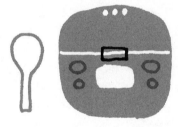

CHICKEN TACOS

serves 4

The Ingredients

    4 boneless, skinless chicken breast halves
    1 (15-ounce) can tomatoes with chiles (Rotel), and their juices
    1 cup frozen corn
    1/3 cup water
    1 (15-ounce) can black beans, drained and rinsed
    corn taco shells
    favorite toppings: shredded cheese, sour cream, lettuce, tomatoes, avocado, ripe black olives

The Directions

Use a 4-quart slow cooker. Put the chicken into the stoneware, and top with the entire can of tomatoes, corn, water, and beans. Cover and cook on low for 7 to 8 hours, or on high for 4 to 5 hours.

Shred the chicken with two large forks, and fill the taco shells. Add your favorite toppings, and enjoy.

The Verdict

I can always count on the kids to eat a lot when they are "in charge" of preparing their own dinner, and a taco bar is a great hands-on, meal-making activity. I appreciate how I can get the meat started early in the day and then shop for the fresh ingredients on my way home.

CHIPOTLE CHICKEN WITH SWEET POTATOES

serves 4

The Ingredients

6 to 8 boneless, skinless chicken thighs

10 ounces sliced mushrooms

1/2 onion, chopped

3 garlic cloves, minced

1 small sweet potato, peeled and chopped in chunks

2 green onions, chopped

1 red bell pepper, diced

1/2 cup chicken broth

1 teaspoon chipotle pepper

1 teaspoon paprika

1/4 teaspoon black pepper

1 cup sour cream

The Directions

Use a 4-quart slow cooker. Put the chicken into the stoneware. Prepare the vegetables, and place on top of the chicken. Pour in the broth, and add the spices. Cover and cook on low for 6 to 8 hours, or on high for 4 hours, or until the chicken is completely cooked and has begun to shred. Before serving, stir in the sour cream, and heat on high for 30 minutes, or until hot. Serve over pasta or brown rice.

The Verdict

This is a wonderful dish. The heat from the chipotle is nicely mellowed by the sour cream and the sweetness from the sweet potatoes. I would serve this to company—it's very yummy.

My kids ate their dinner with the chicken separated from the mushrooms and sweet potato and the rice in its own bowl with butter and Parmesan cheese.

COQ AU VIN

serves 6

The Ingredients

6 slices cooked and crumbled bacon (I used turkey bacon)
6 to 8 chicken thighs
8 ounces sliced baby portobello mushrooms
1 cup baby carrots
1 yellow onion, chopped
3 garlic cloves, chopped or minced
$\frac{1}{2}$ teaspoon kosher salt
$\frac{1}{2}$ teaspoon black pepper
$\frac{1}{2}$ cup chicken broth
$1\frac{1}{2}$ cups red wine (you can use nonalcoholic wine, if you wish)
2 large fresh thyme sprigs

The Directions

Use a 4-quart slow cooker. Cook the bacon on the stovetop or in the microwave and add to the stoneware. Put the chicken (mine was still frozen) on top of the bacon and start layering in the vegetables. Top with salt, pepper, chicken broth, and red wine. Float thyme on top. This is really a no-fuss preparation, just throw it all in. Cover and cook on low for 8 hours. You could cook it on high for 4 hours, but it won't taste as good; the flavors meld better when it is cooked low and slow. Serve with mashed potatoes or your favorite pasta. We used brown rice fusilli.

The Verdict

I hid the leftovers in the back of the fridge behind the cottage cheese so I could eat them all. The chicken has such a great depth of flavor—the bacon provides a nice smoky flavor and the fresh thyme gives it a restaurant aspect that is such a nice surprise. It's purple, which means that it was automatically a hit with my girls. My mom makes this often and prefers to use white wine. It's just as good.

CREAM CHEESE CHICKEN

serves 4

The Ingredients

6 boneless, skinless chicken breast halves, or large thighs

2 tablespoons Italian seasoning

$\frac{1}{2}$ teaspoon celery seed

1 tablespoon onion powder

$\frac{1}{4}$ teaspoon black pepper

1 teaspoon kosher salt

2 garlic cloves, minced

1 tablespoon sugar

2 cups homemade Cream of Mushroom Soup (page 191), or 1 (10-ounce) can condensed cream of mushroom soup

1 (8-ounce) block cream cheese

The Directions

Use a 4-quart slow cooker. Put the chicken into the cooker. Combine the seasonings and sugar in a small dish and pour on top. Add the mushroom soup. Cook on low for 6 to 8 hours, or until the chicken is cooked through. Shred with two large forks, and mix in the cream cheese. Switch the cooker to high, and cook for another 30 minutes, or until the cream cheese has fully melted. Serve over pasta. We had brown rice fusilli.

The Verdict

This is a wonderful dish. My six-year-old reported that it was the very best pasta she's ever had. I let her skip bath time.

"FRIED CHICKEN"

serves 6 to 8

The Ingredients

cooking spray

1 tablespoon seasoned salt

1 tablespoon Italian seasoning

2 teaspoons onion powder

1 teaspoon paprika

1/2 teaspoon black pepper

1/4 cup flour (I used a gluten-free baking mix)

18 thawed drumsticks (or however many will fit nicely into your slow cooker)

4 tablespoons (1/2 stick) butter, melted

The Directions

Use a 6-quart slow cooker. Spray the stoneware with cooking spray. Combine all the seasonings and flour in a ziplock freezer bag. Add the chicken, and tightly seal the bag. Shake until the chicken is nicely coated. Dump chicken into the stoneware. Add the melted butter. Cover and cook on low for 8 to 10 hours, or on high for about 6 hours.

The Verdict

Tasty. I've increased the seasoning since the first time I made the chicken, and like the added flavor. The pieces of chicken on top and near the sides of the crock get a bit crispy, which is an added bonus. I like munching on these cold, and the kids like to dip their drumsticks into barbecue sauce.

HONEY AND APRICOT GLAZED DUCK

serves 6

The Ingredients

4- to 5-pound duck
$\frac{1}{2}$ teaspoon dried oregano
$\frac{1}{4}$ teaspoon black pepper
1 teaspoon garlic salt
$\frac{1}{2}$ teaspoon grated lemon zest
2 teaspoons cornstarch
$\frac{1}{3}$ cup apricot preserves
1 tablespoon gluten-free soy sauce
2 tablespoons honey
2 tablespoons lemon juice

The Directions

Use a 6-quart slow cooker, with a wire rack inside. I used the little rack that came with my rice cooker. Skin the duck, and remove the neck and giblets (ick).

Mix the oregano, pepper, garlic salt, and lemon zest and cornstarch in a small bowl. Rub the mixture all over the duck, inside and out. Place the duck onto rack, breast side up.

Use the same bowl (might as well) to mix the wet ingredients together. Pour over the top of the duck. Cover and cook on high for 4 hours, or until a meat thermometer registers 165° to 180°F.

The Verdict

Duck. It's what's for dinner! I don't eat much duck, but I liked this tremendously. The glaze is quite tasty, and I recommend making a bit more to have for dipping. My kids really liked the sauce a lot, and dipped their "chicken" into it. I told them they were eating duck, but they didn't believe me.

INDONESIAN PEANUT BUTTER CHICKEN

serves 4

The Ingredients

¹⁄₃ cup natural peanut butter
2 tablespoons brown sugar
2 tablespoons gluten-free soy sauce
¹⁄₂ teaspoon sesame oil
2 garlic cloves, chopped
¹⁄₄ teaspoon cayenne pepper
¹⁄₂ teaspoon ground ginger
16 to 18 frozen chicken drumettes
sesame seeds, crushed red pepper flakes (optional garnish)
2 limes, cut in wedges

The Directions

Use a 4-quart slow cooker. Put the peanut butter into the stoneware and turn the cooker to high to begin the melting. Add the brown sugar, soy sauce, sesame oil, garlic, cayenne, and ginger. Stir to combine. Add chicken, and toss to coat. Cover and cook on low for 6 to 8 hours, or on high for 4 to 5 hours. Your meal is done when the chicken is cooked through and has reached the desired tenderness. The longer you cook it, the more tender it will become, but it may fall off the bone if you cook it too long. If your slow cooker isn't at least two-thirds full, keep an eye on it so the peanut butter doesn't burn. You may need to stir it a few times. Garnish with sesame seeds and add red pepper flakes to the grown-up portions, if desired. Serve with white rice and lime wedges.

The Verdict

We really liked this meal. The first time I made it, I didn't add the brown sugar, but you really need it if using all-natural peanut butter. If your peanut butter is already sweetened, you may choose to omit the added sugar. This sauce would taste great on tofu, as well.

LAZY CHICKEN

serves 4 to 6

The Ingredients
3 pounds boneless chicken (or other meat, it really doesn't matter)
1 (25-ounce) jar pasta sauce

The Directions
Use a 4-quart slow cooker. Put the chicken (or other meat) into your slow cooker. Add the entire jar of sauce. If you'd like, you can put a tablespoon or so of water into the empty jar and shake it around to release the remaining sauce. Pour that in, too. Cover and cook on low for 8 hours, or on high for 4 to 5 hours. When finished, shred the meat with 2 large forks, and serve over pasta or rice.

The Verdict
This is my favorite way to slow cook. Before this yearlong challenge, I cooked the "lazy way" at least once a week. I'd get a bag of frozen chicken or a hunk of meat on sale, and plop it into the crock with a jar or bottle of sauce—no need to thaw. I've used barbecue sauce, salad dressing, and bottled meat marinade with fantastic results.

LEMON-AND-HERB-ROASTED CHICKEN

serves 6

The Ingredients

1 (4-pound) whole chicken
½ teaspoon kosher salt
½ teaspoon pepper
1 head garlic, cloves intact and peeled
2 lemons, sliced
3 to 4 sprigs fresh rosemary

The Directions

Use a 6-quart slow cooker. Skin the chicken with poultry shears, and discard the neck and giblets. Salt and pepper the chicken, inside and out. Put the whole cloves of garlic inside the cavity. Place into the crock, breast side down. Place the lemon slices all over the chicken and put a few inside the bird. Lay the sprigs of fresh rosemary on top. Do not add water. Cover and cook on low for 8 hours, or on high for 4 to 6 hours. Carefully remove the chicken from the crock with large tongs—the meat will fall off the bone. Reserve the garlic to serve alongside with some rice or potatoes and fresh vegetables.

MAPLE-DIJON CHICKEN

serves 4

The Ingredients

1 pound boneless, skinless chicken pieces

1 onion, chopped

3 garlic cloves, chopped

1 teaspoon dried thyme

3 tablespoons maple syrup

2 tablespoons Dijon mustard

2 sweet potatoes, peeled and chopped

1 cup chicken broth

2 bay leaves

The Directions

Use a 4-quart slow cooker. Put the chicken into the stoneware and toss with the onion, garlic, thyme, maple syrup, and Dijon mustard. Place the sweet potatoes on top of the chicken. Pour in the broth and add the bay leaves. Cover and cook on low for 5 to 7 hours, or on high for 3 to 5 hours. The chicken is done when it is cooked through and the vegetables reach the desired tenderness.

The Verdict

Anything with the word "Dijon" in the title instantly sounds exquisite and marvelous—even though it's only a $2.99 condiment. Dijon is the show-off in the mustard family. The chicken was tasty and quite moist, and paired nicely with the sweet potatoes. My kids both ate two servings of chicken and some of the sweet potatoes. We didn't have any leftovers.

MARGARITA CHICKEN

serves 4

The Ingredients

4 to 5 boneless, skinless chicken thighs (mine were frozen)

¼ cup Dijon mustard

¼ cup honey

1 tablespoon gluten-free soy sauce

2 garlic cloves, minced

3 tablespoons margarita mix

The Directions

Use a 4-quart slow cooker. Put the chicken into the stoneware. In a small bowl, combine the remaining ingredients. Pour on top of the chicken. Cover and cook on low 7 to 9 hours, or on high 4 to 5 hours. Fresh chicken will not take as long to cook as frozen.

The Verdict

This was delicious! I got the idea from reading a lime chicken recipe Alanna Kellogg posted on her Kitchen Parade Web site, Kitchenparade.com, but we didn't have any limes in the house, only margarita mix. The kids enjoyed it a lot, and Adam and I both had seconds.

MEDITERRANEAN CHICKEN

serves 4

The Ingredients

4 frozen boneless, skinless chicken breast halves
1 (16-ounce) bag frozen artichoke hearts
1 cup pitted green olives
1 (16-ounce) can diced tomatoes with their juices

The Directions

Use a 4-quart slow cooker. Put the chicken into the stoneware, and top with the artichoke hearts, olives, and the entire can of tomatoes. Cover and cook on low for 8 hours, or on high for 4 to 6 hours. Serve with couscous or quinoa.

The Verdict

This is a grown-up version of Lazy Chicken (page 262). The taste is sophisticated, but the preparation takes all of 12 seconds. We love this meal.

MOROCCAN CHICKEN

serves 4

The Ingredients

6 to 8 boneless, skinless chicken thighs
1 cup salsa
1/4 cup chicken broth
2 teaspoons Tabasco sauce
2 teaspoons honey
1 teaspoon ground cumin
1/2 teaspoon ground cinnamon
1/4 teaspoon chipotle chili powder
1/2 teaspoon saffron threads
5 garlic cloves, minced
1/3 cup golden raisins
1/3 cup toasted almonds (I threw raw almonds into the microwave for 2 minutes)

The Directions

Use a 4-quart slow cooker. Put the chicken into the stoneware. In a small bowl, combine the salsa, broth, Tabasco, honey, spices, and garlic. Pour on top of the chicken. Add the raisins and almonds. Cover and cook on low for 6 to 8 hours, or on high for about 4 hours. Serve with quinoa or couscous.

The Verdict

The first time I made this recipe, I was timid with the spices, but these measurements are correct. It's fun for me to be able to put on a meal and taste and tweak throughout the day—the slow cooker provides plenty of tweaking time. My family enjoyed this meal—especially the raisins.

ROTISSERIE-STYLE CHICKEN

serves 4

The Ingredients

1 (4- to 5-pound) whole chicken

2 to 3 teaspoons kosher salt (I used 2)

1 teaspoon paprika

1 teaspoon onion powder

1/2 teaspoon dried thyme

1 teaspoon Italian seasoning

1/2 teaspoon cayenne pepper

1/2 teaspoon black pepper

4 whole garlic cloves (optional)

1 yellow onion, quartered (optional)

The Directions

Use a 6-quart slow cooker. Skin the chicken and get rid of the neck and other stuff from the cavity.

In a bowl, combine the salt, paprika, onion powder, thyme, Italian seasoning, and cayenne and black peppers. Rub the mixture all over the bird, inside and out. If desired, shove 4 whole garlic cloves and a quartered onion inside the bird. Plop the chicken breast-side down into the slow cooker. Do not add water.

Cover and cook on high for 4 to 5 hours, or on low for 8 hours. The meat is done when it is fully cooked and has reached the desired tenderness. The longer you cook it, the more tender the meat will be.

The Verdict

The result? A moist, delicious rotisserie-wanna-be with virtually no fat. I used 2 teaspoons of kosher salt, and the meat was nowhere near as salty as a store-bought rotisserie chicken. I was also surprised at how the meat was not-too-spicy (even the part coated in the spice rub) although I added a good deal of pepper. We were pleased with the flavor, and the kids ate their portions without comment—which is always good.

SALSA CHICKEN

serves 5 to 6

The Ingredients

6 to 9 boneless, skinless chicken thighs, or equivalent bird parts

1 (15-ounce) can black beans, drained and rinsed

1 cup chunky salsa

1 cup frozen white corn

The Directions

Use a 4-quart slow cooker. Put the chicken in the stoneware; my chicken was still frozen. Top with the rinsed black beans, salsa, and corn. Cover and cook on low for 6 to 9 hours, or on high for 4 to 5 hours. Cooking time will vary depending on whether or not your chicken is frozen, and how big the pieces are. If you decide to use boneless, skinless breasts, increase your salsa by $1/2$ cup; breasts are drier than thighs.

The Verdict

This is a really yummy dish, and I liked how low in fat it is. If you don't have enough meat in the house, or would like to stretch the meal, you can add half an 8-ounce block of cream cheese, a cup of sour cream, or a can of cream-of-something soup an hour before serving. The leftovers make a terrific nacho topping.

SLOPPY JOES

serves 4

The Ingredients

1 pound lean ground meat (I used ground turkey)

1 (1.4-ounce) packet Sloppy Joe mix (or use the recipe below to make your own)

1 (6-ounce) can tomato paste

1 cup warm water

FOR THE SLOPPY JOE MIX

1 tablespoon onion flakes

1 tablespoon paprika

2 tablespoons brown sugar

1 teaspoon ground cumin

1 teaspoon kosher salt

1 teaspoon cornstarch

$1/2$ teaspoon garlic powder

$1/4$ teaspoon dry mustard

$1/4$ teaspoon celery seed

$1/4$ teaspoon black pepper

The Directions

Use a 4-quart slow cooker. Put the meat into the stoneware, and add the spice packet (or your own mix), the tomato paste, and the water. Stir well. Cover and cook on low for 6 to 7 hours, or on high for 3 to 5 hours. The meat is done when it is crumbly and fully cooked. Serve on hamburger buns or on top of rice.

(CONTINUED)

The Verdict

I think I was in second grade the last time I had a Sloppy Joe, and was pleasantly surprised how tasty it was; not overly sweet as I had remembered. The kids enjoyed the "ketchup" meat, and liked that they were kind of messy. I made my own hamburger buns out of a box of gluten-free sandwich bread mix.

SPANISH BRAISED CHICKEN

serves 4 to 6

The Ingredients

1 tablespoon butter

4 to 6 large boneless, skinless chicken breast halves

1/2 teaspoon kosher salt

1/4 teaspoon black pepper

1/2 teaspoon dried thyme

3 bell peppers, sliced (I used red and orange)

1 medium yellow onion, sliced crosswise into rings

2 garlic cloves, chopped

1/2 cup dry sherry (you could use apple juice)

2 teaspoons orange juice

12 large pitted green olives, chopped

The Directions

Use a 6-quart slow cooker. Plug in the cooker and turn it to low. Put butter in the bottom of the stoneware. Add the chicken (mine was frozen). Sprinkle salt, pepper, and thyme on top of chicken. Add bell peppers, onion, and garlic. Top with the sherry and orange juice. Sprinkle the chopped green olives over the top. Cover and cook on low for 6 to 8 hours.

The Verdict

I cooked our chicken for 6 hours, and the meat was cooked, but a bit dry inside. I then chopped each breast in half, and added it back to the pot for another hour. The chicken was then quite juicy.

SWEET-AND-SOUR CHICKEN WITH MANGO LETTUCE WRAPS

serves 4

The Ingredients

1½ pounds boneless, skinless chicken breast pieces

1 (10-ounce) jar apricot jam

3 tablespoons gluten-free soy sauce

1 tablespoon sesame oil

1 teaspoon red chili paste

2 garlic cloves, chopped

½ red onion, chopped

½ teaspoon kosher salt

¼ teaspoon black pepper

1 (1-inch) piece fresh ginger, peeled and grated

2 whole jalapeño peppers

2 cucumbers, peeled, seeded, and diced

2 mangoes, peeled and chopped

romaine lettuce leaves

2 limes

2 tablespoons sesame seeds

The Directions

Use a 4-quart slow cooker. Put the chicken into the stoneware. Add the jam, soy sauce, sesame oil, and chili paste. Add garlic, onion, salt, black pepper, and ginger. Toss in the whole jalapeño peppers and the cucumbers. Cover and cook on low for 6 to 8 hours, or high for 4 to 5 hours. Cut the mangoes now while the kitchen is still dirty and put them in a container for use later.

When chicken has fully cooked, shred the meat with two large forks, and spoon ½ cup at a time on large romaine lettuce leaves. Add the mango, a squeeze of fresh lime, and a sprinkle of sesame seeds.

The Verdict

Three out of four of us liked this a lot. That is a successful meal, by my judgment, and the one who didn't like it wouldn't have liked anything that night. Seriously. She was in a funk. The whole jalapeños lend a bit of spice and smokiness without being overpowering.

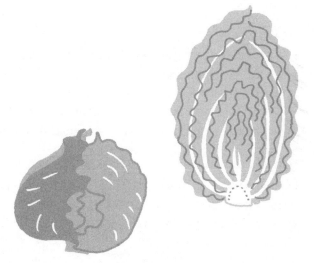

STUFFED PEPPERS

serves 4

The Ingredients

1 pound lean ground turkey or beef (I used ground turkey)
1 cup cooked rice
1 (14-ounce) can fire-roasted tomatoes, drained
1/2 cup chopped onion
1 teaspoon gluten-free Worcestershire sauce
2 tablespoons ketchup
1 teaspoon black pepper
6 large bell peppers (I used red and orange)
1/3 cup water

The Directions

Use a 6-quart oval slow cooker. In a mixing bowl, combine the ground meat with the rice, tomatoes, onion, Worcestershire sauce, ketchup, and black pepper. Set aside. Wash the bell peppers, and cut off and reserve the very tops. Remove the membrane and seeds from each pepper, and stuff with the meat mixture. Replace the tops, and nestle the peppers into your slow cooker. Add 1/3 cup of water around the pepper bases. Cover and cook on low for 6 to 8 hours, or on high for 3 to 4 hours.

The Verdict

I made these on a day we planned to have dinner out, expecting to only take a tiny taste. Instead, I devoured two and had only a small appetizer and water at the restaurant. These are delicious, without a hint of grease—a fear I had.

TURKEY BREAST

serves 4 to 6

The Ingredients

4- to 6-pound turkey breast (bone in or out; your choice)
kosher salt
black pepper
1 onion, chopped coarsely
8 tablespoons (1 stick) butter
2 cups white wine, or you can use broth

The Directions

Use a 4-quart slow cooker. If desired, cut off turkey skin with poultry shears, and discard. (I did this; I freak out about skin.) Season liberally with salt and pepper, and put into the stoneware. Wash your hands well. Add the onion to pot, pushing some pieces down the sides, and put a few in the rib cavity. Add the butter. Pour the wine over the top. I know it's suggested not to cook with wine that you wouldn't drink, but it's okay because I drink cheap wine. Cover and cook on low for 7 to 9 hours, or on high for 4 to 6 hours. Use an instant-read meat thermometer to test doneness—it should register a minimum of 165°F. Remove from cooker, and let sit for about 20 minutes before carving.

The Verdict

I used my mom's "famous" and "secret" family recipe that she got from her friend Mark. I love this turkey—it's moist and juicy, even though there isn't any brown meat. If you'd like, you can throw in some turkey legs along with the breast. The rule of thumb is usually 1 pound of turkey per person. Gobble gobble.

TURKEY CUTLETS IN MANGO SALSA

serves 4

The Ingredients

2 fresh mangoes

2 fresh peaches

1 (15-ounce) can tomatoes and chiles (Rotel) (no need to drain)

$1/4$ cup water

1 tablespoon dried minced onion

1 pound turkey breast cutlets

The Directions

Use a 4-quart slow cooker. Peel and cut the fruit in large dice. Mother Nature certainly had a sense of humor when she developed mangoes—those things are ridiculously hard to cut. In a mixing bowl, combine the canned tomatoes and chiles with the diced fruit, water, and dried onion flakes. Lay the pieces of turkey in the bottom of your slow cooker, slightly staggered so they don't stick together. Pour your newly made salsa on top. Cover and cook on low for 6 to 7 hours, or on high for 4 to 5. Serve with rice and salad. This salsa tastes wonderful over pork chops, too.

WHOLE ENTIRE CHICKEN

serves 6

The Ingredients

1 (3- to 5-pound) whole chicken
1/4 teaspoon kosher salt
1/4 teaspoon black pepper
1/4 cup prepared Italian salad dressing

The Directions

Use a 6-quart slow cooker. Pull the skin off the chicken. This could be considered optional, but skin grosses me out, and I wouldn't be able to eat the chicken if there was skin on it. Salt and pepper the bird, inside and out. Put the chicken into the slow cooker, breast-side down. Pour on the salad dressing. Cover and cook on low for 7 to 8 hours, or on high for 4 to 5 hours. The chicken will be quite tender, and will fall off the bones.

The Verdict

I make this chicken to use in other recipes. There isn't quite enough flavor to eat it on its own; we usually dip it into barbecue sauce. I freeze the meat to use in soups, casseroles, or for sandwiches, and save the carcass for homemade broth.

MEATLESS MAINS

*A*lthough many of the soup and bean recipes I've shared can be made vegetarian, the following dishes can be considered main courses, without an ounce of flesh. Don't be scared to try tofu in the slow cooker; it holds up much better than you would think, especially when pan-fried a bit before it is added to the pot.

EGGPLANT "PARMESAN" WITH FETA

GINGER TERIYAKI TOFU

HONEY AND ORANGE TOFU

INDIAN SPINACH AND TOFU

RATATOUILLE

STUFFED PORTOBELLO MUSHROOMS

STUFFED TOMATOES

SWEET-AND-SOUR TOFU

TOFU IN PEANUT SAUCE

VEGETARIAN CURRY

VEGETARIAN NO-NOODLE LASAGNA

EGGPLANT "PARMESAN" WITH FETA

serves 4

The Ingredients

1 (26-ounce) jar pasta sauce
1 large eggplant
$1/4$ cup bread crumbs (I used brown rice bread crumbs)
2 teaspoons Italian seasoning
$1/2$ teaspoon kosher salt
$1/4$ teaspoon black pepper
$1/4$ cup olive oil
$3/4$ cup crumbled feta cheese

The Directions

Use a 4-quart slow cooker. Pour 1 cup of the jarred pasta sauce into the bottom of the stoneware. Wash the eggplant and slice into $1/2$-inch-thick pieces; no need to peel. Combine bread crumbs, Italian seasoning, salt, and pepper in a shallow dish and set aside. Use a pastry brush to paint both sides of each eggplant slice with olive oil. Dredge each slice in the bread crumb mixture. Stagger-stack the eggplant pieces in your stoneware on top of the pasta sauce. Pour the rest of the pasta sauce on top. Add the crumbled feta. Cover and cook on low for 4 to 6 hours, or high for 3 to 4 hours. This doesn't take very long to cook. Serve with your favorite pasta.

The Verdict

Although I call this eggplant "Parmesan," there isn't actually any Parmesan cheese at all—unless you sprinkle some on the top before eating. I have also omitted the layers of mozzarella and opted for feta, which instantly lightens the dish and creates a fun, tart flavor. I really like eggplant. A lot of people (like the three others in my house) don't like it, but I could eat it every day.

GINGER TERIYAKI TOFU

serves 2 to 3

The Ingredients
    1 (16-ounce) block extra-firm tofu
    1/4 cup cornstarch
    1 tablespoon butter or olive oil
    1/2 white onion, sliced crosswise
    1 teaspoon ground cinnamon
    1/2 teaspoon fennel seed
    1/2 teaspoon ground ginger
    1/2 teaspoon ground cloves
    1/2 teaspoon crushed red pepper flakes
    1/2 cup gluten-free teriyaki sauce
    1 tablespoon gluten-free Worcestershire sauce

The Directions
Use a 2-quart slow cooker. Drain and press the tofu to release any extra moisture. Cut the tofu into 1-inch pieces, and shake in a plastic bag with the cornstarch. Pan-fry the coated tofu in some butter or olive oil until it's golden on all sides. Put into the stoneware. Add the onion, spices, and sauces. Toss the tofu in the mixture to coat thoroughly. Cover and cook on low for 6 hours. Serve with brown rice and steamed or roasted vegetables.

HONEY AND ORANGE TOFU

serves 2 to 3

The Ingredients

1 (16-ounce) block extra-firm tofu
1/4 cup cornstarch
1 to 2 tablespoons butter
2 garlic cloves, minced
1/4 cup gluten-free soy sauce
1/4 cup orange juice
1/4 cup honey
4 cups fresh broccoli florets

The Directions

Use a 4-quart slow cooker. Drain the tofu well, and chop into bite-size chunks. Shake with the cornstarch in a plastic ziplock bag until coated. Pan-fry on the stove in butter until the tofu is a golden color and the outside begins to crisp. Set aside.

In a mixing bowl, combine garlic, soy sauce, orange juice, and honey. Put the tofu into the stoneware, and pour over the sauce. Top with the fresh broccoli florets. Cover and cook on low for 3 to 5 hours. Serve with brown rice or quinoa.

The Verdict

This is a phenomenal sauce that makes anything taste good. If you are scared to try tofu, this is a good beginner recipe. And since tofu is so good for you, it's totally okay to have a pint of Ben & Jerry's for dessert.

INDIAN SPINACH AND TOFU

serves 4

The Ingredients
1 (16-ounce) block extra-firm tofu
¼ cup cornstarch
1 tablespoon butter
2 (10-ounce) boxes frozen spinach, drained (I used one chopped, and one whole leaf)
1 yellow onion, diced
3 garlic cloves, chopped
1 (15-ounce) can garbanzo beans, drained
1 (2-inch) piece fresh ginger, peeled and grated
½ teaspoon kosher salt (plus more to taste)
1 teaspoon ground cumin
1 teaspoon curry powder
1 tablespoon ground coriander
½ teaspoon chile powder
½ teaspoon garam masala
½ cup water

The Directions
Use a 4-quart slow cooker. Drain tofu by squeezing it between some paper towels or a clean dish cloth to get as much of the liquid out as you can. Cut into 1-inch cubes and toss with cornstarch in a plastic ziplock bag. Fry in butter until golden brown. While the tofu is browning, place the drained spinach into your stoneware insert. Add the onion, garlic, garbanzo beans, ginger, salt, and spices. Stir in the ½ cup of water. Add the tofu to the top of the spinach. Cover and cook on low for about 4 hours; it won't take very long to cook. Serve over white rice, and scoop up with naan, pitas, or corn tortilla wedges.

RATATOUILLE

serves 12

The Ingredients

1 large eggplant

1 zucchini

1 yellow summer squash (it looks like a yellow zucchini)

½ yellow onion

1 yellow bell pepper

1 orange bell pepper

1 teaspoon Italian seasoning

1 teaspoon kosher salt

½ teaspoon black pepper

3 garlic cloves, minced

1 (15-ounce) can peeled whole tomatoes, drained

1 (15-ounce) can diced fire-roasted tomatoes and their juices

2 tablespoons olive oil

½ cup water

The Directions

Use a 6-quart slow cooker. Chop all the vegetables in bite-size chunks. I didn't peel anything, but you can if you'd like. Layer the vegetables in the slow cooker, and cover with seasonings, tomatoes, oil, and water. Cook on low for 5 to 6 hours, or on high for 3 to 4 hours. Your meal is done when the vegetables reach the desired tenderness and the flavors have mingled. The vegetables will create more liquid on their own, but the finished result isn't overly soupy.

The Verdict

I liked this more than I thought I would. Ratatouille is a traditional French vegetable stew made with vegetables which are growing in the summer garden. This ratatouille was made with vegetables from the neighborhood supermarket. This stew does not have rats in it, nor did little rats come out of the woodwork to sit on my shoulder while I was chopping vegetables. My children were sorely disappointed.

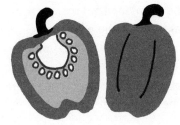

STUFFED PORTOBELLO MUSHROOMS

serves 2

The Ingredients

4 large portobello mushrooms

1½ cups cherry tomatoes, chopped

¼ cup bread crumbs (I used some made from brown rice bread)

4 tablespoons olive oil

¼ cup balsamic vinegar

⅓ cup shredded Parmesan cheese

1 tablespoon dried basil

½ teaspoon kosher salt

½ teaspoon black pepper

The Directions

Use a 6-quart oval slow cooker. With a paring knife, carefully cut the stems off the mushrooms. Chop the stems, and put them in a mixing bowl. Use a spoon to scoop out the centers of each mushroom, and add to the bowl. Add the tomatoes, bread crumbs, 3 tablespoons olive oil, the vinegar, Parmesan, basil, salt, and pepper. Mix well and set aside. Spread the remaining 1 tablespoon of olive oil in the bottom of your stoneware. Put mushroom caps on top of the oil. It's okay if they are a bit on top of each other, or lean them up onto the sides of the crock. Spoon the filling mixture on top of the mushrooms. Cover and cook on low for 4 to 7 hours. Serve with basmati rice.

The Verdict

Portobello mushrooms are nice big, meaty mushrooms that can mimic the texture of meat in your mouth. They are amazing, and hold up well during slow cooking. I loved every bit. The kids weren't so sure and had salami and cheese. Adam ate his along with a steak he barbecued for himself.

STUFFED TOMATOES

serves 2

The Ingredients

    6 large vine-ripened tomatoes
    ¼ cup cream cheese, softened
    ¼ cup goat cheese
    ¼ cup feta cheese, crumbled
    1 garlic clove, chopped
    2 tablespoons chopped fresh basil
    ¼ cup water

The Directions

Use a 4-quart slow cooker. Cut the core out of each tomato; this is much more difficult than I thought it would be—wear an apron. In a bowl, cream together the cheeses with the chopped garlic and basil. Stuff the cheese mixture into the cored tomatoes. Pour the ¼ cup of water into the stoneware, and nestle in the tomatoes. Cover and cook on low for 2 to 4 hours. These will not take long at all. If you overcook them a bit, it's not the end of the world. They will just begin to lose their shape and you'll get a stewed tomato covered with yummy cheese.

The Verdict

I ate them all. We were going out to dinner, and were meeting Adam at the restaurant. The kids already had on nice(ish) clothes and I didn't want tomato juice on them. So I took one for the team and ate them all myself.

SWEET-AND-SOUR TOFU

serves 4

The Ingredients

1 (16-ounce) block extra-firm tofu, drained
1 tablespoon cornstarch
1 tablespoon butter
4 cups fresh vegetables, chopped (I used bell peppers, carrots, and broccoli)
1/2 white onion, chopped
1 (10-ounce) jar gluten-free sweet-and-sour sauce
1/2 tablespoon water
crushed red pepper flakes (optional garnish)

The Directions

Use a 4-quart slow cooker. Cut the tofu into 1-inch chunks, and place into a ziplock freezer bag with the cornstarch. Seal and shake well to coat the tofu. Pan-fry on the stovetop over medium heat in butter, resisting the urge to flip often.

While the tofu is cooking, wash and trim the vegetables and add to the stoneware. When the tofu is finished, add it also. Pour the entire bottle of sweet-and-sour sauce on top of the tofu and vegetables. Add the 1/2 tablespoon of water to the empty sauce jar, and shake. Pour it over the top of the contents in the crock, and toss gingerly. Cover and cook on low for about 3 hours. Your meal is ready when the vegetables have reached the desired consistency. We like the veggies to have a crunch, so I don't let it cook very long. The broccoli was not too crisp, but the onion, bell pepper, and carrot were still al dente. Serve with rice, and add crushed red pepper flakes to the grown-up servings, if desired.

TOFU IN PEANUT SAUCE

serves 4

The Ingredients

1 (16-ounce) block extra-firm tofu, cubed

1/4 cup cornstarch

1 tablespoon butter

1/2 cup natural peanut butter

2 tablespoons gluten-free soy sauce

3 tablespoons margarita mix (or lime juice)

1/2 teaspoon ground ginger

3 garlic cloves, chopped

1/4 teaspoon crushed red pepper flakes

1 (12-ounce) bag baby spinach

The Directions

Use a 2-quart slow cooker. Although I despise precooking things before slow cooking, tofu is best when lightly browned. I've found the best way is to cube it, then toss with a tablespoon or so of cornstarch in a plastic ziplock bag until well coated. Pan-fry on the stovetop over medium heat in butter, resisting the urge to flip often. Add to the slow cooker along with peanut butter, soy sauce, margarita mix, ginger, garlic, and red pepper flakes. Cover and cook on low for 3 to 4 hours. Fifteen minutes before serving, cram the contents of an entire bag of baby spinach inside and cover. The spinach will wilt. Serve over basmati rice.

VEGETARIAN CURRY

serves 6

The Ingredients

2 (15-ounce) cans garbanzo beans, drained and rinsed
1 red bell pepper, seeded and diced
1 potato, diced
1/2 cup diced carrots
1/2 cup diced celery
1 (16-ounce) can diced tomatoes with their juices
2 cups vegetable broth
3 garlic cloves, minced
2 tablespoons curry powder
1/2 teaspoon ground coriander
1/4 teaspoon cayenne pepper
3/4 cup plain yogurt
1 cup frozen peas

The Directions

Use a 4-quart slow cooker. Put garbanzo beans into the stoneware. Add the vegetables and the entire can of tomatoes. Pour in the broth, and stir in the garlic and spices. Cover and cook on low for 8 to 10 hours. Stir in yogurt and frozen peas 30 minutes before serving, and turn the cooker to high. Serve the curry over freshly cooked basmati rice, and have corn tortilla wedges or naan on hand for scoopers.

VEGETARIAN NO-NOODLE LASAGNA

serves 6

The Ingredients

- 1 large eggplant
- 3 yellow squash
- 1 (26-ounce) jar of your favorite pasta sauce
- 1 (12-ounce) container ricotta cheese
- 1 pound sliced mushrooms
- 1 (10-ounce) bag baby spinach
- 8 slices mozzarella cheese
- 2 cups shredded Italian cheese mix
- 2 tablespoons warm water

The Directions

Use a 6-quart slow cooker. Cut the eggplant and squash lengthwise in long slices about ¼ inch thick; no need to peel. These are going to be your noodles. Set aside.

Pour ¼ cup of the pasta sauce into the bottom of your stoneware. Layer in a few pieces of eggplant and squash. Smear some ricotta cheese on top. Add a handful of mushrooms and baby spinach, and a few slices of mozzarella cheese. Pour in some more pasta sauce. Continue layering food until your slow cooker is full and you have run out of ingredients. Top with the rest of the pasta sauce and the shredded cheese. Put the water into the empty pasta sauce jar, cover, and shake. Pour the remaining sauce on top of everything. Cover and cook on low for 5 to 8 hours. The lasagna is done when the vegetables have reached their desired tenderness and the cheese has melted. Serve with garlic bread sticks, yum!

MEAT

*S*low-cooked meat is marvelous—you can get a lesser-quality hunk on sale, and come home to a melt-in-your-mouth meal at the end of a long day. All of these meat meals were tested by my family, aside from the pork dishes. I am allergic to pork, and I'm uncertain if the kids are, so we didn't eat any. Instead, I gifted any pork I made to friends and family, who reported their verdicts.

3-PACKET POT ROAST

A-1 AND DIJON STEAK

ASIAN PEANUT BUTTER PORK

BARBECUE BEEF AND BEAN SANDWICHES

BARBECUE RIBS

BARBECUED PULLED PORK

BLUE CHEESE AND DRIED CHERRY MEATLOAF

BLUE CHEESE AND STEAK ROLL-UPS

CAJUN PULLED PORK

CHILE VERDE

COCONUT BEEF

CORNED BEEF

CRANBERRY PORK ROAST

FAJITAS

FLANK STEAK STUFFED WITH APPLE, FETA, AND ALMONDS

FRENCH DIP SANDWICHES

GINGER BEEF WITH ONIONS AND GARLIC

HAGGIS

HAMBURGER PATTIES

HICKORY-SMOKED BRISKET

HIRINO PSITO

JALAPEÑO POT ROAST

JAVA ROAST

LAMB CHOPS

LAYERED DINNER: STEAK, POTATOES, AND CORN ON THE COB

LEG OF LAMB

LEG OF LAMB WITH PRUNES

LEMON PEPPER RIBS

MAPLE HAM

MARINATED MEAT

MEATLOAF

MOLE

ORANGE-APRICOT PORK CHOPS

ORANGE CHIPOTLE RIBS

PEKING PORK CHOPS

PEPPERCORN STEAK

PINEAPPLE PORK TENDERLOIN

POMEGRANATE BEEF

POT ROAST GLAZED WITH RED WINE AND CRANBERRIES

RED RIBS

ROAST BEEF

ROPA VIEJA

SAUSAGE AND VEGETABLE MEDLEY

SMOKY SPICED LAMB CHOPS

SUN-DRIED TOMATO AND FETA TRI-TIP

USING THE SLOW COOKER AS A SMOKER: SMOKED BRISKET

VEAL MARSALA

VEAL PICCATA

3-PACKET POT ROAST

serves 8

The Ingredients

1 (3-pound) chuck roast
1 (1-ounce) packet salad dressing and seasoning mix
1 (1-ounce) packet of Italian salad dressing mix
1 (1-ounce) packet McCormick Grill Mates Peppercorn & Garlic (see Note)
3 cups water

The Directions

Use a 4-quart slow cooker. Trim the roast of any visible fat and place it into the stoneware. In a small bowl, combine contents of the 3 seasoning packets. Sprinkle over the meat. Flip the meat over a few times to get it covered with the seasoning on all sides. Add about 1 cup of water. Cook on low for 8 hours, or on high for 4 to 5 hours. The meat will be more tender if you cook it low and slow.

Add 2 cups of warm water to the crock, 20 to 30 minutes before eating, and increase the heat to high. The meat only needs 1 cup of water to cook properly, but the spices are too concentrated to only have 1 cup of water in the pot when it's time to eat. Waiting to add the water until the end will help the meat retain its shape, and the added water will make a nice juicy gravy.

The Verdict

So simple and easy, and it makes awesome gravy. If you wait until the packets are on sale, and stick with chuck roast, this is a very inexpensive meal that can be stretched for a few days.

Note: The original recipe called for a packet of beef gravy or au jus, but all of the gravies and au jus packets contain wheat starch. Please read labels carefully a few times if you avoid gluten.

A-1 AND DIJON STEAK

serves 4 to 6

The Ingredients

2 tablespoons A-1 steak sauce

2 tablespoons Dijon mustard

4 to 6 steaks (inexpensive cuts are fine), or a hunk of tri-tip you cut into 4 to 6 steaks

1/4 cup white wine (I had Pinot Grigio in the house)

The Directions

Use a 4-quart slow cooker. Combine the A-1 sauce and Dijon mustard in a little bowl. Paint the sauce mixture on all sides of each piece of meat. Put the meat into the slow cooker. Add the wine. Cover and cook on low for 6 to 8 hours. Serve with potatoes, rice, French fries, or what your family traditionally wants to eat with steak.

The Verdict

Sometimes the easiest recipes taste the best, which can be kind of a bummer if you usually put in a lot of time and effort chopping, mixing, and tasting. The kids ate their servings eagerly—the meat was tender and tasted marvelous. I drizzled the collected crock drippings on top of rice pilaf we had as a side.

ASIAN PEANUT BUTTER PORK

serves 4

The Ingredients

1 onion, sliced in rings
1 ($1\frac{1}{2}$- to 2-pound) pork tenderloin
$\frac{1}{4}$ cup brown sugar, firmly packed
$\frac{1}{4}$ cup gluten-free soy sauce
3 tablespoons white wine vinegar
3 tablespoons water
2 garlic cloves, chopped
$\frac{1}{2}$ cup creamy natural peanut butter
2 tablespoons chopped peanuts (optional garnish)
1 lime, cut in wedges (optional garnish)

The Directions

Use a 4-quart slow cooker. Put the onion slices into the bottom of your stoneware and place the pork on top. Add the brown sugar, soy sauce, vinegar, water, garlic, and peanut butter. No need to stir—the peanut butter needs to melt before you can do so. Cover and cook on low for 8 hours, or on high for 4 to 6 hours. One hour before serving, flip the meat over to allow the other side to soak up the peanut-buttery goodness. Garnish with chopped peanuts, and serve with lime wedges. Lime juice and peanut butter is a delicious combination.

The Verdict

I received this recipe from a reader who makes it monthly for a potluck gathering. The day I cooked it, I packed the meat up for my friend Stephanie and her family. When asked what she thought, she told me that she had a problem. Her husband, Bill, was home from work and ate it all, and she and the kids didn't get to try any. I'm thinking that means he liked it.

BARBECUE BEEF AND BEAN SANDWICHES

serves 6

The Ingredients

1 (3-pound) chuck roast (mine was frozen)
1 yellow onion, sliced in rings
3 garlic cloves, chopped
1 (16.5-ounce) can barbecue baked beans
2 tablespoons water
¼ cup prepared barbecue sauce
sliced cheese (optional)
jalapeño pepper slices (optional)

The Directions

Use a 4-quart slow cooker. Place the meat into the stoneware. Add the onion and garlic. Pour the beans on top. Put 2 tablespoons of water into the empty bean can and swish it around. Pour that in, too. Add the barbecue sauce. Cover and cook on low for 8 to 12 hours, or until the meat shreds easily with a fork. Serve on rolls, buns, rice cakes, or over rice. If desired, top with slices of your favorite cheese and sliced jalapeños.

The Verdict

We all really liked this meal. The kids ate their meat right off the plate with a fork, and Adam and I had ours on top of lightly salted rice cakes. I loved the sliced jalapeños—there was a perfect mix of spicy tang and sweetness from the barbecue sauce. The meat was very tender and fell apart, just as I like it.

BARBECUE RIBS

serves 6

The Ingredients

5 pounds ribs (I used beef short ribs)
1 yellow onion, diced
2 green onions, sliced
8 garlic cloves, minced
$1/4$ teaspoon black pepper
1 (18-ounce) bottle barbecue sauce

The Directions

Use a 6-quart slow cooker. I have browned the ribs in the oven before putting them in the cooker, but I no longer see the use. The raw meat will cook just fine in the slow cooker, and I like saving steps. Toss them in, and add the onion, green onions, garlic, black pepper, and barbecue sauce. Cover and cook on low for 8 to 10 hours, or on high for 4 to 6 hours. The meat will be quite tender and will fall off the bone. Floss after eating.

BARBECUED PULLED PORK

serves 6

The Ingredients

4 pounds boneless pork shoulder

1 onion, sliced in rings

2 cups ketchup (this is the contents of a 24-ounce bottle)

$1/2$ cup warm water

$1/4$ cup apple cider vinegar

$1/4$ cup brown sugar, firmly packed

1 teaspoon gluten-free Worcestershire sauce

1 teaspoon Tabasco sauce

$1/2$ teaspoon kosher salt

The Directions

Use a 6-quart slow cooker. Trim the meat, and place it into the stoneware. Add the onion rings. Squeeze in the ketchup, and then pour the $1/2$ cup warm water into the ketchup bottle and shake. Pour the ketchup-y water into your crock. Add vinegar, brown sugar, Worcestershire sauce, Tabasco, and salt. Cover and cook on low for 8 to 10 hours, or until meat shreds easily with a fork. Serve over rice, or make sandwiches on rolls or sliced bread. I cooked this overnight and had a hard time sleeping because it smelled so good.

BLUE CHEESE AND
DRIED CHERRY MEATLOAF

serves 4

The Ingredients

1 pound of lean ground beef or turkey
½ cup dried cherries
½ cup blue cheese, crumbled (make sure the cheese is certified gluten free)
1 teaspoon seasoned salt
½ teaspoon black pepper
1 teaspoon onion powder
1 tablespoon chopped fresh basil (optional)
½ cup bread crumbs (I have bread crumbs made from a loaf of brown rice bread)
1 large egg
cooking spray

The Directions

Use a 4- or 6-quart slow cooker. I used a 4-quart round, because I chose to make a glob of meatloaf and cook it directly in the stoneware, but you can use a glass or metal 9×5×3-inch loaf pan placed inside of a 6-quart oval if you'd like. In a large mixing bowl, combine the meat, cherries, cheese, salt, pepper, onion powder, basil, if using, bread crumbs, and egg. Spray the inside of your stoneware (or loaf pan) well with cooking spray. Put the meat into the pot and shape into a large round blob in the center, or press into the loaf pan. Cover and cook on high for 4 hours, or on low for 7 to 8 hours. The meatloaf is done when it is cooked thoroughly and has browned on top and darkened on the edges. Using two spatulas, lift the meatloaf out of the pot and let it stand on a cutting board for 15 minutes before cutting.

The Verdict

Whoa, mama! This is not your grandma's meatloaf. This is decadent. This is gourmet. This is super duper easy, yet you will get tons of praise and be granted bragging rights. My friend Jennifer was with me when I mixed the meatloaf, and she is to thank for the added spices. I would have stuck to just the blue cheese and the cherries, and it would have been terribly bland. Thanks, Jen!

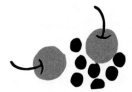

BLUE CHEESE AND STEAK ROLL-UPS

serves 4

The Ingredients

1/2 cup red wine
1/4 cup gluten-free soy sauce
2 tablespoons gluten-free Worcestershire sauce
4 garlic cloves, minced
1 1/2 pounds round tip, pounded thin, and cut in 4 pieces
8 ounces of blue cheese (make sure the cheese is certified gluten free)

The Directions

Use a 4-quart slow cooker. Make a marinade with the wine, soy sauce, Worcestershire sauce, and minced garlic. Add the meat and marinate in a plastic ziplock bag overnight.

In the morning, dump the contents into your slow cooker. Slice the blue cheese into strips. A piece at a time, take the meat out of the marinade mixture and place strips of cheese all over it. Roll it up, and repeat with the remaining pieces of meat. Return the meat to the stoneware, seam-side down. Cover and cook on low for 4 to 5 hours. It will not take long to cook.

The Verdict

This is good. Very good. Unless you don't like blue cheese. And you're a vegetarian. Or from Mars. For the rest of you, this is a scrumptious and (dare I say it) gourmet slow-cooked meal.

CAJUN PULLED PORK

serves 6

The Ingredients

4 pounds boneless pork shoulder or butt (surely there has to be a nicer name for this)
1 tablespoon brown sugar
1 teaspoon ground cumin
1 teaspoon garlic powder
1 teaspoon onion powder
1 teaspoon cayenne pepper
1 teaspoon smoked paprika
1 teaspoon black pepper
1/2 cup chopped onion
1 tablespoon butter
1 to 2 tablespoons hickory liquid smoke
2 cups water

The Directions

Use a 6-quart slow cooker. Put the meat into a large plastic ziplock bag with the brown sugar and seasonings. Seal well and shake to coat. Pour the contents of the bag into the stoneware. Top with the chopped onion, butter, and liquid smoke. Pour in the water. Cover and cook on low for 8 to 10 hours, or until meat shreds easily with two forks. Serve on toasted buns, on rice, or in large romaine lettuce leaves.

The Verdict

I made this up after I spent a day watching the Food Network, and Emeril's "bamming" got to me—I felt like doing some bamming of my own. It's a bit spicy for kids, but eating it in a sandwich with mayo, mustard, and cheese downplays the spice. My friend Georgia fed it to her four kids, and they liked it a lot. This would also make excellent burrito filling.

CHILE VERDE

serves 8

The Ingredients

4 pounds chuck roast or pork shoulder/butt (I used a chuck roast)
1 green bell pepper, seeded and diced
1 small onion, diced
10 tomatillos (peel off the outer wrapper, if they have one)
1 (4-ounce) can diced chiles (mine were mild, your choice)
1 (14.5-ounce) can diced tomatoes with juices
4 cloves garlic, minced
2 teaspoons kosher salt
2 teaspoons cumin
2 teaspoons sage
1 tablespoon oregano
½ teaspoon red pepper flakes (or more, to taste)
¼ cup chopped cilantro leaves

The Directions

Use a 6-quart slow cooker. Trim any visible fat from the meat, and plop into your stoneware. Add diced bell pepper and onion. If your tomatillos have the leafy outer skin, take the skin and stem off, and dice finely or pulse in a food processor (I used a handheld chopper). Pour in the chiles and tomatoes. Add the garlic and seasonings, and stir a bit to get the spices down the sides of the meat. Add chopped cilantro to the top. Cover and cook on low for 8 to 10 hours, on high for 6 hours, or until meat shreds easily with a fork. After 7 hours on low, my meat was still pretty tough, so I chopped it into large chunks and put it back in the pot for another 2 hours. By then, it had shredded nicely for me. Serve with rice, corn tortillas, shredded cheese, and a dollop of sour cream.

The Verdict

Delicious. Three out of the four of us ate this happily, and the other had a quesadilla. The meat was super tender, and had a good flavor. If you'd like more heat, you can add more red pepper or top with some jalapeño slices at the table. If your slow cooker releases a lot of steam through a vent hole, put a layer of foil over the stoneware, then put the lid on. You want a lot of moisture to tenderize the meat. Be super careful when removing the foil—the steam will be quite hot.

COCONUT BEEF

serves 6

The Ingredients

2 pounds stew meat
juice of 1 lime
1 (14-ounce) can coconut milk
1 yellow onion, cut in chunks
2 garlic cloves, chopped
2 teaspoons brown sugar
1 teaspoon curry powder
1/2 teaspoon ground coriander
1 teaspoon ground cumin
1 1/2 tablespoons chili paste
1 (1-inch) piece fresh ginger, peeled and grated

The Directions

Use a 4-quart slow cooker. Put the meat, lime juice, and coconut milk into the stoneware. Follow with the onion and garlic. Add the brown sugar, spices, and grated ginger. Toss the meat a bit in the liquid and spices to coat. Cover and cook on low for 8 hours, or on high for 4 hours. The coconut milk will be yellow from the curry, and will separate a bit, but a quick stir will turn it all creamy again. Serve over white or brown rice.

The Verdict

I used really cheap stew meat for this recipe, and was concerned it wouldn't tenderize as much as I'd like since I only had enough time to cook on high for 4 hours. I didn't need to worry—the meat was tender and infused with a great creamy coconut flavor.

CORNED BEEF

serves 6

The Ingredients

1 pound potatoes, chopped
1 bunch celery, chopped
2 cups carrots, chopped
3 pounds corned beef, with seasoning packet
$1/2$ cup water

The Directions

Use a 6-quart slow cooker. Cut the vegetables into 2-inch chunks and put on the bottom of the stoneware. Trim the fat off the meat, and put the meat on top. Add the seasoning packet and the water. Cover and cook on low for 8 to 10 hours, or on high for 4 to 6 hours. Corned beef is much more tender when it is cooked slowly.

The Verdict

Corned beef is not my favorite, but I married an Irishman so I cook it once in a while. It seems to make him happy, and when he's happy he folds laundry and takes out the garbage.

Adam likes how moist the meat gets when slow-cooked, without being too gelatinous the way it sometimes gets when boiled. My kids wouldn't touch corned beef if Santa served it on a magic carpet, so they had some canned soup. If you are gluten-free, read the package ingredients carefully.

CRANBERRY PORK ROAST

serves 4 to 6

The Ingredients

2 1/2- to 3-pound pork loin roast or rib roast
1 teaspoon ground ginger
1/2 teaspoon dry mustard
1/2 teaspoon kosher salt
1/4 teaspoon black pepper
2 tablespoons cornstarch
1 cup fresh or frozen cranberries
1/2 cup granulated sugar
1/2 cup brown sugar, firmly packed
1/3 cup raisins
1 garlic clove, chopped
1/3 cup cranberry juice
1/2 small lemon, thinly sliced

The Directions

Use a 4-quart slow cooker. Put the meat in a plastic ziplock bag with the ginger, mustard, salt, pepper, and cornstarch. Shake to coat. Pour the contents into your stoneware. Add the cranberries, sugars, raisins, and garlic. Pour in cranberry juice, and top with the lemon slices. Cover and cook on low for 8 hours, or high for about 4 hours. Serve with rice or pasta.

The Verdict

One of my Web site readers wrote "this is hands down our family's favorite slow cooker recipe." My friend who tried it liked it a lot, and her husband said the meat was perfectly cooked and juicy. Her nine-year-old, Austin, reported "I didn't really like the cranberries so much, but I thought they really brought out the flavor of the pork." Oh my. He's adorable.

FAJITAS

serves 4

The Ingredients

2 pounds thinly cut stir-fry beef (you could use chicken)

1 onion, sliced in rings

1 orange bell pepper, cut in strips

1 yellow bell pepper, cut in strips

1 or 2 packets of fajita seasoning mix (I said one or two because I've found that it's awfully spicy if I use 1 packet per pound of meat as directed on the label—use what is right for your family and double check labels for gluten)

$1/2$ cup water

tortillas (brown rice or corn)

favorite toppings such as: lime wedges, shredded cheese, diced tomatoes, avocado slices, sour cream, salsa

The Directions

Use a 4-quart slow cooker. Put meat in crock with onion and bell peppers. Sprinkle in seasoning, and add water. Stir. Cover and cook on low for 8 to 9 hours, or on high for 6 hours. The meat is done when it reaches desired tenderness. I like to cook on low for as long as possible, because I don't like to chew forever. Serve with your favorite fajita fixins'. We really like squeezing some fresh lime over the top of the meat before doctoring it up.

The Verdict

My family adores Mexican food. My kids will eat anything with cheese and sour cream on it, and avocado was their very first food. Fajitas are fun to make (I like the name—they sound much fancier than tacos for some reason), and are easy to prepare with the help of the slow cooker. I get the meat going in the morning, and then head out for fresh ingredients at some point during the day, or ask Adam to stop on his way home from work.

FLANK STEAK STUFFED WITH APPLE, FETA, AND ALMONDS

serves 4

The Ingredients

3 pounds flank steak
1/2 cup honey
1/2 cup gluten-free soy sauce
3/4 cup feta cheese, crumbled
2 garlic cloves, chopped
1 green apple, diced (no need to peel)
1/3 cup raw almonds, chopped

The Directions

Use a 4-quart slow cooker. Put the flank steak in a plastic ziplock bag with the honey and soy sauce and marinate overnight.

In the morning, combine the feta cheese, garlic, green apple, and chopped almonds in a mixing bowl. Pour the flank steak and marinade into the stoneware. Remove the meat from the marinade, and put it on a cutting board. Put a handful or two of the cheese filling in the middle of the flank, and roll it up. Return the meat to the crock, seam-side down. If you'd like to secure the meat with twine or skewers, go for it. Cover and cook on low for 6 to 7 hours, or on high for about 4 hours. Slice carefully, and serve. If the meat unrolls a bit, you can stick it back together with toothpicks to present nicely. Or don't worry about it—it's just going to get eaten anyway. If you are left with extra garlic, feta, apple, and almond mixture, it makes a great salad topping.

The Verdict

This is a good meal. A very good meal. A meal that I never in a gazillion years would have ever attempted to make (or think up) without a wild and crazy slow-cooking challenge. Each one of us cleaned our plates.

FRENCH DIP SANDWICHES

serves 4

The Ingredients

2 tablespoons butter
2 pounds lean top round, cut in strips
3 garlic cloves, minced
1 yellow onion, cut in rings
3 cups beef broth
1 (12-ounce) bottle beer (Redbridge is gluten-free)
$1/4$ cup dry sherry
$1/2$ teaspoon black pepper
$1/2$ tablespoon sugar
1 teaspoon gluten-free Worcestershire sauce
bread rolls
cheese slices

The Directions

Use a 4-quart slow cooker. Put the butter into the bottom of the stoneware and turn the cooker to high. Add the meat, garlic, and onion, and swirl around in the butter. Pour in the broth, beer, and sherry. Add the black pepper, sugar, and Worcestershire sauce. Cover and cook on low for 7 to 9 hours. Serve on rolls. I made rolls from a gluten-free bread mix, and added cheddar cheese to the sandwiches. (Traditionally, Gruyère is used.)

Serve the sandwiches on plates with a small bowl of broth. Dip the sandwich into the broth before each bite for a nice juicy flavor and consistency.

GINGER BEEF WITH ONIONS AND GARLIC

serves 4

The Ingredients

1 tablespoon olive oil

1 to 2 pounds lean beef, cut in strips

1 yellow onion, cut in rings

1 head garlic, peeled (about 10 cloves)

1 (1-inch) piece fresh ginger, peeled and grated

1/2 teaspoon black pepper

1/2 cup chicken broth

The Directions

Use a 4-quart slow cooker. Put the olive oil into the stoneware, and toss with the meat. Add the onion, and whole garlic cloves. Put in the ginger and black pepper. Pour in the chicken broth. Cover and cook on low for 6 to 8 hours, or on high for 4 hours. Serve over pasta. I chose brown rice fusilli. This will give you stinky breath. Consider yourself warned.

HAGGIS

serves 8

The Ingredients

$1/2$ pound ground beef

$1/2$ pound ground lamb

1 chopped red onion (doesn't need to be diced, largish chunks are okay)

1 cup certified gluten-free rolled oats

pinch each of ground nutmeg, cloves, and cinnamon

$1/2$ teaspoon cayenne pepper

$1/2$ teaspoon black pepper

1 teaspoon kosher salt

1 large egg

cooking spray

$1/2$ cup chicken broth

The Directions

Use a 4-quart slow cooker. In a large mixing bowl, mix all the ingredients, except the cooking spray and the broth, the same way you'd make a meatloaf. Spray the stoneware with cooking spray, and place the meat blob inside. Shape with your hands into a round lump. Pour in the broth. Cover and cook on low for 6 to 7 hours, or on high for about 4 hours. The haggis is fully cooked when it has browned on the edges and is beginning to brown on top. Don't overcook it and risk having it dry out. Use large spatulas to carefully remove it from the cooker and set it on a cutting board. Let rest for a full 30 minutes before slicing.

(CONTINUED)

The Verdict

Haggis is pretty much a Scottish meatloaf, which is traditionally cooked in a sheep's stomach, or pluck, to keep it all together. The pluck isn't eaten—it's just used as a casing. I actually bought a pluck from our local butcher to try it out, but after 45 minutes of fiddling around with the box of innards, I still couldn't figure out which part was the stomach—the butcher had given me all the entrails. So this is an Americanized version—no pluck needed. I loved the flavors of the clove and nutmeg, and liked the kick of the cayenne. It was salty, but not too salty, and it reminded me of the haggis I ate in Scotland when I was twelve. This was served at a family party, and all who tasted really enjoyed it.

HAMBURGER PATTIES

serves 2

The Ingredients

    aluminum foil or a wire rack that fits into your stoneware
    2 frozen, preformed hamburger patties
    1/8 teaspoon seasoned salt
    sliced cheese (optional)

The Directions

Use a 6-quart oval slow cooker. Insert a wire rack into the stoneware, or make a rack out of aluminum foil by weaving foil "worms" together. Place the frozen meat on top of the rack. Sprinkle the seasoned salt on top. Cover and cook on high for 60 to 90 minutes, or until the meat is cooked through. Add the sliced cheese, if desired, 15 minutes prior to serving. Drain on paper towels, and serve on a bun or a rice cake with desired toppings.

The Verdict

School was out for the summer when I prepared these burgers, which meant many more meals at home for me and the kids. Usually the "cooked" lunches around here are canned chili or soup, but I thought I'd give hamburgers in the slow cooker a whirl to see what happened. The result was a fun lunch the kids gobbled down without grease splatters on my stovetop, or me needing to learn how to turn on the barbecue. That thing scares me.

HICKORY-SMOKED BRISKET

serves 6

The Ingredients

3 to 4 pounds beef brisket, or chuck roast
½ tablespoon celery salt
½ tablespoon garlic powder
½ teaspoon black pepper
¼ cup A-1 steak sauce
1 to 2 tablespoons hickory liquid smoke (or more, to taste; I initially used ½ cup but that's too much)

The Directions

Use a 4-quart slow cooker. Put the meat into the stoneware, and rub the spices on all sides. Add the A-1 sauce and liquid smoke. Cover and cook on low for 8 to 10 hours, or on high for 4 to 6 hours. Slow and low is better; the meat will shred nicely when cooked for a long period of time. Serve over mashed potatoes or polenta.

The Verdict

It tastes like wet beef jerky—which is a good thing. Our house smelled like we were in the middle of a national forest (one that allows campfires) while the meat was cooking.

HIRINO PSITO

serves 6

The Ingredients

3- to 4-pound boneless pork shoulder or butt
1 teaspoon dried sage
1 teaspoon dried rosemary
1 1/2 teaspoons kosher salt
1/2 teaspoon black pepper
1 tablespoon brown sugar
10 whole garlic cloves
1 tablespoon gluten-free Worcestershire sauce
1/4 cup Dijon mustard
1/4 cup honey
1/2 cup dried cranberries
3 bay leaves
1 cup beer (Redbridge is gluten-free)

The Directions

Use a 6-quart slow cooker. Put the meat into the stoneware, and sprinkle on the sage, rosemary, salt, pepper, and brown sugar. Flip the meat over a few times in the stoneware so the herbs and spices are kind of stuck to all sides. Peel the garlic cloves and add whole. Add the Worcestershire sauce, mustard, honey, and cranberries. Top with the bay leaves. Pour in the beer (drink the rest). Cover and cook on low for 8 to 10 hours, or until meat shreds easily with a fork. Serve over rice or pasta, or on your favorite sandwich rolls.

The Verdict

Adam declared this recipe the "winner." I didn't know we were actually conducting a contest, but whatever. He happily ate the meat for lunch for almost a whole week.

JALAPEÑO POT ROAST

serves 6

The Ingredients

3 pounds chuck roast (mine was frozen)
1 (10.75-ounce) can cream-of-something (or 2 cups homemade, page 191, or stovetop alternative, page 248)
2 to 4 tablespoons jarred jalapeño slices
1 (15-ounce) can black beans, drained and rinsed
1 yellow onion, sliced in rings
1 to 2 cups plain nonfat yogurt or sour cream

The Directions

Use a 4-quart slow cooker. Put meat into crock, and add the cream-of soup, jalapeño slices, black beans, and onion rings. Cover and cook on low for 8 to 10 hours.

After cooking, remove the meat with tongs. Scoop out a cup of the liquid, and put it into a mixing bowl with yogurt or sour cream. Mix well. Pour the mixture back into the cooker, and stir until the yogurt or sour cream has dissolved completely. Slice the meat, and return it to the crock.

The Verdict

It's up to you how spicy you'd like this meal to be. I used 4 tablespoons (1/4 cup) of the sliced jalapeños, and then used 2 cups of plain yogurt to mellow the flavor. I liked it like that, and so did my family. There was definitely a kick, but it wasn't too crazy. If you're worried about the heat, stick with 2 tablespoons sliced jalapeños, and then slowly add yogurt at the end to taste.

JAVA ROAST

serves 6

The Ingredients

1 yellow onion, sliced in rings

1 red bell pepper, seeded and chopped

8 ounces sliced mushrooms

4–5 garlic cloves, chopped

3-pound chuck roast, trimmed of fat

¾ cup brewed coffee

1 tablespoon gluten-free Worcestershire sauce

3 tablespoons red wine vinegar

½ teaspoon kosher salt

¼ teaspoon black pepper

4 ounces cream cheese

The Directions

Use a 4-quart slow cooker. Put the onion, pepper, mushrooms, and garlic into the stoneware and lay the meat on top. Add the coffee, Worcestershire sauce, red wine vinegar, salt, and pepper. Cover and cook on low for 7 to 8 hours, or on high for 4 to 5 hours. Carefully remove the meat from the pot, and scoop out some of the broth. Mix this broth with the cream cheese until smooth. Stir the mixture into the remaining broth. Return the meat to the pot and serve with gravy.

The Verdict

Yummy! If I didn't know coffee was in there, I wouldn't have guessed what that hint of flavor was. I liked how the gravy was dark brown and rich. Adding the cream cheese thickened it up nicely and gave a pleasant creamy texture. The coffee really tenderizes the meat, and it becomes fork-tender more quickly than other roast recipes.

LAMB CHOPS

serves 4

The Ingredients

1 tablespoon olive oil
4 to 6 lamb chops
packaged spice rub (I used McCormick Roasting Rub)
½ cup water

The Directions

Use a 4-quart slow cooker. Pour 1 tablespoon of olive oil into the bottom of the stoneware and spread it around. Cover all sides of each lamb chop with your favorite spice blend. The one I used contained salt, garlic, cracked black peppercorns, rosemary, and crushed red pepper. Put the chops on top of the olive oil, and add water. Cover and cook on low for 7 to 10 hours, or on high for 4 to 5 hours.

The Verdict

My lamb chops were frozen solid when I plugged in the slow cooker, yet by the end of the day they were juicy and fork-tender. We had these on a terribly stormy night in front of a real fire made with a real Duraflame.

LAYERED DINNER:
STEAK, POTATOES, AND CORN ON THE COB

serves 4

The Ingredients

- 1½ pounds rib-eye steak
- 1 tablespoon of your favorite seasoning rub (I used McCormick's Roast Rub)
- 1 onion, sliced in rings
- ¼ cup tequila (or broth, apple juice, etc.)
- 2 tablespoons gluten-free Worcestershire sauce
- 2 to 4 baking potatoes (I used brown, but sweet potatoes would work well, too)
- 2 to 4 ears of fresh corn
- aluminum foil

The Directions

Use a 6-quart or larger slow cooker. Rub the seasoning blend on all sides of the meat, and add to the stoneware. Top with the onion rings. Add the tequila and Worcestershire sauce. Wash the potatoes and wrap individually with foil. Add to the pot, on top of the meat. Shuck the corn, and wrap each ear in foil. Add to the pot. It doesn't seem to matter if the potatoes are closer to the meat or the corn. The new slow cookers heat from the sides as well as from the bottom, so everything will cook through regardless of its location. Cover and cook on high for 5 to 7 hours, or on low for about 8 hours.

The Verdict

It was so neat to make a complete meal in one appliance that wasn't a soup, stew, or casserole. I was able to fit 2 large potatoes and 4 ears of corn along with the meat. Although I used the above ingredients, you can play around with the meat and vegetables you have on hand to create your own family-pleasing meals.

LEG OF LAMB

serves 8

The Ingredients

1 (4-pound) boneless leg of lamb
1/2 teaspoon black pepper
1/2 teaspoon kosher salt
1/2 teaspoon dried rosemary
1/2 teaspoon garlic powder
1/2 cup water

The Directions

Use a 4-quart slow cooker. Rub the seasonings all over the lamb, or use a preseasoned piece of meat. We really like the frozen leg of lamb from Trader Joe's, and use that quite often. If you don't have access to a Trader Joe's, this seasoning blend will work fantastically. Place the meat in the stoneware and add the water. Cover and cook on low for 8 hours, or on high for 4 to 6 hours. The meat is done when it is cooked through and has reached the desired tenderness. I like my lamb to fall apart, so I opt for cooking it on low for a full 8 hours.

The Verdict

Lamb has the tendency to dry out, which is just not a possibility when slow cooked. Each time I slow cook lamb, I marvel at just how good it is. I will not attempt to prepare lamb any other way.

LEG OF LAMB WITH PRUNES

serves 6

The Ingredients

1 (4-pound) boneless leg of lamb
1 teaspoon dried rosemary
1 teaspoon ground cumin
1 teaspoon kosher salt
1 teaspoon black pepper
4 garlic cloves, chopped
2 cups dried plums (prunes!)
½ cup dry white wine (you can use apple juice)
1 cinnamon stick
2 tablespoons cornstarch (optional)

The Directions

Use a 4-quart slow cooker. Put the meat inside the cooker, and rub it on all sides with the seasonings. Add the garlic and prunes. Pour in the wine, and toss in a cinnamon stick. Cover and cook on low for 8 hours, or on high for about 4 hours. I'd go with the longer cooking time and lower heat, though.

When the lamb is done, if you'd like, remove the meat from the stoneware, and make a gravy out of the accumulated juices by whisking in some cornstarch. The prunes will be awfully squishy, and can blend right in. Serve with mashed potatoes or polenta with the gravy drizzled over the top.

LEMON PEPPER RIBS

serves 4

The Ingredients

  4 pounds beef or pork ribs
  2 tablespoons garlic powder
  2 tablespoons kosher salt
  2 tablespoons black pepper
  juice of 3 lemons

The Directions

Use a 6-quart slow cooker. Cut the ribs to fit your stoneware. In a small bowl, combine the garlic powder, salt, and pepper. Rub the rack of ribs with the dry mixture, covering all sides. Put the ribs into the slow cooker. If you have extra seasoning, sprinkle it on top. Juice lemons (use one of those handheld juicer things, to make sure all the juice gets out) onto the ribs. Cover and cook on low for 7 to 10 hours, or on high for about 5 hours. The meat will be more tender if you cook it on low.

The Verdict

I saw Senator John McCain barbecue these ribs on TV during the 2008 presidential campaign, and was interested in seeing how they held up in the slow cooker. I was nervous that they'd get awfully tough and burn without liquid, but that couldn't have been further from the truth. The meat was flavorful, tender, and juicy. The lemon gave a neat tartness I've never had with ribs before. The kids ate a ton, and there were happy noises at the table. These ribs are fantastic.

MAPLE HAM

serves 10

The Ingredients
    7 to 8 pound bone-in spiral-cut ham
    1 cup dark brown sugar, firmly packed
    ½ cup all-natural maple syrup
    1 cup pineapple juice

The Directions

Use a 6-quart slow cooker. Unwrap the ham, and discard flavor packet. Place the ham into the stoneware, flat-side down. Rub the brown sugar on all sides. Pour on the maple syrup and pineapple juice. Cover and cook on low for 6 to 8 hours.

Remove the ham carefully and let rest on a cutting board for 15 to 20 minutes before carving.

The Verdict

Ham smells crazy-good when it's slow cooking. I had to pack up the kids and head to the library for the day so we could concentrate and not drool all over ourselves. I packed most of the meat up for my brother and sister-in-law and some for my dad. They all loved it, and my dad said it tasted better than "normal ham." Adam ate the meat for dinner, and then the next day in a sandwich. The kids and I had frozen *taquitos*. It's tough being allergic to pork.

MARINATED MEAT

serves 4

The Ingredients

3 to 4 pounds frozen marinated meat, or fresh marinated meat from a butcher
1/2 cup warm water

The Directions

Use a 4-quart or larger slow cooker. Put the meat into the crock, and add the water. Cover and cook on low for 7 to 10 hours, or on high for 4 to 8 hours. The cooking time will vary depending on the variety and cut of meat, and whether it is fresh or frozen.

The Verdict

This is a fail-proof meal. I like to buy already-marinated meat when it's on sale, but you can also make your own by freezing meat in plastic ziplock bags after you've liberally applied your own spice blend, barbecue sauce, teriyaki sauce, or other prepackaged marinade mixture. Always check ingredients thoroughly to search for hidden allergens.

MEATLOAF

serves 6

The Ingredients

1 pound lean ground turkey

1/2 pound lean ground beef

1 red bell pepper, seeded and chopped

1/4 cup raw brown rice

1 (14.5-ounce) can tomatoes with Italian seasoning and their juices

1 tablespoon A-1 steak sauce

1 packet onion soup mix

1 large egg

1/4 cup ketchup

The Directions

Use a 4- to 6-quart slow cooker. In a mixing bowl, combine all the ingredients except for the ketchup. Mix with your hands until everything is well incorporated and there aren't any seasoning clumps. If using an oval 6-quart cooker, put the meat mixture into a glass or metal 9×5×3-inch loaf pan, and put it into the slow cooker. Otherwise, put the meat directly into your crock, and form a roundish lump with your hands. Spread the ketchup all over the top of your meatloaf. Cover and cook on low for 8 hours, or on high for about 4 hours. The meat is done when it is browned and fully cooked when you cut into it. Use paper towels to soak up any collected grease. Let sit for 20 to 30 minutes before slicing.

The Verdict

Moist and delicious. My parents came over for dinner and we all really enjoyed our meal. The kids dipped their meat into barbecue sauce. Every time I make meatloaf the mix is slightly different—feel free to use your own secret family recipe. Slow-cooked meatloaf is much juicier than oven-baked, which allows you to use a leaner meat without sacrificing moisture or flavor.

MOLE

serves 8

The Ingredients

¼ cup raw sunflower or sesame seeds (I used sunflower because I had them; sesame is traditional)

½ cup raw slivered almonds

2 pounds beef, chicken, or pork (I used beef)

¼ teaspoon ground cloves

1 tablespoon chili powder

½ teaspoon ground coriander

¼ teaspoon anise seeds

1 dry California chili pod

1 yellow onion, chopped

⅓ cup raisins

1 cup water

1 cinnamon stick

3 garlic cloves, minced

1 (14-ounce) can diced tomatoes and their juices

1 (6-ounce) can tomato paste

¼ cup tequila (or dry white wine, or apple juice)

1 to 2 ounces unsweetened chocolate (I used 2 and liked it; some readers thought it was too bitter)

salt

The Directions

Use a 6-quart slow cooker. Don't freak out about the number of ingredients, it'll be worth it. In a small pan, brown the raw seeds and almonds on the stovetop. Set aside to cool. Put the meat into the stoneware. Cover with the seasonings. Put the dry chili pod into the pot with meat, onion, raisins, and water. Add the toasted nuts, seeds, cinnamon stick, garlic, tomatoes, tomato paste, tequila, and chocolate. Cover and cook on low for about 8 hours. Shred the meat with forks, and serve over rice and with corn tortillas. Salt to taste.

The Verdict

Mole is pronounced mol-AY. This will not stop the "holy moly" jokes. This is such a satisfying meal. The kids mostly ate corn tortillas and butter, but I will make it again, and soon. This is great company food—the flavor is so rich and full-bodied—you get a bit of a crunch from a nut here, and a sweet burst from a raisin there. It's incredible.

ORANGE-APRICOT PORK CHOPS

serves 4 to 6

The Ingredients

6 pork chops
1 cup apricot jam
3 tablespoons brown sugar
1 teaspoon kosher salt
1/2 teaspoon black pepper
1/2 teaspoon ground cinnamon
1/4 teaspoon ground ginger
1/4 teaspoon ground cloves
1 (11-ounce) can mandarin oranges (and their juice!)

The Directions

Use a 4-quart slow cooker. Put the pork chops into the stoneware. In a small bowl, combine the jam, brown sugar, salt, and spices. Spoon over the pork chops. Pour the entire can of mandarin oranges evenly over the top. Cover and cook on low for about 8 hours, or on high for about 4 hours. Serve with rice to soak up the yummy juice.

The Verdict

This is such a great sauce. My friend Stephanie reported that her kids ate a ton of these pork chops, and her nine-year-old ate the meat without ketchup (unheard of in her home), and her thirteen-year-old sucked the bones clean, she liked them so much.

ORANGE CHIPOTLE RIBS

serves 4

The Ingredients

3 pounds ribs (I used beef short ribs)
1/2 cup ketchup
1/4 cup orange marmalade
1/4 cup apple cider vinegar
2 tablespoons gluten-free soy sauce
3 tablespoons brown sugar
4 garlic cloves, minced
2 teaspoons chipotle chili powder
1/4 teaspoon ground cumin
1/4 teaspoon ground ginger

The Directions

Use a 6-quart slow cooker. I didn't brown or precook my meat at all. It was thawed, however. If you are using frozen meat, it will take longer to cook. Put the ribs into the slow cooker. In a small bowl, combine the ketchup, orange marmalade, vinegar, soy sauce, brown sugar, garlic, and spices. Pour the sauce mixture on top. Cover and cook on low for 8 to 9 hours, or on high for 5 to 6 hours. The meat is done when it has reached the desired tenderness and is no longer pink. I prefer the meat to fall off the bone, and to eat it with a knife and fork. If you'd rather gnaw on the bones, pull them out after 4 hours on high or 6 to 7 hours on low.

The Verdict

Barbecuing ribs in the slow cooker is the way to go. The meat is much more tender and flavorful, and you don't get that charred meat taste in your mouth that reminds you (me) of the "Marlboro Man." The kids have finally begun to appreciate ribs. They still ate hot dogs for their main dinner, but ate enough of the ribs to need sauce scrubbed off their faces with a washcloth.

PEKING PORK CHOPS

serves 6

The Ingredients

6 pork chops
¼ cup brown sugar, firmly packed
1 teaspoon ground ginger
1 teaspoon five-spice powder
½ cup gluten-free soy sauce
¼ cup ketchup
4 garlic cloves, chopped

The Directions

Use a 4-quart slow cooker. Put the chops into the stoneware. In a small bowl, combine the sugar, spices, soy sauce, ketchup, and garlic. Pour evenly over the top of chops. Cover and cook on low for 6 to 8 hours, or on high for about 4 hours. Serve with rice and veggies and ladle the sauce on top. These chops freeze and reheat well—yay!

PEPPERCORN STEAK

serves 4

The Ingredients

4 to 6 steaks (use whatever is on sale, it's going to tenderize nicely)

2 chopped bell peppers (I used one yellow, one green)

1 yellow onion, chopped

8 ounces sliced mushrooms

1 cup tomato sauce

1/2 cup gluten-free Worcestershire sauce

1/4 cup water

1 tablespoon Italian seasoning

1/4 teaspoon black pepper

The Directions

Use a 4-quart slow cooker. Put the meat into the stoneware; mine was still frozen solid. Cover with the chopped vegetables. Pour in the tomato sauce, Worcestershire, and water. Add the Italian seasoning and black pepper; no need to stir. Cover and cook on low for 7 to 9 hours, or on high for 4 to 6. I cooked our dinner for 6 hours on high.

The Verdict

I liked this! I liked how the steak lifted out of the juices without falling apart, and could be sliced like a steak cooked in the oven or on the grill. The flavor of the tomato sauce and the Worcestershire was great—rich and peppery. This makes a lot of sauce. I'd imagine you could use the remaining sauce as a soup base or to make a fabulous gravy.

PINEAPPLE PORK TENDERLOIN

serves 4 to 6

The Ingredients

3 pounds pork tenderloin
2 tablespoons brown sugar
1/2 teaspoon Italian seasoning
1/2 teaspoon kosher salt
1/2 teaspoon black pepper
3 tablespoons cornstarch
2 garlic cloves, chopped
1 orange bell pepper, seeded and sliced
1 red bell pepper, seeded and sliced
2 tablespoons gluten-free soy sauce
1/2 cup apple juice
16 ounces frozen cubed pineapple

The Directions

Use a 4-quart slow cooker. Combine the meat, sugar, Italian seasoning, salt, pepper, and corn-starch in a plastic ziplock bag. Seal and shake well to coat. Pour the contents of the bag into the stoneware. Add the garlic and peppers. Pour in the soy sauce, apple juice, and frozen pineapple. Cover and cook on low for 7 to 9 hours, or on high for 4 to 6 hours. Serve with rice or pasta.

The Verdict

Oh, this is good. I made 3 pounds, and packed it up to give away to two different families. My friend Georgia has four children, and she said they all loved it. The peppers retained their color and shape—the key to slow cooking with softer veggies is to put them on top of the meat so they aren't simmering in liquid all day.

POMEGRANATE BEEF

serves 8

The Ingredients

1 tablespoon olive oil
1 onion, sliced
$1/4$ teaspoon ground cinnamon
1 teaspoon herbes de Provence
$1/2$ teaspoon kosher salt
3 pounds beef roast (I get what's on sale)
4 garlic cloves, chopped
1 (14-ounce) can fire-roasted crushed tomatoes
1 cup unsweetened pomegranate juice
$1/4$ cup balsamic vinegar
2 tablespoons maple syrup
$1/2$ cup golden raisins

The Directions

Use a 6-quart slow cooker. Swirl the olive oil into the bottom of the stoneware. Add the onion. Rub the cinnamon, herbs, and salt on all sides of the meat and add to the stoneware with the garlic, the whole can of tomatoes, pomegranate juice, balsamic vinegar, and maple syrup. Sprinkle the raisins on top. Cover and cook on low for 8 hours, or on high for 5 hours. The meat is done when it has reached the desired tenderness. Serve with mashed potatoes or polenta, and drizzle with the sauce.

The Verdict

This is one of the best slow-cooked meat dishes ever. It comes from Karina Allrich, who writes at glutenfreegoddess.blogspot.com. I served this at a family dinner with four generations represented. Everybody loved it. The sauce is tangy and sweet and the meat is packed with flavor.

POT ROAST GLAZED WITH RED WINE AND CRANBERRIES

serves 8

The Ingredients

1/4 cup flour (I used a gluten-free baking mix)

1 teaspoon kosher salt

1 teaspoon black pepper

1 tablespoon dried onion flakes

2 pounds top round

3 garlic cloves, minced

1/2 cup dry red wine

2 tablespoons gluten-free Worcestershire sauce

1/4 cup gluten-free soy sauce

3 tablespoons maple syrup

1/2 cup dried cranberries

The Directions

Use a 4-quart slow cooker. Make a dredge with the flour, salt, black pepper, and onion flakes. Rub the dry mixture on all sides of the meat. Discard the rest of the dry mixture, and place the meat into the stoneware. Add the garlic and liquid ingredients; no need to stir. Sprinkle on the cranberries. Cover and cook on low for 8 to 10 hours, or on high for 4 to 6 hours. Serve with mashed potatoes or polenta.

The Verdict

This is definitely not an everyday boring pot roast. The sauce is a bit peppery, but my kids didn't find it overly seasoned. My six-year-old said it was "the best steak she's ever had," and my three-year-old dipped her pieces in ketchup. Because that's what three-year-olds do.

RED RIBS

serves 4

The Ingredients

2 pounds boneless ribs (beef or pork; I used beef)
1 (8-ounce) can sliced bamboo shoots, drained
1 (8-ounce) can sliced water chestnuts, drained
2 teaspoons ground ginger
4 garlic cloves, minced
1/4 to 1/2 teaspoon crushed red pepper flakes
2 cups sliced mushrooms
1/2 cup dry sherry
3/4 cup beef broth
6 tablespoons gluten-free soy sauce
1/4 cup honey
1 cinnamon stick

The Directions

Use a 4-quart slow cooker. Put the meat into the stoneware, and add the bamboo shoots, water chestnuts, ginger, garlic, red pepper flakes, and mushrooms. Pour in the sherry, broth, soy sauce, and honey. Stir to distribute the flavors. Throw a cinnamon stick on top.

The Verdict

I am glad that I added only a bit of the red pepper flakes, because there was not one whine of "this is too spicy"—I actually would have preferred some more heat, but was glad to know that the kids ingested some protein other than peanut butter. These ribs are tasty, without being too sweet.

ROAST BEEF

serves 8

The Ingredients

1 large yellow onion, sliced in rings

5 pounds bone-in, rib-eye steak

6 garlic cloves, peeled

2 tablespoons cornstarch

1 teaspoon kosher salt

1 teaspoon black pepper

1 tablespoon gluten-free Worcestershire sauce

$\frac{1}{2}$ cup beef stock or broth

The Directions

Use a 6-quart slow cooker. Spread the onion slices into the bottom of your stoneware. Trim excess fat off the meat, and make six little slits with a serrated knife. Insert a garlic clove into each slit, spacing evenly, if you can. Add the dry ingredients to a plastic ziplock bag with the meat. Seal well, and shake. Place the meat onto the onion. Add the Worcestershire sauce and broth. Cover and cook on high for 4 hours, or on low for 6 to 8 hours, or until the meat has reached the desired temperature (140°–160°F) with an instant-read meat thermometer. (140° is medium; 160° is well done.) Let the meat stand for 15 minutes before slicing. If you'd like, you can combine crock drippings and cornstarch to make a gravy on the stovetop.

The Verdict

This was great; the meat was tender and had a nice, mild garlicky flavor. You can use a less-expensive cut of meat, but you'll need to cook it longer to get it tender, and it won't slice as nicely. There is nothing wrong with that at all—just a heads up.

ROPA VIEJA

serves 6

The Ingredients

1 tablespoon ground cumin
1 teaspoon smoked paprika
1 teaspoon kosher salt
$\frac{1}{2}$ teaspoon black pepper
$\frac{1}{4}$ teaspoon cayenne pepper
3 pounds beef or pork (get what's on sale: stew meat, chuck roast)
1 large red onion, chopped
2 red bell peppers, chopped
3 celery stalks, chopped
3 garlic cloves, chopped
$\frac{1}{2}$ cup fresh cilantro leaves
2 yellow apples, peeled and grated
$\frac{1}{2}$ cup chicken broth
$\frac{1}{4}$ cup apple cider vinegar

The Directions

Use a 6-quart slow cooker. Combine the cumin, paprika, salt, and peppers in a bowl. Rub the spice mixture all over the piece (or pieces) of meat you are using. Put the meat into the stoneware. Dump any extra spice left in the bowl on top. Add the vegetables, garlic, cilantro, grated apples, chicken broth, and vinegar. Cover and cook on low for 10 hours, or until meat shreds easily with a fork. Ropa Vieja means "old clothes"—the meat and vegetables should be shredded and fully intertwined. The longer and slower you cook this, the better. Serve over brown or white rice, with a ladle full of broth.

SAUSAGE AND VEGETABLE MEDLEY

serves 4 to 6

The Ingredients

    4 cups vegetables (I used carrots, celery, broccoli, cauliflower)
    2 cups sliced mushrooms
    2 potatoes, cubed
    6 fully cooked sausage links (I used half Italian-seasoned chicken and half chipotle-spiced
        chicken sausages)
    2 cups chicken broth
    1/3 cup dry white wine
    1 large handful baby spinach

The Directions

Use a 4-quart slow cooker. Cut the vegetables into 2-inch chunks and place at the bottom of your slow cooker. Slice the sausage, and add on top (if serving young children, opt for the sweeter chicken and apple or similar sausage). Pour in the broth and wine. Cover and cook on low for 8 hours, or on high for 4 hours. Add a handful of baby spinach and turn to high for 15 minutes before serving. This is one my family's favorite meals—it's a regular in the rotation.

SMOKY SPICED LAMB CHOPS

serves 4

The Ingredients

1 medium yellow onion, sliced in rings
1 teaspoon ground cumin
1 teaspoon smoked paprika
1 teaspoon ground coriander
4 large lamb chops (mine were frozen)
1 red bell pepper, seeded and sliced
1 yellow bell pepper, seeded and sliced
1/2 cup chicken broth, or beef stock
kosher salt
black pepper

The Directions

Use a 4-quart slow cooker. Put the onion rings into the bottom of your crock. In a small bowl, combine the spices. Rub the spice mixture on all sides of the lamb chops, and nestle the chops on top of the onion. Toss bell peppers on top. Pour the broth over. Cover and cook on low for 7 to 8 hours, or on high for 4 to 6 hours. I cooked our meat on high for 6 hours. It was well cooked, and quite tender. If I had taken it out about an hour earlier, it wouldn't have fallen off of the bone so easily—which is really the only problem with cooking too long. Season with salt and pepper to taste, and serve with rice or quinoa.

The Verdict

Adam and I really enjoyed the flavors. I mistakenly had the "yes, the lamb at the store is from actual baby sheep—like the ones at the petting zoo" conversation, which meant the kids ate rice, garbanzo beans, and avocado slices. Oops.

SUN-DRIED TOMATO AND FETA TRI-TIP

serves 6

The Ingredients

2 pounds tri-tip (or bottom roast)
1 (8-ounce) jar sun-dried tomatoes, packed in oil, drained
8 ounces feta cheese
$\frac{1}{3}$ cup dry white wine

The Directions

Use a 4-quart slow cooker. Put the meat into the crock, and add the drained sun-dried tomatoes. Crumble the feta cheese over the top. Add the wine. Cover and cook on low for 6 to 10 hours. The cooking time will vary depending on if your meat is frozen or fresh, and how tender you like the meat. I cooked our frozen meat for 6 hours on low; it held shape and needed to be cut with a knife.

The Verdict

So super easy to prepare, yet tastes restaurantish—this was one of Adam's favorites. My kids love feta, and happily eat any meal including it (because feta sounds like feet, and eating feet is always fun). We ate this on a warm evening in the backyard with a big green salad, and had sandwiches with the meat for lunch the next day.

USING THE SLOW COOKER AS A SMOKER: SMOKED BRISKET

serves 4 to 6

The Ingredients

1 to 2 cups mesquite wood chips, soaked

parchment paper

3 to 4 pounds beef brisket, or comparable hunk o' meat

2 teaspoons favorite spice rub (I used McCormick's Roasting Rub)

1/2 cup water or beer

The Directions

Use a 6-quart slow cooker. Soak the wood chips in a bowl of water for at least 30 minutes. Spread out a good-sized length of parchment paper on the counter, and put the drained wood chips on it. Fold over the edges of the paper to enclose the wood chips and make a packet that fits inside your removable stoneware completely. Place the packet in the stoneware. With scissors, cut teeny tiny holes here and there in the top level of the parchment paper to let the smoky steam escape.

Rub all sides of your meat with spice rub. Put it in the crock, directly on top of the parchment paper packet (lots of Ps, there). Cover with water or beer. I stuck with water. Put the lid on and cook on low for 8 to 10 hours. The meat is done when it is cooked through and has reached desired tenderness. I wanted ours to fall apart, and cooked it on low for 9 hours.

The Verdict

It worked! The parchment didn't disintegrate, and the wood chips never touched the meat. The brisket was flavorful and had a definite smoky flavor in each bite. My spice rub was quite peppery, so after the first few bites, I mostly tasted pepper, but the smoke was infused. The kids loved it, and called it "the best steak my mom has ever made in the Crock-Pot." It cracks me up that they included the "in the Crock-Pot" part.

VEAL MARSALA

serves 4

The Ingredients

1 tablespoon olive oil

½ cup flour (I used gluten-free baking mix)

½ teaspoon kosher salt

½ teaspoon ground black pepper

½ teaspoon dried oregano

1 pound veal (or chicken) cutlets, pounded thin

2 green onions, sliced

2 cups mushrooms, sliced

1 tablespoon balsamic vinegar

½ cup Marsala wine

4 tablespoons (½ stick) butter, melted

The Directions

Use a 4-quart slow cooker. Drizzle the olive oil in the bottom of your stoneware. In a shallow dish, combine the flour with the salt, pepper, and oregano. Lightly dust each piece of veal with the flour mixture and place it into the slow cooker. Top the veal pieces with the green onions and mushrooms. Add the vinegar, wine, and melted butter. Cover and cook on low for 4 to 7 hours, or on high for 2 to 3 hours. Veal cooks quickly; keep an eye on it.

VEAL PICCATA
serves 4

The Ingredients
½ cup flour (I used a gluten-free baking mix)
½ teaspoon kosher salt
½ teaspoon black pepper
2 pounds veal cutlets, pounded thin
4 tablespoons (½ stick) butter, melted
½ cup diced onion
2 tablespoons dry white wine
2 tablespoons sugar
juice of 2 lemons
8 ounces sliced mushrooms
½ cup drained capers

The Directions
Use a 4-quart slow cooker. In a shallow dish, combine the flour, salt, and pepper. Dredge each piece of veal in the flour mixture, shaking off the excess. Stagger-stack the veal pieces in your crock. In a mixing bowl, combine the melted butter, diced onion, white wine, sugar, and the juice of 1 lemon. Pour over the top of the veal. Add the sliced mushrooms and capers. Cover and cook on low for 4 to 5 hours. Veal doesn't take long to cook. Before serving, squeeze the other lemon onto the veal. Serve with your favorite pasta.

The Verdict
The first time I made this, I didn't dredge the veal, and was slightly off with my lemon and caper taste. Dredging the veal is important, or it sticks together in a weird lump. You can make this with thin pieces of chicken, also, adjusting the cooking time longer by about 2 hours. This tastes great—the capers provide a fun tang that my kids really like.

TAKEOUT FAKE-OUT

One of the side effects of my "Year of Slow Cooking" was that we didn't eat out much. Previously, many a Saturday night would involve looking through the takeout menu drawer (it's not weird to have a whole drawer of menus, is it?) and trying to agree upon what to order. Since I needed to cook in the slow cooker daily, I had no choice but to try to re-create the dishes we were craving at home. The results were amazing: tasty, wonderful meals that completely satisfied our takeout cravings without the worry of gluten contamination.

BROCCOLI BEEF

CHICKEN MAKHANI (INDIAN BUTTER CHICKEN)

CHIMICHANGAS

CHOW MEIN

DOLMAS

FALAFEL

FRIED RICE

GYROS

HOT AND SOUR SOUP

INDIAN CURRY

KOREAN RIBS

LAMB VINDALOO

LEMON CHICKEN

LETTUCE WRAPS

MONGOLIAN BEEF

PEKING DUCK

PHILLY CHEESESTEAK

PHO

TAMALES

TANDOORI CHICKEN

THAI COCONUT SOUP

THAI CURRY

VIETNAMESE ROASTED CHICKEN

BROCCOLI BEEF

serves 4

The Ingredients

¼ cup gluten-free soy sauce

2 tablespoons dry white wine

2 tablespoons apple cider vinegar

2 teaspoons sesame oil

2 garlic cloves, minced

1 tablespoon brown sugar

½ teaspoon crushed red pepper flakes

1 pound thin beef, cut in strips (I used rib-eye)

1 (16-ounce) bag frozen broccoli florets, thawed

The Directions

Use a 4-quart slow cooker. Pour the liquid ingredients into the stoneware. Stir in the garlic, sugar, and pepper flakes. Slice the meat and add to the sauce. Toss with spoons to thoroughly coat the meat. Cover and cook on low for 6 to 8 hours. Add the broccoli, and turn to high. Cover and cook 30 minutes, or until broccoli has heated through. Serve over white or brown rice.

The Verdict

This is a very tasty rendition of an Asian-inspired broccoli beef that is gluten-free and doesn't leave you feeling as if you just ingested a tanker full of oil. One kid ate two helpings and the other ate one piece of broccoli and three bowls of rice.

CHICKEN MAKHANI
(INDIAN BUTTER CHICKEN)

serves 4

The Ingredients

15 cardamom pods (sewn together!)
2 pounds boneless, skinless chicken thighs
1 onion, sliced
6 garlic cloves, chopped
2 teaspoons curry powder
1/2 teaspoon cayenne pepper
2 teaspoons garam masala
1/2 teaspoon ground ginger
4 tablespoons (1/2 stick) butter
1 (6-ounce) can tomato paste
2 tablespoons lemon juice
1 (14-ounce) can coconut milk
1 cup plain yogurt (to add at the end)
kosher salt

The Directions

Use a 6-quart or larger slow cooker. Carefully sew together the cardamom pods using a needle and thread. You can put them in a little cheesecloth bundle, instead, if you have that in the house. Put the chicken in the stoneware, and add the onion, garlic, and all the spices. Plop in the butter and the tomato paste. Add the lemon juice and coconut milk. Cover and cook on low for 8 hours, or on high for 4 hours. The chicken should shred easily with two forks when fully cooked. Stir in the plain yogurt 15 minutes before serving, and discard the cardamom pods. Salt to taste and feel free to tweak the amount of garam masala and curry to your own taste—it's fine to add more at the end of cooking. Serve with basmati rice.

CHIMICHANGAS

serves 6

The Ingredients

1½ pounds lean beef or pork (I used top round)
½ teaspoon kosher salt
½ teaspoon black pepper
1 onion, diced
½ cup water
1 (15-ounce) can tomatoes and chiles (Rotel), drained
1 (15-ounce) can diced tomatoes, drained
brown rice or flour tortillas
6 tablespoons olive oil
favorite toppings: shredded cheese, sour cream, guacamole, salsa

The Directions

Use a 4-quart slow cooker. Trim away any visible fat from the meat, and salt and pepper both sides. Put it into your cooker with the diced onion and water. Cover and cook on low for 8 to 10 hours. After the meat has cooked all day, remove it from the stoneware. Empty the liquid, reserving 1 cup. Slice the meat into thin strips, or shred with two forks. Put the meat back in the crock with the reserved liquid and both cans of drained tomatoes. Turn to high and cook for 30 minutes to warm the contents.

When the meat is hot, you can make chimichanga packets by adding scoopfuls of meat to the center of a steamed tortilla. Fold the bottom and top of the tortilla, then the sides. The edges need to overlap a bit so the meat doesn't escape. Heat 1 tablespoon of olive oil in a large skillet on the stovetop. When it is superhot, carefully put the chimichanga into the oil, seam-side down. Fry until golden brown (about 1 minute), then flip and fry the other side. Repeat the process until you run out of meat and tortillas.

Top with desired fixin's.

The Verdict

We all enjoyed eating our "crunchy burritos." Since we're gluten-free, there is no way to have chimichangas unless we make them at home. The slow cooker ensures that the meat is tender and juicy and provides ample time to shop for and prepare fresh ingredients.

CHOW MEIN

serves 6 to 8

The Ingredients

1 to 2 pounds raw meat, sliced (I used 1 pound chicken breast)

2 yellow onions, chopped

2 cups chopped celery

2 cups water

¼ cup cornstarch

¼ cup gluten-free soy sauce

3 tablespoons molasses

1 red bell pepper, seeded and chopped

1 (6.5-ounce) can bamboo shoots, drained

1 (16-ounce) can whole baby corn ears, drained

1 cup fresh bean sprouts

1 pound spaghetti or chow mein noodles (I used brown rice spaghetti)

olive oil

kosher salt

black pepper to taste

The Directions

Use a 4-quart slow cooker. Put the meat into the stoneware, and add chopped onion, celery, and two cups of water. Cover and cook on low for 6 to 7 hours, or on high for 4 hours. Shred the meat carefully with two forks.

In a small bowl, combine the cornstarch, soy sauce, and molasses. Mix until smooth with no clumpy balls of cornstarch. Set aside. Add the bell pepper to the pot. Add the bamboo shoots, corn, and bean sprouts. Stir in the sauce mixture. Cover the slow cooker again and cook on high for about 1 hour, or until the flavors have melded, and the vegetables have reached the desired tenderness.

Before serving, cook pasta according to package instructions in heavily salted water. When the pasta is al dente, drain and set aside. Heat the olive oil in a large frying pan or wok, and add a bit of salt and pepper. On high heat, toss the cooked pasta in the olive oil, allowing it to sizzle and get a tiny crust on some of the noodles. Serve the noodles with the slow-cooked vegetables and meat.

The Verdict

This was one of the best chow mein dishes I've ever had. I loved how the noodles weren't squishy and how the vegetables remained crisp and the sauce was perfectly seasoned. My parents dropped by and they really liked it a lot.

DOLMAS

serves 12

The Ingredients

½ pound ground turkey breast
½ pound ground lamb
1 cup cooked white rice
1 large egg
1 teaspoon ground allspice
1 teaspoon dried dill
½ cup chopped fresh parsley
2 lemons
1 (8-ounce) jar grape leaves (near the pickles in the grocery store)

The Directions

Use a 6-quart slow cooker. In a mixing bowl, combine the ground meat, rice, egg, allspice, dill, parsley, and juice from 1 lemon. Mix well with your hands to combine. Drain and rinse the grape leaves. Put a small amount of the meat mixture into each leaf, and roll to form a little packet. I'm pretty sure the vein-y part of the leaf is supposed to be inside, with the shiny side facing out. I didn't do this at first, but they do roll better if done that way. Place the wrapped packet into your stoneware. Repeat, until you run out of filling or leaves. It's okay to stagger-stack. I was able to make 24 before I ran out of filling. Squeeze the juice from the other lemon over the top. Cover and cook on high for 2 to 3 hours, or until meat is fully cooked.

The Verdict

These are supereasy, fun to make, and even more fun to eat. I was floored at how many my kids ate—they really liked them a lot. These are an excellent appetizer to serve to guests. Dolmas can be made a day ahead of time and are served chilled or at room temperature.

FALAFEL

serves 2

The Ingredients

1 (15-ounce) can garbanzo beans, drained
1¼ teaspoons kosher salt
¼ teaspoon black pepper
2 teaspoons ground cumin
1 teaspoon ground coriander
¼ to ½ teaspoon cayenne pepper
1 tablespoon dried parsley
½ onion, chopped
2 garlic cloves, minced
1 large egg
juice of 1 lemon
½ to ¾ cup bread crumbs (I used crumbs from a loaf of brown rice bread)
2 tablespoons olive oil, for greasing the crock

The Directions

Use a 4-quart oval slow cooker. Take a deep breath. It looks like there are a lot of ingredients, but this comes together awfully quickly. I seriously only spent 25 minutes in preparation. Pour the garbanzo beans into a mixing bowl and smash with a fork. Set aside. Using a food processor or blender, pulse together the salt, pepper, all of the spices, parsley, onion, garlic, egg, and lemon juice. Pour on top of the smashed garbanzo beans. Use a fork to mix, and add bread crumbs slowly until the mixture is wet and sticky but can be formed into balls nicely. I needed ¾ cup of bread crumbs.

Pour olive oil into the bottom of your stoneware. Form squished golf-ball sized patties of falafel—you should be able to make 8 or 9. Dip each side into the olive oil and then nestle into your

(CONTINUED)

slow cooker. It's okay if they overlap, or are on top of each other. Cook on high for 2 to 5 hours. Ours cooked on high for 3$\frac{1}{2}$ hours—you will know that the falafels are done when they turn a brownish-golden. You can flip them halfway through the cooking time if you feel like it, but they will brown on top even without flipping. Stuff into folded corn tortillas, or pita bread with lettuce, tomato slices, and tzatziki sauce. (Recipe on page 360.)

The Verdict

I never would have imagined that a delicate falafel would turn out so nicely in a slow cooker. I am thrilled that this worked and even more thrilled that my kids didn't run screaming from the kitchen when I showed them what we were having for dinner—although they did choose to eat plain pasta. This is a great meal to have on a hot summer day.

FRIED RICE

serves 4

The Ingredients

2 cups leftover rice or quinoa

3 tablespoons butter

2 tablespoons gluten-free soy sauce

2 teaspoons gluten-free Worcestershire sauce

1/2 teaspoon black pepper

1/4 teaspoon kosher salt

1/2 yellow onion, diced

1 cup fresh or frozen vegetables (I had a bit of asparagus, some carrots and peas)

1 cup cooked meat, diced (I had leftover chicken and three-quarters of a cheeseburger patty from a restaurant)

1 large egg, whisked

1 teaspoon sesame seeds for garnish (optional)

The Directions

Use a 4-quart slow cooker. Put all ingredients into the stoneware and stir well. Cook on high for 2 to 3 hours, or on low for 3 to 4 hours. You only need to heat everything through and cook the egg. After slow cooking daily, I had tons of little plastic containers taking up valuable real estate in the fridge, and this used every last bit.

GYROS

serves 4 to 6

The Ingredients

FOR THE GYRO MEAT

1/2 chopped onion

3 garlic cloves, minced

1/2 pound ground lamb

1/2 pound ground turkey

1 teaspoon paprika

2 teaspoons dried oregano

juice of 1 lemon

FOR THE TZATZIKI SAUCE

1 small cucumber, peeled, seeded, and chopped

1 cup plain nonfat yogurt

1 tablespoon olive oil

3 garlic cloves, minced

2 tablespoons chopped fresh mint

juice of 1 lemon

EXTRA STUFF (OPTIONAL)

pita bread (we used corn tortillas)

lettuce

tomatoes

feta cheese

pitted black olives

The Directions

Use a 4-quart slow cooker. Put the onion and garlic into your cooker. In a small mixing bowl, combine the two kinds of ground meat with the paprika and oregano. Make a little meatloaf with your hands. Put the meatloaf log on top of the onion and garlic in the slow cooker. Pour the lemon juice over the top. Cover and cook on low for 3 to 4 hours, or on high for about 2 hours. While you are waiting for the meat to cook, make up a batch of the yummy tzatziki sauce and chill in the fridge. Remove the meat from the crock and slice thinly on a cutting board. Serve with pitas (or corn or brown rice tortillas) along with the tzatziki sauce and whatever other desired fixings you have chosen.

The Verdict

A hundred million years ago, my very first job was working in the education department at the local zoo. I think I spent pretty much every dollar I made across the street at a gyro stand. I have fond memories of those gyros, which flooded back with each bite. These were so much fun, and cooked perfectly—lots of flavor and moisture, with no grease.

HOT AND SOUR SOUP

serves 2

The Ingredients

1 cup cubed extra-firm tofu
1 (16-ounce) package sliced mushrooms
1 can bamboo shoots, drained
1 can sliced water chestnuts, drained
2 cups water
2 cups chicken broth
1 teaspoon sesame oil
2 tablespoons gluten-free soy sauce
2 tablespoons rice wine vinegar (and more later to taste)
1/4 teaspoon crushed red pepper flakes (and more later to taste)
1 green onion, sliced

The Directions

Use a 4-quart slow cooker. Put the cubed tofu into the slow cooker. Add all the vegetables except for the green onion, the water, and the broth. Add the sesame oil, soy sauce, vinegar, and red pepper flakes. Cover and cook on low for 6 to 8 hours, or on high for 4 hours.

Taste and adjust the seasoning. If you need more of the sour flavor, add more rice wine vinegar. If you need more of the hot flavor, add more red pepper flakes. I like my soup very hot and sour, so I added another tablespoon of the vinegar and another 1/4 teaspoon of the red pepper flakes. Garnish with the sliced green onion.

The Verdict

This is my favorite soup to eat when I'm sick. You can add chicken or pork in addition to or in lieu of the tofu, if you'd like.

INDIAN CURRY

serves 8

The Ingredients

2 tablespoons curry powder

1 teaspoon ground coriander

1 teaspoon ground cumin

1-inch piece fresh ginger, peeled and grated

3 garlic cloves, minced

1 (14-ounce) can coconut milk

1/2 teaspoon Tabasco sauce

1 tablespoon tomato paste

4 to 6 frozen skinless, boneless chicken thighs

1 (15-ounce) can garbanzo beans, drained and rinsed

1 yellow onion, chopped

1 green bell pepper, seeded and chopped

1/2 an eggplant, chopped (I didn't peel)

1 sweet potato, peeled and chopped

The Directions

Use a 6-quart slow cooker. Assemble the spices, ginger, garlic, coconut milk, Tabasco sauce, and tomato paste. Combine the sauce ingredients in the bottom of your cooker. The sauce will be a lovely yellow. Add the chicken, flipping it over a few times to coat nicely. Pour in the garbanzo beans. Wash and chop all the vegetables, and then add them to the crock. Don't worry about stirring them into the sauce. Let them sit on top of the chicken and steam away. Cover and cook on low for 7 to 9 hours, or on high for 4 to 6 hours. Stir carefully to combine all the flavors.

(CONTINUED)

The Verdict

Rachael Ray gave me this recipe, along with a Thai Curry (page 379). It's delicious. We had family over for dinner, and they all really enjoyed it, and took home leftovers. This was really good, and as with many dishes made in the slow cooker, the flavors are even more pronounced the next day.

KOREAN RIBS

serves 4

The Ingredients

4 pounds ribs (I used beef short ribs)
1 cup brown sugar, firmly packed
1 cup gluten-free soy sauce
$\frac{1}{2}$ cup water
5 whole jalapeño peppers

The Directions

Use a 6-quart or larger slow cooker. Put the ribs into the crock. Add the brown sugar, soy sauce, water, and the whole jalapeños (don't cut them! leave them whole!).

Cover and cook on low for 8 hours, flipping once. If you are out of the house all day, flip when you get home so the other side of the ribs gets saturated while you change your clothes and set the table. Serve with rice and vegetables.

The Verdict

Oh. Em. Gee. These are the best ribs in the history of the universe. I got the recipe from Stefania Pomponi Butler, who writes the CityMama blog. I've made them a handful of times now, the meat is tender, and the sauce just cannot be beat. If you feel brave, you can try eating the cooked jalapeños. Otherwise, feel free to toss. Serve with rice and steamed vegetables.

LAMB VINDALOO

serves 6

The Ingredients

3 pounds boneless leg of lamb or stew meat
1 medium yellow onion, chopped
6 garlic cloves, minced
1/2 teaspoon ground cloves
1 teaspoon dried ginger
1/2 teaspoon cayenne pepper
1 tablespoon ground coriander
1 tablespoon ground cumin
1 teaspoon ground cinnamon
1/4 cup apple cider vinegar
2 chopped potatoes ("aloo" means potato)
1 (14-ounce) can stewed tomatoes

The Directions

Use a 6-quart slow cooker. Trim the excess fat from the lamb, and cut the meat into 1-inch chunks, or use lamb stew meat. Put into a ziplock freezer bag with the onion, garlic, and dry spices. Close bag tightly and shake to coat lamb with the spices. Refrigerate overnight.

In the morning, dump the marinated meat into the cooker, and add the apple cider vinegar, chopped potatoes (I didn't peel), and canned tomatoes. Cover and cook on low for 8 to 10 hours. Serve with rice and corn tortillas or naan. This freezes well, and the flavors are even more pronounced in the leftovers.

LEMON CHICKEN

serves 4

The Ingredients

1½ pounds boneless chicken, cut in 2-inch chunks

½ cup flour (I used a gluten-free baking mix)

olive oil, for browning the chicken (optional)

1 tablespoon kosher salt

6 ounces (½ can) frozen lemonade concentrate, thawed

3 tablespoons brown sugar

1 teaspoon balsamic vinegar

3 tablespoons ketchup

The Directions

Use a 4-quart slow cooker. I hate precooking food before putting it into the slow cooker, but this is one of those times when it's a good idea. The browning will provide a bit of texture to the outside of the chicken pieces not achieved through slow cooking alone. Dredge the chicken pieces in flour and dump excess. Brown the chicken on the stovetop in a bit of olive oil. There's no need to fully cook, just get a bit of crust on the outside of the chicken. Place the chicken into the stoneware. Add the other ingredients, and toss gently to coat with sauce. Cover and cook on low for 6 hours, or on high for 3 to 4 hours. Serve over white rice.

The Verdict

This completely satisfied my family's Chinese takeout cravings. It's a marvelous dish. I'd suggest adding a pinch of red pepper flakes to the grown-up servings for a bit of a kick. The kids ate a ton of this, and asked for more. You can make an orange chicken version by using frozen orange juice concentrate instead of lemonade.

LETTUCE WRAPS

serves 8

The Ingredients

1 pound chicken breast
½ yellow onion, chopped
5 garlic cloves, chopped
¼ cup chopped water chestnuts (optional)
¼ cup gluten-free soy sauce
¼ cup dry white wine
2 tablespoons balsamic vinegar
½ teaspoon ground ginger
⅛ teaspoon ground allspice
16 romaine lettuce leaves
plum sauce

The Directions

Use a 4-quart slow cooker. Chop the chicken into teeny tiny chunks, and put into the slow cooker. Add the onion, garlic, and water chestnuts, if using. Mix in the liquid ingredients and spices. Cover and cook on low for 6 hours, or on high for 3 to 4 hours. Serve in lettuce leaves with plum sauce. For a gluten-free plum sauce recipe, see page 371.

The Verdict

I've been told that these taste remarkably similar to the variety offered at P.F. Chang's. We served them to company, and all the grown-ups thoroughly enjoyed their servings. The kids were all too busy running around like wild turkeys to stop and have a taste.

MONGOLIAN BEEF

serves 4

The Ingredients

3 pounds flank steak

1/4 cup cornstarch (to dredge meat—don't add to sauce mixture)

1 cup gluten-free soy sauce

1/2 cup dry white wine

1/2 cup dry sherry

1 tablespoon white wine vinegar (optional—I forgot to add it!)

2 teaspoons sesame oil

2 teaspoons molasses

2 teaspoons ground ginger

1/2 teaspoon black pepper

1 teaspoon crushed red pepper flakes

1/4 cup brown sugar, firmly packed

1 tablespoon natural peanut butter (if allergic, use black bean paste)

6 garlic cloves, minced

4 green onions, sliced

2 teaspoons dried minced onion (or 1/2 fresh onion, diced very small)

The Directions

Use a 4-quart slow cooker. There are a lot of ingredients listed because I didn't want to use a bottled hoisin sauce. Slice the meat into thin strips and toss in a ziplock freezer bag with the cornstarch. Set aside. Add all liquids and dry spices, brown sugar, and peanut butter to your slow cooker, and mix well. Add the garlic and three of the sliced green onions; reserve 1 green onion for garnish. If you are using fresh onion, add that now, too. Put the meat into the crock, and toss gently to coat.

(CONTINUED)

Cover and cook on low for 4 to 6 hours. Flank steak is thin and has very little fat, and will cook quickly. There isn't a lot of liquid in this dish, so if your cooker tends to cook hot, please check after 3 hours. The meat is done when it is no longer pink and has reached the desired tenderness. Serve over steamed or Fried Rice (see page 359 for slow-cooked version), and garnish with the sliced green onion.

The Verdict

Delicious. This is so good—before this challenge I would not have attempted to make something so "complicated" in a slow cooker. But really, the only complicated thing was figuring out what flavors would work and assembling the ingredients—the actual cooking and food preparation was a snap, and the kitchen was clean and mopped by 12:00 noon. This is much better for your wallets than delivery or take-out, and much, *much* less greasy. It's also gluten-free!

PEKING DUCK

serves 6

The Ingredients

    5 green onions
    1 (4-to 5-pound) duck
    1 (1-inch) piece ginger, peeled
    4 whole star anise
    2 teaspoons five-spice powder
    1 teaspoon ground cinnamon
    1/2 teaspoon ground nutmeg
    2 tablespoons gluten-free soy sauce
    1 tablespoon honey

The Directions

Use a 6-quart slow cooker, and insert a cooking rack of some sort in the bottom of the stoneware. I used a steamer rack that came with a rice cooker. Lay the green onions on top of the rack. Skin the duck the best you can, and remove the neck and giblets. Stuff the ginger inside the cavity, along with the star anise. In a small bowl, combine the dry spices. Rub all over the bird, inside and out. Place the duck inside your cooker, breast-side up. Drizzle with the soy sauce and honey. Cover and cook on high for 4 hours. Serve with rice and plum sauce (see Note).

    Note: I made an easy plum sauce by combining: 1/3 cup plum jam; 1 tablespoon gluten-free soy sauce; 1 tablespoon sugar; and 1 teaspoon garlic powder.

PHILLY CHEESESTEAK

serves 4

The Ingredients

1 pound sliced tri-tip
1 red bell pepper, seeded and sliced
1 yellow bell pepper, seeded and sliced
1 orange bell pepper, seeded and sliced
1/2 yellow onion, sliced
1/4 cup dry white wine
1 tablespoon gluten-free Worcestershire sauce
sandwich rolls
8 slices of cheese (provolone, Swiss, or pepper Jack)

The Directions

Use a 4-quart slow cooker. Put the sliced meat into the stoneware, and top with the bell peppers and onion. Toss the meat and vegetables with the white wine and Worcestershire sauce. Cover and cook on low for 8 hours, or on high for 4 hours. Serve on rolls with slices of cheese. If desired, bake open sandwiches on a baking sheet in the oven at 400°F for 12 to 15 minutes, or until cheese is melty.

The Verdict

I've never been to Philadelphia, which means I've never had an authentic cheesesteak. I've ordered them in restaurants on numerous occasions and each time, I seem to get a different variation. I made this recipe up with stuff we had around the house, and we all really enjoyed them. I made the rolls out of a box of gluten-free sandwich bread mix.

PHO

serves 6

The Ingredients

    6 cups beef broth or stock

    1 pound thin sliced beef (I used stir-fry meat from the butcher)

    2 green onions, sliced

    2-inch piece of fresh ginger, peeled and grated

    1 teaspoon fish sauce (anchovies, salt, water; it smells horrible)

    ¾ teaspoon ground anise

    1 cinnamon stick

    ½ teaspoon black pepper

    ½ teaspoon kosher salt

    1 (8-ounce) package thin rice noodles

    bean sprouts, chopped cilantro, basil, and lime wedges (optional garnishes)

The Directions

Use a 6-quart slow cooker. Pour the broth into the stoneware. Add the meat, green onions, ginger, fish sauce, and all the spices and salt. Cover and cook on low for 8 hours, or on high for 4 to 6 hours. It's done when the meat is fully cooked and tender. Add the entire package of rice noodles to the slow cooker 15 minutes before serving, pushing the noodles down with a wooden spoon. Cover and cook on high until the noodles are soft and translucent. Ladle into bowls, and serve with optional garnishes on the side, to add at the table.

The Verdict

This has a very nice mellow flavor. I loved the hint of anise (tastes like black licorice) and the cinnamon. If using a homemade stock (see page 172), you'll need to add salt to taste. Pho is pronounced "fuh," but that didn't stop the "Fee-fi-fo-fum" jokes around the dinner table.

TAMALES

makes approximately 20

The Ingredients

1 (6-ounce) package dried corn husks (I went to a Mexican grocer)

FOR THE FILLING
1 (3½-pound) store-bought rotisserie chicken, or 3 pounds shredded beef or pork
½ yellow onion, diced
1 garlic clove, minced
1 (4-ounce) can chopped mild green chiles
1 teaspoon ground cumin
½ teaspoon kosher salt
1 (15-ounce) can corn, drained
1 cup shredded cheddar cheese (optional)

FOR THE TAMALE DOUGH
4 cups masa harina
2½ cups beef broth
2 teaspoons baking powder
1 teaspoon kosher salt
1⅓ cups lard or vegetable shortening

The Directions

Use a 6-quart oval slow cooker. Combine the chicken with the onion, garlic, green chiles, cumin, salt, and drained corn in your stoneware. Cook on low for 6 hours, or on high for about 4 hours. The onions need to be translucent before going into the tamales. If you don't have time for this step, skip the garlic and onion, and combine the chicken with the other ingredients in a mixing bowl. Set aside.

Soften the corn husks by soaking them in very hot water until they are pliable. To make the masa, combine the dough ingredients in a large bowl, and beat on medium to high speed until the dough is spongy. Check the dough by dropping a little ball of it into a glass of water. It should float. If it doesn't, continue to beat the dough.

Take a piece of masa dough a bit larger than a golf ball in size, and spread it into a wet corn husk. The dough should be about ¼ inch thick—you do not want to see the corn husk through the dough. Add a bit of filling, and some cheese. Fold the corn husk over to join the edges of the masa. If you need to add more dough, do so—no filling should peek through. Fold all corn husk edges into the center and place into the bottom of an empty 6-quart slow cooker, seam-side down. Repeat until you run out of filling, dough, or corn husks.

When finished, put the lid on and cook on high for 4 to 6 hours, or until a tester tamale looks and tastes done. The tamales on the edges will cook a bit faster. Once your tester looks good (I used the same one, and kept rewrapping it and adding it back when it wasn't ready), unplug the slow cooker and keep the lid off. Don't unwrap any others until they've set for about 15 minutes. My tamales were cooked at 6 hours, but I began checking every 45 minutes at 4 hours.

The Verdict

I was thrilled that these worked so well! They are definitely labor-intensive, but pack an awfully impressive presentation. I brought them to my daughter's second grade class, and the children ate them after reading *Too Many Tamales* by Gary Soto and Ed Martinez. Fifteen of the eighteen kids enjoyed them, and the other three were polite with their "no thank-you"s.

TANDOORI CHICKEN

serves 6

The Ingredients

3 to 4 pounds chicken (I used a whole chicken, but boneless, skinless thighs would work quite well)

1 cup plain yogurt, divided (you could use sour cream instead)

1 teaspoon ginger

1 teaspoon coriander

½ teaspoon cayenne pepper (or more to taste)

¼ teaspoon ground cloves

¼ teaspoon black pepper

1 tablespoon cumin

1 teaspoon kosher salt

5 to 6 drops red food coloring (optional)

6 cardamom pods, or ¼ teaspoon ground cardamom

6 cloves garlic (I tossed them in whole)

1 lemon, juiced

The Directions

Use a 6-quart slow cooker. Skin the bird (assuming you are using a whole chicken) and toss out the neck and the stuff from inside. (Shudder a few times.) In a small mixing bowl, combine ½ cup yogurt with all dry spices, salt, and the red food coloring. Smear all over the chicken, inside and out. Put the cardamom pods inside the bird, and lower it into the stoneware. Toss whole garlic cloves on top, and squeeze on the lemon juice. Cover and cook on low for 6 to 8 hours, or on high for 4 hours. Serve with basmati rice.

After removing the meat from the pot, stir in the remaining ½ cup of yogurt to make a yummy sauce to pour over the meat and rice.

The Verdict

I did some research on tandoori chicken and learned that a lot of times, the way the red coloring is achieved in restaurants is through food coloring. The more food coloring you add, the redder the chicken. I find this highly amusing, yet no one else in my family finds it as funny as I do. But imagine: The chicken could be blue!—or chartreuse!—and still taste same!

Anyway—if you don't want to use food coloring, don't. But you won't get red chicken. The meat was spicy where it was coated in the blend, but otherwise just slightly infused with a smoky flavor. I was able to peel some non-spicy meat off the bones, for the kids (which they dipped in barbecue sauce), and Adam and I piled our plates high with the meat on top of rice with lots of the tandoori sauce. If I was going to make this for company, I'd use boneless, skinless thighs. The bones got in my way.

THAI COCONUT SOUP

serves 4

The Ingredients

    4 cups chicken or vegetable broth
    4 limes (3 juiced, 1 for garnish)
    1/2 teaspoon lime zest
    1 teaspoon sugar
    3 tablespoons fish sauce
    1 (1-inch) piece fresh ginger, peeled and grated
    1 (14-ounce) can coconut milk
    1/2 to 2 teaspoons red chili paste
    1/2 pound extra-firm tofu, cubed
    1 red bell pepper, seeded and sliced in strips
    2 garlic cloves, minced
    4 ounces sliced shiitake mushrooms, cut in quarters
    1 large vine-ripened tomato, coarsely chopped

The Directions

Use a 4-quart slow cooker. Although there are a lot of ingredients listed, this soup comes together quite quickly. Pour the broth into the cooker. Add the juice of three of the limes, and the lime zest. Stir in the sugar, fish sauce, grated ginger, and coconut milk. You now have your soup base. Add the red chili paste to taste, 1/2 teaspoon at a time, until you have reached the desired heat. I ended up using 1 1/2 teaspoons, but you can always add more after cooking, so go slow and don't overdo it. Add the tofu, bell pepper, and garlic. Coarsely chop the shiitake mushrooms and tomato. Stir in carefully, so you don't break up the tofu or the tomatoes. Cover and cook on low for 4 to 5 hours, or on high for 2 to 4 hours. Garnish with fresh lime slices. This is an elegant soup, fit to serve to your very best friends, which we did.

THAI CURRY

serves 6

The Ingredients

1 (14-ounce) can coconut milk

1 tablespoon gluten-free soy sauce

1 tablespoon brown sugar

1 tablespoon Thai red or green chili paste, plus more if needed

1 teaspoon fish sauce

1 (1-inch) piece fresh ginger, peeled and grated

2 to 3 garlic cloves, chopped

6 boneless, skinless chicken thighs

1 yellow onion, chopped

1 red bell pepper, seeded and chopped

1 green bell pepper, seeded and chopped

½ large eggplant, chopped (no need to peel)

1 sweet potato, chopped in 1-inch chunks

The Directions

Use a 5- to 6-quart slow cooker. Combine the sauce ingredients: the coconut milk, soy sauce, brown sugar, chili paste, fish sauce, ginger, and garlic in the bottom of your stoneware. Taste. If you think you need more chili paste, add some, a bit at a time (it's spicy stuff!). Add chicken pieces to the sauce, flipping them over a few times so they get nice and saucy. Add the vegetables to the mix. Cover and cook on low for 6 to 8 hours, or on high for 4 to 6 hours. This is done when the chicken is fully cooked and the vegetables have reached the desired tenderness. Serve over white rice.

(CONTINUED)

The Verdict

Rachael Ray gave me this recipe, along with an Indian Curry (page 363), when I appeared on her show. The prep time was right about 20 minutes, and although it looks like a bunch of ingredients, it comes together easily. This dish is full of flavor that is so on-the-money. It was not too spicy, and the kids ate a good amount. It pairs wonderfully with the Thai Coconut Soup (page 378).

VIETNAMESE ROASTED CHICKEN

serves 4

The Ingredients

4 to 6 chicken thighs (my thighs had skin and bones)
1½ tablespoons gluten-free soy sauce
1½ tablespoons fish sauce
1½ teaspoons sugar
½ teaspoon black pepper
4 garlic cloves, chopped
1 tablespoon canola oil

The Directions

Use a 4-quart slow cooker. Put the chicken into the stoneware. Combine the sauce ingredients in a small bowl, and pour over the top. My chicken was frozen solid, and I worried that the flavor wouldn't sink in as nicely as it would if I had marinated it for a while—but it was fine. Cover and cook on low for about 6 hours, or on high for 3 to 4 hours. The cooking time depends on how thick your chicken pieces are, and if they are fresh or frozen.

The Verdict

Make this. Eat this. This is not a boring dry chicken meal; this is the opposite. This chicken is juicy, full of flavor, and downright adventurous. The meat was moist and tender and the sauce has an amazing flavor. We ate it over white rice and practically licked the remaining sauce out of the crock.

SNACKS & FONDUE

*S*nack time means fun time when you plug in the slow cooker for a fondue party or for making slow-cooked versions of childhood favorites. It's really hard not to smile while munching on a bowl full of Cracker Jack, or a Rice Krispies treat. Please note that children under age four should not be given nuts, seeds, popcorn, chunky peanut butter, or any other food that may cause choking. If you own only a large slow cooker, you can still make the listed fondues by simply inserting an oven-safe dish (Corningware, Pyrex) into your stoneware to create a smaller cooking vessel.

APPLESAUCE

CANDIED WALNUTS

CHEX PARTY MIX

CHOCOLATE AND MARSHMALLOW FONDUE

CHOCOLATE FONDUE

CRACKER JACK

CRANBERRY-ORANGE DIP

CRUNCHY ROASTED GARBANZO BEANS

FANCY CHEESE FONDUE

NUTS AND BOLTS TRAIL MIX

PEANUT BUTTER FONDUE

PIZZA FONDUE

PUMPKIN PIE DIP

PUPPY CHOW/MONKEY MIX

RICE KRISPIES TREATS

ROASTED AND SPICED NUTS

APPLESAUCE

serves 4

The Ingredients

4 large apples, peeled, cored, and cut in quarters
juice of 1 lemon
¼ cup water
1 teaspoon vanilla extract
½ teaspoon ground cinnamon
1 tablespoon brown sugar

The Directions

Use a 4-quart slow cooker. Plop the apple pieces into your stoneware. Add the lemon juice and water. Pour in the vanilla and add the cinnamon and brown sugar. Cover and cook on low for 4 to 6 hours. When the apples are very tender, mash them with a potato masher or a large fork. My apples were quite tender after 6 hours, and I was able to use a fork.

The Verdict

This is a great snack on a foggy day. If you feel adventurous, toss in a handful of raisins or dried cranberries. They will swell and pack a juicy punch.

CANDIED WALNUTS

serves 4

The Ingredients
2 cups walnut halves
2 tablespoons salted butter
1/4 cup brown sugar, firmly packed

parchment paper

The Directions
Use a 2-quart slow cooker. Plop all the ingredients into your stoneware, and cook on high for 1 hour.

After 1 hour, mix well, and pour onto a layer of parchment paper to cool and dry. The nuts will be hot—keep little fingers away for at least 15 minutes. When cool, the nuts will crisp up and are ready to be used.

The Verdict
Candied nuts are terribly easy and inexpensive to make in the slow cooker. You can make them in bulk and freeze them in little ziplock bags to defrost at your convenience for salad toppings, trail mix, or just to munch on. I tried walnuts instead of candied pecans on the baked Brie with Pecans and Cranberries (page 24) and was quite pleased with the woody flavor walnuts provide.

CHEX PARTY MIX
serves 10

The Ingredients
3 tablespoons butter
$1/2$ teaspoon onion powder
$1/2$ teaspoon seasoned salt
$1^1/2$ tablespoons gluten-free Worcestershire Sauce
5 cups General Mills Rice Chex Cereal (clearly labeled gluten-free)
1 to 2 cups dry roasted peanuts (salted or not, your choice)
2 cups pretzel sticks (I used Glutino)

The Directions
Use a 6-quart slow cooker. Put the butter into the stoneware, and turn the cooker to low. Add the onion powder, seasoned salt, and Worcestershire sauce. Add the dry ingredients. Toss to coat. Cover and cook on low for 2 to 3 hours, stirring every 45 minutes or so. Dump out onto a baking sheet to cool.

The Verdict
This is seriously addicting. I've made Chex Mix numerous times in the slow cooker, and love that I can turn it on and wander off for a while, rather than staying put in the kitchen. I consistently burn my party mix when I cook it in a traditional oven. This snack is requested often in our house.

CHOCOLATE AND MARSHMALLOW FONDUE

serves 4

The Ingredients

    7 ounces milk chocolate

    3 ounces white chocolate

    1 tablespoon almond extract (or you could use Amaretto)

    $^1/_4$ cup heavy cream

    1 cup marshmallow fluff

The Directions

Use a 1-quart or smaller slow cooker. Break chocolate into the stoneware and add the almond extract or Amaretto and heavy cream. Scoop the marshmallow fluff from the jar, and push it in with your fingers (so you can then lick them). Cover, and cook for about 90 minutes, stirring every 30 minutes or so. Serve with cut-up fruit, almonds, and graham crackers. I used gluten-free animal crackers.

The Verdict

The best part of this (for me) was that I sent Adam to the store to get the chocolate and he came home with the good stuff: Cadbury and Ghirardelli. I totally would have cheaped out, and he didn't. I love that man. This stuff rocks. Make sure you brush your teeth afterward.

CHOCOLATE FONDUE

serves 4

The Ingredients

1½ cups chocolate chips (semisweet, dark, milk, or white. Your choice.)
½ cup heavy cream
1 teaspoon vanilla extract

OPTIONAL
You can doctor this up with:
1 tablespoon Grand Marnier
1 tablespoon rum
1 tablespoon Peppermint Schnapps
1 tablespoon Baileys Irish Cream
1 teaspoon peppermint, orange, or coconut extract
pinch of espresso powder

The Directions

Use a 1-quart or smaller slow cooker. Put the chocolate chips into the stoneware. Add the heavy cream and vanilla, and cover. Plug in and cook for about 1 hour. Stir. Serve with apple chunks, banana slices, cubes of pound cake, strawberries, or marshmallows. Or all of them, and invite me over!

The Verdict

You can't not have fun while dipping stuff in chocolate. If you don't have fun dipping stuff in chocolate, seek help. This is simple and easy and wonderful and amazing. The kids liked the marshmallows the best, surprise, surprise.

CRACKER JACK

serves 8

The Ingredients

1 cup brown sugar, firmly packed
1/2 cup light corn syrup
2 tablespoons molasses
4 tablespoons (1/2 stick) butter
1 cup popcorn kernels
1 air-popped popcorn machine
parchment paper
1 1/2 cups salted cocktail peanuts
1 teaspoon kosher salt

The Directions

Use a 6-quart slow cooker. Put the sugar, corn syrup, molasses, and butter into your cooker and set on high for 1 to 3 hours, or until the mixture is hot and bubbly. While waiting, pop the popcorn in the air-popper. Spread out long pieces of parchment paper on the countertop or table. When the sugar mixture is bubbly, carefully mix in the popcorn and peanuts. You may need to add a bit at a time and ladle the hot syrup over the top. Spread the popcorn and peanuts out on the parchment paper and sprinkle with the kosher salt. Store in an airtight container.

CRANBERRY-ORANGE DIP

serves 4

The Ingredients

1 (8-ounce) block cream cheese
2/3 cup shredded Swiss cheese
1/2 teaspoon orange zest
2 tablespoons apple juice
1/2 cup sweetened dried cranberries

The Directions

Use a 1-quart or smaller slow cooker. Plug in the cooker to warm it up. Shove the block of cream cheese into the stoneware. You may need to squish it in with a spoon, but I promise it will fit. Add the Swiss cheese, orange zest, and apple juice. Cover and let cook for 45 minutes to 1 hour. When the cheeses have fully melted, stir in the dried cranberries. Serve with your favorite crackers or apple slices.

The Verdict

This looks like a big pile of fluffy snow.

CRUNCHY ROASTED GARBANZO BEANS

serves 6

The Ingredients

2 (15-ounce) cans garbanzo beans, drained and rinsed
1 tablespoon lemon juice
1 teaspoon kosher salt
1/4 teaspoon cayenne pepper

The Directions

Use a 4-quart slow cooker. Place the garbanzo beans into the stoneware. Pour on lemon juice, and add salt and cayenne. Toss well to distribute the flavors. Prop the lid of your crock open with a wooden skewer or chopstick to release any condensation, and cook on low for 8 to 10 hours, or until the garbanzo beans have shriveled up and have a crunch. I cooked my batch on low for 9 hours overnight. Store in the refrigerator.

The Verdict

These are fun to munch on, beyond healthy, slightly addictive, and super easy to make. Every once in a while you will get a soggy-ish bean, but the crunch of the beans is nice. They are reminiscent of corn nuts, without fear of damaging teeth. The kids decided they look like shrunken brains.

FANCY CHEESE FONDUE

serves 6

The Ingredients
¼ cup each of three "fancy" cheeses. I used goat, Gruyère, and Swiss
¼ cup dry white wine
½ teaspoon ground nutmeg

The Directions
Use a 1-quart or smaller slow cooker. Shred the hard cheeses and put into the mini cooker. Add the goat cheese. Pour in the white wine and sprinkle the nutmeg on top. No need to stir—it will melt together. Cook for 45 minutes, then stir. Cover again and heat until the cheeses have melted and are bubbly. Serve with bread, crostini, crackers, or your favorite dipping vegetables.

I made crostini out of a loaf of brown rice bread. All I did was brush olive oil on both sides of each slice, and sprinkle with kosher salt and pepper. I baked them at 400°F until golden, flipping once.

NUTS AND BOLTS TRAIL MIX

serves 6

The Ingredients

2½ cups unsalted nuts (I used almonds and walnut halves)
1½ cups pretzel sticks (I used gluten-free pretzels)
1 cup dried cranberries
2 tablespoons butter, melted
1½ teaspoons water
1 teaspoon vanilla extract
½ cup sugar
parchment paper

The Directions

Use a 6-quart slow cooker. Put the nuts, pretzels, and cranberries into the stoneware. Combine the melted butter with the water, vanilla, and sugar. Pour the mixture over the top of dry ingredients. Stir well to coat. Cover and cook on high for 2 to 3 hours, stirring every 30 minutes. When the pretzels have browned and the nuts are toasty, pour the mix out onto a parchment–lined baking sheet to cool. Store in an airtight container.

The Verdict

I was worried that the pretzels would taste stale after being coated, but once they cooled, they regained their original crunch. This tastes delicious and makes a fantastic after-school snack.

PEANUT BUTTER FONDUE

serves 4

The Ingredients

3/4 cup natural peanut butter
1/4 cup brown sugar, firmly packed
1 teaspoon vanilla extract
1/4 cup heavy cream or half-and-half
4 large marshmallows

The Directions

Use a 1-quart or smaller slow cooker. Scoop the peanut butter into the stoneware. Add the brown sugar, vanilla, and cream. Push the marshmallows into the mixture. Don't bother to stir now; the peanut butter will just stick to the spoon. Cover and cook for about 1 hour. Stir well. Heat some more if it isn't all melty. Serve with apple slices and celery sticks, and eat in bed while watching *Oprah*.

PIZZA FONDUE

serves 4

The Ingredients

10 pieces pepperoni, diced
1 cup pasta sauce
$1/2$ teaspoon Italian seasoning
1 cup shredded Italian cheese blend

The Directions

Use a 1-quart or smaller slow cooker. Count out 10 pieces of pepperoni, then eat the rest of the package. Put the pasta sauce into the mini cooker, and plug it in. Add the Italian seasoning and diced pepperoni. Shove in the cup of shredded cheese. Cover and cook for 45 minutes or so. Stir well and serve with tortilla chips, bread sticks, or bread cubes.

PUMPKIN PIE DIP

serves 6

The Ingredients

> 4 ounces cream cheese
> 1/4 cup sour cream
> 1 cup canned pumpkin pie filling
> 1 tablespoon chopped walnuts (optional)

The Directions

Use a 1-quart or smaller slow cooker. Add the cream cheese to the stoneware, and top with the sour cream. Pour in the pumpkin pie filling. Cover and cook for about 1 hour, then stir well. If the cream cheese hasn't fully melted, cook a bit longer. Garnish with the chopped walnuts, if desired.

The Verdict

I served this with gluten-free gingersnaps, pretzels, and apple slices. It was a big hit; it tasted like pumpkin cheesecake. This would be fun to serve along with Pumpkin Spice Lattes (page 15) at a pumpkin-carving party.

PUPPY CHOW/MONKEY MIX

serves 12

The Ingredients

 1 cup chocolate chips

 4 tablespoons (½ stick) butter

 1 box (10.6-ounce) EnviroKidz Peanut Butter Panda Puffs (if you don't have access to Panda Puffs, you can substitute with your favorite cereal and add ½ cup peanut butter to the mixture; of course, if you are gluten-free, you will stick to GF cereal)

 1 cup dried cranberries

 ½ cup unsalted sunflower seeds

 1 cup almonds

 parchment paper

 1 cup confectioners' sugar

 3 (1-gallon) plastic ziplock freezer bags

The Directions

Use a 6-quart or larger slow cooker. Put the chocolate chips and butter (add peanut butter now, if using) into your stoneware. Turn the cooker to low for 90 minutes, or to high for about 45 minutes. When the chocolate chips are beginning to lose shape, stir in the cereal, cranberries, seeds, and almonds. Turn off the slow cooker. Spread out a big length of parchment paper on your countertop. Add ⅓ cup confectioners' sugar to each freezer bag. Shake about one-third of the chocolaty cereal into each bag. Spread out on the parchment paper to cool. Get hugs.

The Verdict

This is a snack for good kids. Really good kids. If you want your kids to finish their homework promptly, make their beds, or rub your back, say you're going to make Puppy Chow/Monkey Mix. Thankfully we packed up half of this to send home with some friends, or I would have eaten my weight in it—this makes a lot.

RICE KRISPIES TREATS

serves 10 to 12

The Ingredients

   3 tablespoons butter
   4 cups mini marshmallows
   6 cups Rice Krispies (or similar) cereal
   parchment paper or aluminum foil

The Directions

Use a 6-quart slow cooker; it needs to be large enough to stir the ingredients easily. Put the butter and the marshmallows into your stoneware and turn the cooker to high. Add the cereal. Cover and let cook for 1 hour.

While waiting, prepare an 11×9-inch cake pan with parchment paper or greased foil. When the time has elapsed, stir well. If the marshmallows and butter haven't fully melted, cook for another 30 minutes on high. Spread the contents into the prepared pan, and let cool fully before cutting into squares.

The Verdict

This is the best way I've found to make Rice Krispies treats (we don't use the real stuff, but Barbara's Organic Gluten-Free Brown Rice Treats doesn't sound quite as nice). I like that the kids can be in charge of making the whole thing without me being worried they'll burn themselves on the stove, and that for the hour the marshmallows and butter are melting they are on their absolute best behavior.

ROASTED AND SPICED NUTS

serves 12

The Ingredients

cooking spray
1 cup raw, unsalted pecans
1 cup raw, unsalted almonds
1 cup raw, unsalted pistachios (no shells, just the meat)
1/2 cup raw, unsalted pumpkin seeds
1 teaspoon curry powder
1 teaspoon dried rosemary
1/4 teaspoon cayenne pepper
1/2 teaspoon kosher salt
1 1/2 tablespoons maple syrup

The Directions

Use a 6-quart slow cooker. Spray the inside of your stoneware with cooking spray. This is the only grease/butter, which creates a fantastic non-oily nut. Put in your nuts/seeds, and add the spices and the maple syrup. Toss well to coat. Cover and cook on high for 2 hours, stirring every 20 minutes or so. The nuts will burn if you don't stir them (don't worry if a few get burned; they still taste good and get that rustic homemade look). Spread the nuts out on a layer of foil or wax paper to completely cool, and store in an airtight container.

The Verdict

We all really liked these, and so did my dad. The kids ate a bunch, then fanned their tongues because of the slight kick from the cayenne. Both the maple syrup and cayenne are there, but they are not overpowering, which is sort of scary because you can eat a bucket load. These make a fantastic gift, unless your recipient is allergic to nuts. Then you should make something else.

DESSERTS

*S*ome of my favorite dishes I've ever prepared in the slow cooker have been the desserts. Our family was blown away by the chocolate mousse, cheesecake, crème brûlée, and the apple dumplings. You must give them a try.

APPLE CRISP

APPLE DUMPLINGS

BANANAS FOSTER

BLUEBERRY BUCKLE

BREAD PUDDING

CARAMEL APPLES

CHEESECAKE

CHERRIES JUBILEE

CHOCOLATE-COVERED STRAWBERRIES
   AND APPLES

CHOCOLATE FRITO CANDY

CHOCOLATE MOUSSE

CRÈME BRÛLÉE

DULCE DE LECHE

PEACH COMPOTE

PEACH PIE

PEANUT (NOT BRITTLE) CANDY

PEANUT CLUSTERS

PUMPKIN PUDDING (CRUSTLESS PUMPKIN PIE)

RICE PUDDING

ROCKY ROAD CANDY

STUFFED AND BAKED APPLES

TAPIOCA PUDDING

APPLE CRISP

serves 6

The Ingredients

cooking spray

9 smallish apples

4 tablespoons (½ stick) butter

¼ cup orange juice

⅓ cup brown sugar, plus another 2 tablespoons for crumb topping

2 tablespoons vanilla extract

1 cup crumb topping stuff (I used gluten-free gingersnap crumbs mixed with crushed gluten-free cereal. You can use anything you'd normally use for a crumb topping: oats, smashed cereal, graham crackers, cookies, etc.)

The Directions

Use a 4-quart slow cooker. Spray the inside bottom and sides of your stoneware with cooking spray. Peel, core, and slice the apples and plop them into the crock. Cube the butter and dot on top. Add the orange juice, ⅓ cup brown sugar, and vanilla. Toss to combine with the apples. Smash up your topping of choice and combine with the remaining 2 tablespoons of brown sugar. Sprinkle on top of the apple concoction. Cover and cook on high for 3 hours, or until the apples are sufficiently tender. If you like your crumb topping crunchy (I do!), broil the uncovered stoneware on the lowest rack of your oven for 4 to 7 minutes, or use a kitchen torch. Serve with vanilla ice cream.

APPLE DUMPLINGS

serves 6 to 8

The Ingredients

cooking spray
2 cans refrigerated crescent rolls, or gluten-free substitute (recipe follows)
2 Granny Smith apples, peeled and sliced in thin wedges
8 tablespoons (1 stick) butter
1 cup sugar
1 teaspoon ground cinnamon
1 teaspoon vanilla extract
1 cup Mountain Dew soda

The Directions

Use a 6-quart slow cooker. Spray your stoneware with cooking spray. If you are using the refrigerated crescent rolls, roll out the little triangles and fill each one with an apple slice or two and roll it up. If you are using the gluten-free dough, do the same thing. Pile the crock high with all of your little dumpling guys.

Melt the butter in a bowl in the microwave, and stir in the sugar, cinnamon, and vanilla. Pour over dumplings, making sure to get it down into the nooks and crannies. Then add 1 cup of Mountain Dew—it will make a delightful bubbly sound! Cover, but prop lid with a wooden spoon or chopstick, and cook on high for 4 to 5 hours, or until the dough is brown and cooked through. Serve with ice cream, or eat as is. The leftovers make a great breakfast.

(CONTINUED)

GLUTEN-FREE CRESCENT DOUGH

The Ingredients

8 tablespoons (1 stick) butter, at room temperature

1½ cups sour cream

2 cups gluten-free baking mix (I use Pamela's brand)

2 teaspoons xanthan gum (although the baking mix has this already, I added extra for more of a rise)

¼ teaspoon kosher salt

½ teaspoon cream of tartar

1 teaspoon baking soda (add even though the baking mix has it already)

2 tablespoons sugar

plastic wrap

The Directions

In a large mixing bowl, combine all the dough ingredients and mix with a handheld or stand mixer until a ball of dough forms. Dump the dough onto a layer of plastic wrap. Wrap tightly, and refrigerate for at least 2 hours.

When the time has elapsed, pinch off sections of dough and flatten with your hands, then roll the apples inside as described in the recipe. The dough will be lumpier and thicker than traditional crescent roll dough; that's okay.

BANANAS FOSTER

serves 4

The Ingredients

    3 overripe bananas
    4 tablespoons (¹/₂ stick) butter
    ¹/₃ cup brown sugar, firmly packed
    1 teaspoon vanilla extract
    ¹/₄ cup brandy

The Directions

Use a 2-quart slow cooker. Place the bananas into a plastic ziplock bag, and smash. Squeeze the banana pulp into the stoneware. Add the butter, brown sugar, vanilla, and brandy. Cover and cook on low for 3 to 4 hours, or on high for 1 to 2 hours. Serve over vanilla ice cream.

The Verdict

I didn't light this on fire. I wasn't interested in testing out our insurance policy, and we don't live on a cruise ship. It was very tasty, and I stirred the leftovers into my morning oatmeal. The kids ate their ice cream plain—the bananas tasted a bit alcoholy.

BLUEBERRY BUCKLE

serves 4

The Ingredients

FOR THE FILLING

$1/2$ tablespoon lemon juice

$1/4$ cup nonfat plain yogurt

$1/2$ cup flour (I used a gluten-free baking mix)

3 tablespoons granulated sugar

1 large egg

2 cups fresh blueberries (if you do not have access to fresh, use unsweetened frozen)

FOR THE CRUMB TOPPING

2 tablespoons granulated sugar

2 tablespoons dark brown sugar

$1/4$ cup of flour (I used a gluten-free baking mix)

$1/4$ teaspoon ground cinnamon

2 tablespoons butter, melted

cooking spray

The Directions

Use a 6-quart slow cooker and an oven-safe dish or individual ramekins. In a large glass bowl, mix all ingredients for the filling, except the blueberries. Wash and stem the blueberries, then toss into the bowl with the filling. Set aside. In a different glass bowl, add the dry ingredients to the melted butter, and mix. The crumbs will be moist and crumbly.

Place the oven-safe dish or individual ramekins into your stoneware. Spray the dish or ramekins with cooking spray. Divide the blueberry filling evenly among the ramekins, or into the inserted dish, and top with the crumb topping. Cover and cook on high for 3 to 5 hours, removing the lid of the slow cooker during the last 45 minutes or so to crisp up the topping. Your dessert is finished when the crumb topping has set.

BREAD PUDDING
serves 6

The Ingredients
2 large eggs
2 cups soy milk (or 2 percent or lower cow's milk)
1/4 cup brown sugar, firmly packed
1 teaspoon vanilla extract
1/2 teaspoon ground cinnamon
6 slices thick bread (I used brown rice bread), cubed
1/4 cup dried raisins or cranberries
butter, for greasing stoneware
2 tablespoons raw sugar (optional)

The Directions
Use a 2-quart slow cooker. In a mixing bowl, whisk together eggs, milk, brown sugar, vanilla, and cinnamon. Add bread cubes. Stir in the dried fruit. Pour the mixture into a greased stoneware insert. Cover (no need to prop open lid) and cook on low for 3 to 5 hours, or on high for 2 to 3 hours. Your bread pudding is finished when the top has browned, and you can push on the pieces of bread without too much liquid squirting out. If desired, add raw sugar to the very top and caramelize with a kitchen torch. I appreciate how I can use the end pieces of a loaf of bread and sneak in some ground-up flax without notice.

CARAMEL APPLES

makes 4 large apples

The Ingredients

    1 (14-ounce) bag caramel candies
    2 tablespoons water
    4 wooden popsicle sticks
    4 large apples
    1/2 cup chopped nuts, or sprinkles
    parchment paper

The Directions

Use a 2-quart slow cooker. Unwrap the caramel candies, and add them and 2 tablespoons of water to the crock. Cover and cook on high for 1 to 2 hours, checking every 20 minutes or so. The caramel is ready when it is shiny and can be stirred easily. Insert popsicle sticks into the stem end of the apples. Use a spoon to ladle the caramel over each apple, and swirl to completely cover the whole thing. Dip each apple into chopped nuts or sprinkles, if desired. Let cool on parchment paper. They are super messy—get the wipies ready!

CHEESECAKE

serves 8

The Ingredients

FOR THE CRUST

1 cup graham cracker crumbs (I used gluten-free animal crackers)

3 tablespoons melted butter

2 tablespoons brown sugar

FOR THE FILLING

1 (16-ounce) block cream cheese, at room temperature

3/4 cup granulated sugar

2 large eggs, at room temperature

1 tablespoon flour (I used a gluten-free baking mix)

1/4 cup heavy cream

1 teaspoon good vanilla extract

The Directions

Use a 6-quart slow cooker and a heat-resistant dish that will fit all the way into your stoneware for the cheesecake. You are going to create a bain-marie, or water bath. I used a 1½-quart Corningware dish and it fit nicely into my 6-quart oval. In a plastic ziplock bag, beat the crackers into crumbs with a rolling pin. Put a cup of the crumbs into a medium bowl, and add the melted butter and brown sugar. Stir until the mixture is wet and crumbly. Press the crumbs into the bottom of the dish.

In a separate bowl, cream the cheese, sugar, eggs, flour, cream, and vanilla with a handheld or stand mixer. Pour the cheese mixture on top of the crust. Lick the bowl. Add ½ to 1 cup of water to the bottom of your slow cooker. Lower the dish into the stoneware, being careful not to slosh

(CONTINUED)

water into your cheesecake. Cover and cook on high for 2 to 3 hours, checking after 1 hour. Your cheesecake is done when the edges are no longer shiny and have set. Touch the cheesecake lightly—you shouldn't get a bunch of gook on your finger. Unplug the cooker. Let the cheesecake sit in the cooling cooker for an hour, before removing and transferring it to the refrigerator. Chill in the refrigerator for about 2 hours before cutting and serving.

The Verdict

This was a complete success. I couldn't get enough. I had weird hallucinations of being a cross between Homer Simpson—"Mmmm. Cheesecake"— and Rose from the *Golden Girls*—"Nothing can't be fixed with cheesecake." I was quite pleased that the texture was moist and gooey, yet perfectly set and just like a good-quality cheesecake.

CHERRIES JUBILEE

serves 4

The Ingredients

 1 tablespoon cornstarch
 2 tablespoons butter, melted
 2 (15-ounce) cans pitted black cherries in heavy syrup, *not* pie filling
 2 tablespoons sugar
 1/4 teaspoon lemon zest
 1/4 cup brandy (optional)
 vanilla ice cream

The Directions

Use a 2-quart slow cooker. Whisk the cornstarch with the melted butter until fully incorporated. Drain the cans of cherries, and add to the stoneware. Pour in cornstarch mixture. Add the sugar and lemon zest; no need to stir. If you're going to add brandy, do so now. Cook on high for 2 hours, and serve hot over vanilla ice cream. I made two batches, one with and one without brandy. The brandy batch tasted like there was brandy in it; I wouldn't serve that one to children.

CHOCOLATE-COVERED STRAWBERRIES AND APPLES

serves 8

The Ingredients

16 ounces chocolate chips
6 green apples, sliced
1 pound strawberries
parchment paper

Use a 2-quart slow cooker. Pour the chocolate chips into the crock. Cover and cook on high for 30 minutes to 1 hour.

While the chocolate is melting, wash and prepare the fruit, and line a few baking sheets with parchment paper. Check on the chocolate chips after 30 minutes. You will know the chocolate is ready to stir when it gets really shiny and begins to break down. You can start stirring even if the chip forms are still visible.

Dip fruit pieces into the melted chocolate. Put the covered fruit onto parchment paper–lined baking sheets and place in the refrigerator to harden. This doesn't take long—I think we only waited about 20 minutes.

You can go totally fancy and have one slow cooker for semisweet chocolate, one for white, and one for milk. You can make little swirls with the different chocolates and double-dip to create culinary masterpieces. I'd really like to do this one day.

CHOCOLATE FRITO CANDY

serves 10

The Ingredients

2 cups Fritos, smashed
2 cups pretzels (I used gluten-free), smashed
4 tablespoons (1 stick) butter
½ cup brown sugar, firmly packed
2 tablespoons natural peanut butter (optional if you have allergies)
1 (12-ounce) bag chocolate chips
½ cup chopped peanuts (optional) (I used honey roasted because that's what I had)
parchment paper

The Directions

Use a 6-quart slow cooker. Put the Fritos and pretzels in a large ziplock freezer bag and smash until crumbly. Set aside. Line a 13×9-inch baking sheet with parchment paper. Set that aside, too.

Put the butter, brown sugar, peanut butter, and chocolate chips into your slow cooker, set on high, and cook for 1 to 2 hours, or until everything is really melty and you can mix it well.

Stir in pretzel and Frito pieces. Using oven mitts (Use them! The crock is hot!), dump the hot candy out onto your lined baking sheet and spread it out with a wooden spoon. Sprinkle the peanut pieces on top. Put sheet in the refrigerator for about 1 hour, or until the candy has set completely. Break the candy into pieces.

The Verdict

Whoa, mama! Man, these are amazing and wonderful and scary because they are *so* good you will hide pieces in your robe pockets and sneak into a corner of the garage to eat them by yourself.

CHOCOLATE MOUSSE

serves 6

The Ingredients

    2 cups heavy cream
    4 large egg yolks
    3 tablespoons sugar (I like baker's sugar because the granules dissolve quickly)
    1 teaspoon vanilla extract
    $1/3$ cup cold, strong coffee
    2 cups semisweet chocolate chips
    whipped cream, or berries (optional)

The Directions

Use a 4-quart slow cooker. Put the heavy cream, egg yolks, sugar, vanilla, and coffee into your crock. Mix until combined with a whisk. You don't need to go crazy, just mix well. Add the chocolate chips. Cover and cook on high for about 1 hour, or on low for about 2 hours. You are looking for little bubbles in the surface of the cream and melted chocolate. VERY VERY VERY VERY carefully, pour the mixture into a blender. You'll get about $2^1/2$ to 3 cups of liquid. Blend on high until it "grows" to about 5 to 6 cups, and doesn't seem like it will rise any higher. Pour into serving dishes; I used wine glasses. Chill for 2 hours in the refrigerator. Top with whipped cream or berries, or nothing at all.

The Verdict

It's not bad that I didn't let the kids have any because it had coffee in it, right? That doesn't make me mean, does it? They were already eating cake . . . We served this to company and everyone truly enjoyed it.

    Something to note: the very top has a bit of a skin on it, and there are little bubbles that didn't pop during the cooling process. I've been told this can be remedied by pressing plastic wrap directly on the mousse while it is chilling.

CRÈME BRÛLÉE

serves 4

The Ingredients

2 cups heavy cream

5 egg yolks

1/2 cup granulated sugar (baker's or fine sugar is best)

1 tablespoon vanilla extract

1/4 cup raw sugar

The Directions

Use a 6-quart slow cooker and a heat-resistant dish that fits all the way inside your stoneware. I use a 11/2-quart casserole dish. Add water around the dish, until halfway up the side of the dish. (You are using the slow cooker as a bain-marie, or water bath.)

In a mixing bowl, whip together the eggs, cream, sugar, and vanilla. Pour the mixture into the dish, cover, and cook on high for 2 to 4 hours. The custard should be set with the center still a bit jiggly. Touch the surface lightly with your finger to check. Unlike an oven, it will be difficult to overcook this. Try not to worry.

Very carefully (use oven mitts!) remove the dish and let cool completely on the countertop, then chill in the refrigerator for 2 to 3 hours. Before serving, sprinkle raw sugar over the top and brown with a kitchen torch, or place under the broiler for 3 to 5 minutes, or until sugar has browned. Chill again before serving.

The Verdict

This is the dish I prepared on *The Rachael Ray Show*. I love that I can make such a decadent dish at home and eat it without having to spend $40 on a restaurant dinner. I've made it quite a few times and it always comes out perfectly.

DULCE DE LECHE

serves 2 to 8

The Ingredients

2 (14-ounce) cans sweetened condensed milk
oven-safe ramekin(s)
water

The Directions

Use a 4-quart slow cooker. Find an oven-safe dish to insert into your stoneware. You can use individual ramekins or a casserole dish. Carefully pour water all around the dish, until the water reaches three-quarters of the way up the sides of the dish. Open the cans of sweetened condensed milk and pour into the inserted dish(es). Cover and cook on low for 8 hours.

The Verdict

Mmm. Caramel pudding. I cook this overnight and serve it to the kids for breakfast with apple slices. Because that turns caramel into health food. Yes, it does.

PEACH COMPOTE

serves 6

The Ingredients

3 to 4 fresh peaches (I used 3 large ones)
1/3 cup brown sugar, firmly packed
1/4 cup brandy
2 tablespoons butter
1/2 teaspoon ground cinnamon
1 teaspoon vanilla extract

The Directions

Use a 2-quart slow cooker. Pit and slice (I didn't peel) the peaches, and put into the stoneware. Cover with the brown sugar, brandy, butter, cinnamon, and vanilla. There is no need to melt the butter beforehand. Cover and cook for about 90 minutes to 2 hours. Serve over vanilla ice cream. The leftovers are fantastic stirred into oatmeal.

PEACH PIE

The Ingredients

2 (15-ounce) cans sliced peaches with juice
2 tablespoons melted butter
1 teaspoon vanilla extract
1½ cups baking mix (I used a gluten-free baking mix)
½ cup brown sugar, firmly packed
½ teaspoon ground cinnamon
¼ teaspoon ground nutmeg
¼ teaspoon ground allspice

The Directions

Use a 4-quart slow cooker. Put the peaches into the stoneware. In a separate bowl, mix the melted butter with the vanilla and the dry ingredients. Stir with a fork to combine; it will be crumbly. Pour the mixture on top of the peaches, and press down with your hands (or a spatula if you don't want to get gooky). Cover and cook on high for 4 hours. The pie is done when it has begun to brown on the edges and the fruit is bubbly and has caramelized a bit.

The Verdict

Even though the top looked awfully crumby, the topping ended up being baked and a bit chewy like a traditional pie crust. I believe this simple dough can be used with any variety of fruit, canned or fresh, or with canned pie filling. We just happened to have a case of canned peaches in the garage.

PEANUT (NOT BRITTLE) CANDY

makes 3 pounds

The Ingredients

4 tablespoons (¹/₂ stick) butter

3 cups sugar (baker's sugar has finer granules and will dissolve well)

1 cup light corn syrup

2 teaspoons vanilla extract

2 teaspoons baking soda

4 cups of your favorite nuts (I used 3 cups dry roasted lightly salted peanuts and 1 cup raw almonds)

parchment paper

The Directions

Use a 6-quart slow cooker. Drop the 4 tablespoons of butter into your stoneware. Add sugar and corn syrup on top of the butter. Pour in the vanilla extract. Cover and turn to high for one hour. Line two baking sheets with parchment paper.

After an hour, stir to mix well. Add the baking soda. It will sizzle and make fun noises. Your sugar mixture will be milky-yellow and the sugar might still look granulated; that's okay. Cover again and cook on high for another 30 minutes. Check and stir. Cover and cook again for another 15 to 30 minutes, or until the sugar mixture is brown and looks the color of peanut brittle. Stir in nuts. Then, using oven mitts, carefully (*carefully!* seriously—use the oven mitts!) pour half of the contents of the pot onto each baking sheet and spread out with a spatula. It will be lumpy (that's because there are nuts). Let cool at room temperature for about 1 hour, then tear into pieces.

The Verdict

This tastes just like a PayDay candy bar. Everyone who tried it (ten of us, minus my cousin who for some reason doesn't care for nuts) couldn't get enough. It's quite tasty. Prepare to be amazed.

PEANUT CLUSTERS

makes approximately 150 pieces

The Ingredients
1 (8-ounce) box unsweetened Baker's chocolate
2 (4-ounce) boxes German Baker's chocolate
3 (16-ounce) jars lightly salted roasted peanuts
1 (24-ounce) bag semisweet chocolate chips
1 teaspoon vanilla extract
parchment paper
cooking spray

The Directions
Use a 6-quart slow cooker. Spray the inside of your stoneware with cooking spray, and place the unwrapped baking chocolate and bars of German chocolate in the bottom. Add all the peanuts. Pour in the chocolate chips, and add the vanilla. Cover and cook on low for 3 hours, or high for about 1½ hours.

While the chocolate is melting, lay out a bunch of parchment paper on your countertop or kitchen table. When the chocolate has melted, stir well, and remove from the heat. Use a small ice cream scoop to plop bite-size piles onto the parchment paper. Let cool before eating—it'll take much longer than you want it to. It would be best to leave them overnight so you don't pick at them. Package up and give away as soon as possible, or you'll end up eating them all. Trust me.

The Verdict
These are addictive. The chocolate flavor is quite rich. If you aren't a fan of dark chocolate, use milk chocolate chips. The salty flavor of the nuts is subtle, but is there, and it makes your tongue itch for more. And more. If you are allergic to nuts, try using pretzels. This candy makes a fantastic gift.

PUMPKIN PUDDING
(CRUSTLESS PUMPKIN PIE)

serves 6

The Ingredients

cooking spray
1 (15-ounce) can pure pumpkin purée
1 (12-ounce) can evaporated milk
3/4 cup granulated sugar
1/2 cup Bisquick-type mix (I used a gluten-free baking mix)
2 large eggs
2 tablespoons butter, melted
1 1/4 teaspoons ground cinnamon
1/2 teaspoon ground nutmeg
1/4 teaspoon ground cloves
1/8 teaspoon ground ginger
2 teaspoons vanilla extract
whipped cream, for garnish

The Directions

Use a 4-quart slow cooker. Spray the inside of the stoneware with cooking spray. Set aside. In a mixing bowl, combine all the ingredients, and whisk until fully blended. No need to use a handheld or stand mixer, just some elbow grease. Pour the batter into the prepared stoneware. Cover and cook on high for 3 to 4 hours, or on low for about 6 hours. Check your "pie" after 2 hours on high, or 3 hours on low, then every 30 minutes. When fully cooked, the pie will look just like a finished pumpkin pie—the batter will have browned and cracked in a few places. The center will set enough

(CONTINUED)

for you to touch it without getting gookies on your finger. Let sit in the stoneware until cooled to room temperature, then spoon into serving dishes and top with whipped cream.

The Verdict

Perfect. It tastes fantastic, is gluten-free, and terribly easy to do. My kids aren't huge pie eaters, and have never shown any interest in pumpkin pie. Like, EVER. But my six-year-old convinced me that it's the crust of the pie that she doesn't like, and she likes the filling. And then her younger sister decided to say the exact same thing. This is better than my original plan, which was to pop open a can of pumpkin pie filling and hand out spoons.

RICE PUDDING

serves 12 to 14

The Ingredients

cooking spray
8 cups milk (I used half soy milk, half fat-free cow's)
1 cup long-grain white rice
1 cup sugar

THEN:

3 eggs
1/4 cup heavy cream or half-and-half
2 teaspoons vanilla
1/2 teaspoon cinnamon
1/4 teaspoon salt

The Directions

Use a 4-quart slow cooker. Spray the stoneware with cooking spray, then combine the milk, rice, and sugar. Stir well and cook on low for 4 to 6 hours, or on high for about 4 hours. (It took longer than I expected for my rice to become bite-tender—I did low for 3 hours, then high for another 2 hours.) When the rice has softened, mix together the eggs, cream, vanilla, cinnamon, and salt in a large mixing bowl. Scoop 1/2 cup of the hot rice mixture into the mixing bowl and whisk. Keep adding, 1/2 cup at a time, the rice-and-milk mixture into the egg bowl until about half of the rice-and-milk mixture is gone from the stoneware. Then pour everything back into the stoneware. Stir well. This is called "tempering your eggs"—you have to do this step, or your eggs will scramble on you when you add them to the mix.

Cover and cook on high for 1 hour. Stir well, then take the lid off the slow cooker and unplug it. When the rice pudding is room temperature, you can refrigerate it. Some people like their pudding hot or warm, and some prefer it chilled; it's completely up to you.

ROCKY ROAD CANDY

yields approximately 24 pieces

The Ingredients

1 (16-ounce) bag chocolate chips
1/2 (10-ounce) bag mini marshmallows
1 3/4 cups chopped walnuts

The Directions

Use a 4-quart slow cooker. Pour the chocolate chips into your stoneware. Cover and cook on high for 1 hour, stirring every 20 minutes. While chocolate is melting, line two baking sheets with parchment paper. When fully melted, stir in the marshmallows and walnuts.

Remove the stoneware from the heating element. Using spoons, drop mounds of the chocolate-marshmallow-nut gooeyness onto the prepared baking sheets. Refrigerate to cool and harden. Once cool, you can place the candy in cellophane bags and tie with a ribbon to give as gifts.

STUFFED AND BAKED APPLES

4 to 6 servings (1 apple per person)

The Ingredients

1/3 cup brown sugar, firmly packed
1/2 cup raisins
1/2 cup dried cranberries
1/2 cup walnut or pecan pieces
4 to 6 apples, or as many as you can fit into your slow cooker
1/2 cup water
2 teaspoons vanilla extract

The Directions

Use a 6-quart slow cooker. In a small bowl, combine the brown sugar, raisins, cranberries, and nut pieces. Set aside. Wash and core the apples. Stuff each apple with the filling, and nestle into the stoneware. Pour the water and vanilla around the base of the apples. Cover and cook on low for 6 to 7 hours, or on high for 4 hours. The apples are done when they have reached the desired tenderness you and your family prefer. I cooked ours on high for exactly 4 hours. The apples still had their shape, and were tender enough to cut with two spoons, but the halves were still pick-up-able to munch on (it's really sticky this way).

TAPIOCA PUDDING

serves 8

The Ingredients

    2 quarts 1 percent milk (half-gallon)
    1½ cups sugar
    1 cup small pearl tapioca (not instant)
    3 large eggs
    1 teaspoon vanilla extract

The Directions

Use a 4-quart slow cooker. Combine the milk, sugar, and tapioca pearls in the stoneware. Stir well to mix. Cover and cook on high for 2 to 5 hours. You want the tapioca to be soft and somewhat slimy, but it won't get thick.

In a mixing bowl, whisk the eggs with the vanilla. Measure out ½ cup of the hot milk and tapioca mixture and whisk it into the eggs. Add another ½ cup of the hot milk and tapioca, and whisk that into the eggs, too. Then add yet another. Now you'll have a bowl of yellow tapioca gooeyness. Pour the contents of the bowl into the stoneware, and whisk until it is all thoroughly combined. Cover and cook on high for 30 to 45 minutes, or until the tapioca is pudding-like in consistency. Unplug the cooker and let the pudding sit for about 1 hour to cool. Ladle into serving-size bowls and chill in the refrigerator. Or eat it with a serving spoon, hot, right out of the crock! Your choice.

The Verdict

Adam has fond childhood memories of eating homemade tapioca pudding. I have fond memories of peeling back the foil of a Handi-Snacks and then licking it. Repeatedly. We now have new memories—slow-cooked tapioca. It couldn't taste any better, and was so easy to do.

FUN STUFF

*W*ho would have thought you could recycle crayons in the slow cooker or make Shrinky Dinks? Not me, a year ago, but now I know not only that I can, the results are better than when I used the traditional oven, and without the fear of being badly burned.

AIR FRESHENER

BABY FOOD

BROWNIE-IN-A-MUG

CRAYONS

GLYCERIN SOAP

PLAY DOUGH

RECYCLED CANDLES

SALT DOUGH CREATIONS

SHRINKY DINKS

AIR FRESHENER

The Ingredients

AS AN AIR FRESHENER
water (enough to fill your slow cooker by two-thirds)
drops of essential oil
potpourri scent
2 teaspoons vanilla extract or other desired extract
ground cinnamon and cloves
1 cinnamon stick
lemon slices

AS AN ODOR NEUTRALIZER
water (enough to fill your slow cooker by two-thirds)
baking soda (for a mini slow cooker, I used 3 tablespoons)

The Directions

Use a 1-quart or smaller slow cooker. Pour water into the slow cooker. Add the baking soda. Mix. Plug the cooker in and turn the heat to low (most of the small ones don't have settings, they just plug in). Keep the lid off, and allow the baking soda to do its job of soaking up unpleasant odors.

If you would prefer to use the slow cooker as an air freshener, fill with water, add the other desired ingredients listed above, and "cook" with the lid off.

The Verdict

I tried the odor-neutralizer on Thanksgiving evening. I was tired, and wanted to watch *The Wire*, and was not interested in cleaning the six dirty slow cookers on the counter, but the kitchen smelled funky. I was quite pleased with how the baking soda really did absorb the kitchen odors. After a few hours, I took my mini crock into another room and smelled the water—it smelled strongly of mulled wine. Whoa!

BABY FOOD

servings depend on amount of food cooked

The Ingredients

fresh or frozen fruit or vegetables
(I used yellow squash, sweet potatoes, and frozen green beans)
water

The Directions

Use a separate slow cooker for each variety of baby food. It's okay to use frozen fruit or vegetables; the food is picked at the right time, and all nutrients are preserved perfectly during the freezing process. I used yellow squash, sweet potatoes, and frozen green beans. Wash the vegetables and peel the skin. Cut into chunks. Put the chunks into your slow cooker and cover with the least amount of water needed to fully cook. For the yellow squash, I used ¼ cup of water; frozen green beans (toss in frozen), ¼ cup of water; sweet potatoes, I ended up using ¾ cup of water.

Make baby food on a day that you are home to monitor the food. Each variety will cook differently, depending on the moisture content and the density of the fruit or vegetable.

I used a 4-quart, and two 6-quart slow cookers, and everything was cooked fully within 3 hours.

When the veggies or fruit are quite tender, unplug your cooker. Use a handheld immersion blender, a real blender, or a food processor to purée the food. If you need to add a bit of water to make it thinner for your baby, do so in little drips. Freeze the baby food in ice cube trays, then pop out and store in a freezer bag.

The Verdict

Since I'm a total cheapskate I didn't buy little jars of baby food for my kids. I wasn't concerned about chemicals as much as I was blown away by cost and packaging. The vegetables I bought cost a total of $4.23, and I had enough baby food to feed all the kids on *Jon and Kate Plus 8* for a few days.

BROWNIE-IN-A-MUG

serves 4

The Ingredients

1 (18-ounce) box brownie mix (I used a gluten-free mix)
the stuff your favorite brownie mix tells you to use (eggs, cooking oil, etc.)
cooking spray
4 mugs
vanilla ice cream, whipped cream (optional)

The Directions

I fit 4 mugs into a 6-quart oval stoneware. Don't pick fancy-schmancy mugs—use the ones that you don't think twice about throwing in the dishwasher or heating up in the microwave (ceramic or stoneware, *not* plastic or good china).

Mix up the brownie mix according to the directions listed on the package. Spray each mug with cooking spray. Spoon the brownie mix into each mug, filling it about one-half to two-thirds of the way. The brownie mix I used makes an 8×8-inch pan, so each of my mugs was half filled.

Put mugs in the stoneware—they need to fit completely and touch the bottom. Cover and cook on high for 1½ to 3 hours. You will know the brownies are cooked when they have risen, pulled away at the sides, and an inserted knife comes out clean. Unplug the cooker, and let the mugs sit with the lid off. They will be *terribly hot*. Don't get burned. When the mug is coolish to the touch (after about 30 minutes), top with vanilla ice cream or whipped cream.

The Verdict

It's like it's hot chocolate . . . but it's a brownie! in a mug! baked in your slow cooker! This is a wonderful, fun dessert that will evoke fond memories. We had a ball sitting on a blanket in front of the TV laughing and eating our "hot chocolate."

CRAYONS

makes 6

The Ingredients
old crayons
muffin tin or candy mold that will fit into your stoneware insert
kid helpers

The Directions
Use a 6-quart oval slow cooker—unless the mold you're using can fit into a smaller size. Sort crayons into color families and take the wrappers off; it helps to soak the crayons in some warm water before peeling. Break the crayons into small pieces, and load them into the candy mold or muffin tin. It's best to mound the crayons up a bit; they will melt and shrink down. Put the tin or mold into the stoneware, cover, and turn the cooker on. We cooked our crayons on high for 1½ hours. Once the crayons have melted completely, they're done. Let the hot wax sit in the crock and begin to harden before trying to remove the pan—you don't want hot wax spilled, or to get burned. Refrigerate the pan for 30 minutes, or until the crayons have hardened completely and pull away from the edges. Pop out and enjoy!

The Verdict
What's the best thing to do with old, broken crayons? Recycle them! This is a great rainy (or overly hot) day project that is both fun and useful. The kids and I were surprised at how easily some crayons peeled, and how others needed to soak for quite a while to loosen the wrapper. We also noticed that some crayons sank, while others floated. These were easy to do, and the kids had a ball.

GLYCERIN SOAP

makes 12 bars

The Ingredients

soap-making supplies are available at craft stores

oven-safe dish(es) (ramekins) to put in the crockpot
1 pound glycerin blocks
fragrance (extract or essential oil)
soap coloring
soap mold
a few wooden skewers for stirring

The Directions

Use a 6-quart slow cooker. Do *not* put the soap mold into your stoneware and add glycerin cubes, and turn it on. The mold will melt. And you will be annoyed when your husband says something along the lines of "I thought that might happen."

What you should do instead is put an oven-safe dish (or two) into your stoneware and add the separated blocks. Cover and cook on high for about 1 hour, or until the glycerin is all liquidy. Using oven mitts (trust me), carefully pour liquid glycerin into each mold. Add fragrance and color. A bit of fragrance goes a long way, but you do need quite a few drops of color. Stir with a skewer. Let soap cure for about 1 hour before removing from the form. If you wait until it's fully cool, it pops out of the mold *much* more easily than if you try to rush it (trust me again on this one). Repeat steps until you run out of glycerin.

The Verdict

We really enjoyed making this soap. The kids had fun picking out colors, and liked using their creations. I pushed a foam sticker (minus the backing) into the soap while it was setting for some extra oomph. Something to note: Glycerin soap sweats. It surprised me, but evidently this is normal. Wrap your homemade soap in cellophane bags, not tissue paper, for gift-giving.

PLAY DOUGH

makes enough for 4 children to play

The Ingredients

   2 cups flour (I used rice flour)
   1 cup cornstarch
   1 cup iodized salt
   1/3 cup cream of tartar
   2 cups hot water
   2 teaspoons canola oil
   food coloring

The Directions

Use a 6-quart slow cooker. Plug in your cooker and turn it to low to warm up slowly. Put dry ingredients into the stoneware, stirring to distribute evenly. Add the hot water and oil. Cover and cook on high for 30 minutes. Stir well. Cover again and heat on high another 30 minutes. Repeat the process until the dough begins to form a ball when you stir it. It took about 2 hours in my slow cooker.

Remove the stoneware from the heating element, and stir some more. Dump the dough onto a smooth surface and knead carefully—it's going to be hot. If your dough is overly sticky, add a bit of cornstarch; if it's overly dry, add a touch more hot water. Each time you make play dough, the water required will be a bit different, depending on the humidity in the air.

Once entirely cooled, separate the dough into manageable lumps and push a hole into the center for a few drops of food coloring—let the kids squish the dough around to distribute the desired color. Their hands will be a bit tinted for a few hours . . . Store in a plastic ziplock bag, or tightly sealed plastic container. If sealed properly, the dough will last 3 to 4 months.

(CONTINUED)

The Verdict

Before I had children of my own, I ran preschool centers, and made lots of play dough. This is a fun activity where children can help without the worry of being burned by standing near a hot stove. You can add texture by throwing in a bit of cornmeal or playground sand, add drops of essential oil for scent, or even add a packet of sugar-free Kool-Aid for a bright color and strong kid-approved smell.

RECYCLED CANDLES

The Ingredients

Candle-making supplies are found easily at most craft stores.

old candles in glass containers
3-inch wicks (this size works well for the tiny candles sold at the dollar store, small air freshener candles, etc.)
candle fragrance, essential oil, or cooking extract
candle coloring dye (not food coloring, sigh)

The Directions

Use a 6-quart slow cooker. Freeze jars with trapped candle wax. Use a knife to pop the wax out of the jar/glass container. If your container is tapered, you'll need to chop the wax up with the knife before it can fall out. Cut away the old wick and discard. Chop the wax into small pieces, about ½-inch square or thereabouts. Wash the containers well in soapy water and dry completely. Fill each glass with the chopped wax. Nestle the containers into your stoneware. I got 6 to fit nicely in a 6-quart oval. Cover and cook on high for 2 hours, checking every 30 minutes. When the wax has completely melted, add the color and scent. Food coloring doesn't work—I tried it. Mix with a wooden skewer, and lower in wicks.

Unplug the slow cooker. Let the candles sit in the cooling cooker for about 4 hours, or until they have set enough to move. Do not use for 12 hours. Light and enjoy.

The Verdict

I love candles, especially inexpensive ones scented with food: vanilla, cookie dough, pumpkin pie, apple-cinnamon, coffee, and gingerbread. I am the happiest after lighting a yummy-scented candle. Because of this love, I end up with quite a few candles that don't light anymore, but the jar/glass container still has trapped wax. I am thrilled that I can recycle the trapped wax and make new candles with help from the slow cooker. Nine to ten "old" candles will yield three "new" ones.

SALT DOUGH CREATIONS

The Ingredients

  1 cup salt
  3 cups flour (I used a gluten-free baking mix; rice flour will work too)
  1 cup lukewarm water
  1 tablespoon vegetable oil
  parchment paper
  paint
  Mod™ Podge, or varnish

The Directions

Use a 6-quart slow cooker. Stir the salt, flour, water, and oil together in a big bowl. Mix the dough with a handheld or stand mixer until it reaches a ball. If needed, add 1 tablespoon more water while mixing. The dough will be sticky, but will hold shape when molded. Make a desired shape. We chose to make ornaments with play dough cookie cutters. Use a chopstick to make a hole in the center of the ornaments—you need to have a good amount of dough surrounding the hole so it doesn't crumble when hung. Line the bottom of your stoneware with parchment paper. Place the dough creations onto the paper. Cover and cook on high for 2 to 3 hours, flipping once. Your creations are done when they are hard to the touch and have browned slightly. I did overcook a few, but after a coat of paint you can't tell. After they have cooled completely, paint. Seal with varnish or Mod Podge.

The Verdict

These were a lot of fun for us. My three-year-old kept eating the dough, which was a little weird, but we were all in a good mood and made memories. I like salt dough a lot, and have used it to make hand- and footprints. I liked using the slow cooker because we ended up with NO casualties—none of the pieces cracked, and the slow cooking meant I could fuss with the pieces and move them around with spatulas to ensure an even bake.

SHRINKY DINKS

creates one afternoon of fun

The Ingredients
    1 box of Shrinky Dinks—readily available in most craft and drug stores
    colored pencils (our box came with some, but we used our own, too)
    scissors
    kids
    slow cookers

The Directions
Plug in slow cooker(s) (I ended up plugging in three because we made so many) on the counter to preheat on high while coloring and cutting the Shrinky Dinks. The plastic can be sharp; an adult should do the cutting. Put the cut and colored plastic shape into the slow cooker. If the stoneware is fully hot, it will begin to shrink right in front of you—it will curl, fold up a bit, and create either jubilance or tears. But then it flattens and is fine, and tears will turn to glee. Remove the little piece of shrunken plastic with a spoon or spatula. If it hasn't fully shrunk, the piece will stick a bit to the bottom of the stoneware. This alarmed me, and I pushed it around a bit with a spoon, but I don't think that was necessary. They seem to unstick on their own when the shrinking process is complete—the largest piece took about 10 minutes. If the slow cooker isn't fully heated, it will take longer.

The Verdict
I can't remember the last time the girls and I had so much fun working together on a project. This craft is a great age-equalizer—both my almost-four and almost-seven-year-old could work side-by-side without competition, and I was happy to color a few, too.

ACKNOWLEDGMENTS

This book is a group effort. I would not have been able to do it without all of the help, support, and recipes sent in daily by thousands of readers around the world. Thank you. Thank you for your interest, dedication, and help.

Adam, Amanda, and Molly O'Dea
Bunny and Ken Gillespie
Bill, Perky, Andrew, and Karen Ramroth
Bill and Anna Ramroth
John and Maureen O'Dea
Murielle Rose
The Pellissier Family
The Zocca Family
The Teresi Family
The Lewis Family
The Morrison Family
The Beal Family
The Skyriotis Family
Jenny Lauck
Danielle Tribble
Jennifer Bloom-Smith
Lisa Stone
Jory Des Jardins
Elisa Camahort

Thank you to the following people who helped bring *Make It Fast, Cook It Slow* to life:

Alison Picard
Barbara A. Jones
Leslie Wells
Shubhani Sarkar
Betsy Wilson
David Lott
Nina Shield
Leah Stewart
Allison McGeehon
Ed and Allison O'Keefe
Alison St. Sure
Maria Cohen, *Good Morning America*
Stefanie Javorsky, *The Rachael Ray Show*

Thank you to the following Web sites, which helped put crockpot365.blogspot.com "on the map," and for your inspiration:

5dollardinners.com
amiedanny.blogspot.com
blog.fatfreevegan.com
blogher.com
citymama.typepad.com
cookiemadness.net
dinnerwithjulie.com
fridayplaydate.com
glutenfreegoddess.blogspot.com
headlessfamily5.blogspot.com
hedonia.seantimberlake.com
kalynskitchen.blogspot.com

kitchenparade.com
ninecooks.typepad.com
noappropriatebehavior.blogspot.com
notcalmdotcom.typepad.com
notesfromthetrenches.com
parentdish.com
ravelry.com
rocksinmydryer.typepad.com
simplyrecipes.com
sundaynitedinner.com
surefoodsliving.com
thepioneerwoman.com
threekidcircus.com
todayscreativeblog.blogspot.com
wantnot.net
workitmom.com
wouldashoulda.com

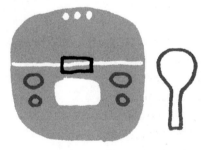

INDEX